The Hardcore Bodybuilder's Source Book

The Hardcore Bodybuilder's Source Book

by Robert Kennedy & Vivian Mason

 Sterling Publishing Co., Inc. New York

Distributed in the U.K. by Blandford Press

Picture Credits: page 256

Designed by Jim Anderson

Edited by Robert Hernandez

Library of Congress Cataloging in Publication Data

Kennedy, Robert, 1938—
    The hardcore bodybuilder's source book.

    Includes index.
    1. Bodybuilding—Miscellanea.   I. Mason, Vivian.
II. Title.
GV546.5.K447 1984   646.7'5   84-8821
ISBN 0-8069-4186-3
ISBN 0-8069-7894-5 (pbk.)

Copyright © 1984 by Robert Kennedy
Published by Sterling Publishing Co., Inc.
Two Park Avenue, New York, N.Y. 10016
Distributed in Australia by Oak Tree Press Co., Ltd.
P.O. Box K514 Haymarket, Sydney 2000, N.S.W.
Distributed in the United Kingdom by Blandford Press
Link House, West Street, Poole, Dorset BH15 1LL, England
Distributed in Canada by Oak Tree Press Ltd.
℅ Canadian Manda Group, P.O. Box 920, Station U
Toronto, Ontario, Canada M8Z 5P9
Manufactured in the United States of America
All rights reserved

Contents

ACKNOWLEDGMENTS

A book of this magnitude is never totally the accomplishment of a single person. Therefore, I would like to thank:

○ all of the companies that quickly responded with the necessary facts, data, and photos

○ the many publication editors (domestic and foreign) who generously furnished me with many magazines

○ Ben Weider and Oscar State for helping me track down names and possible sources of information, while also supplying me with positive reinforcement about the worthwhile nature of this book

○ Doris Barrilleaux for her understanding patience and swiftness in relaying all types of information

○ Kay King-Nealy (New York City AFWB representative) for giving me free space in her newsletter, "The NY Advantage," to promote this project and encourage the participation of the bodybuilding community

○ Candy Csencsits for providing updated AFWB data until the very last minute

○ William Hinbern for allowing me to use his vast library of bodybuilding materials

○ Carlos DeJesus and Lucy Scheerr (New Hampshire AFWB state representative) for providing more information and leads than I requested

○ Greg Zulak for contributing the "Anatomy of the Judging Process" chapter

○ Rickey Dale Crain for providing a bevy of useful facts and data, and much encouragement

○ Jim Anderson for creating the magnificent design

○ Ann Donaldson, Dorothy Mason, Paula Gibbs, Hope Chambers, and Ken Mohr. An explanation of their help could not even begin to do any of them justice.

—Vivian Mason

Bodybuilding is indeed the sport of the '80s—even more specifically, the sport of the future. The phenomenal success of my books *Hardcore Bodybuilding* and *Beef It!* can attest to that. It is also a beautiful art form in regard to sculpting the body and a multi-million-dollar big business. With consistently good media exposure and positive representation and promotion by its leading stars and participants, bodybuilding will surpass all expectations and eventually become a "sport of the people."

Introduction

For those of you who are so sincerely dedicated to the body-building way of life now, it is essential to keep you educated, informed, and enlightened as much as possible, from the beginner to the most advanced student. It is with this in mind that *The Hardcore Bodybuilder's Source Book* was written.

It never fails! At nearly every contest, people will approach me for all kinds of information concerning: training tips and routines; addresses of the stars; the meaning of a training principle called "saturation"; the real name of a bodybuilder nicknamed "The Zipper"; who won the Mr. Olympia title in 1972; the names of companies that sell bodybuilding gear in New York; the title of a particular book written by Bradley Steiner; what exercises to use for developing the abs besides the usual ones; how to understand the judging process; how to obtain decent equipment, leg wraps, and clothing; the name of the New Jersey district chairman of the National Physique Committee; how to get a foreign bodybuilding publication. The list goes on and on.

This book provides the answers to all of your questions and more. It's all here. Yes, this is to be believed! Everything (or almost everything) you always wanted to know about bodybuilding in simple, concise form is now at your fingertips.

A unique feature of *The Hardcore Bodybuilder's Source Book* is the extensive listing of companies and, even more helpful, subdivisions of all of the products (with photos) and a state-by-state breakdown, including a listing of foreign companies.

The majority of the information was culled primarily from magazines, newsletters, newspapers, catalogues, the IFBB, contest promoters, competitors, bodybuilding expositions and fairs, judges, and by word of mouth. The countless hours that it took to compile *The Hardcore Bodybuilder's Source Book* is, I hope, reflected in the quality and consistency that we have tried to maintain throughout this voluminous collection of data.

I don't want the ladies to feel neglected. There's plenty of applicable information for them also, including bodybuilding routines of some of the top female competitors.

The Hardcore Bodybuilder's Source Book is a great reference work that can be utilized in conjunction with almost any other book or magazine on bodybuilding. It is an absolute must for all serious devotees and fans.

Get ready to be thunderstruck by loads of information and photos pertaining to just about everything and everyone in the world of bodybuilding!

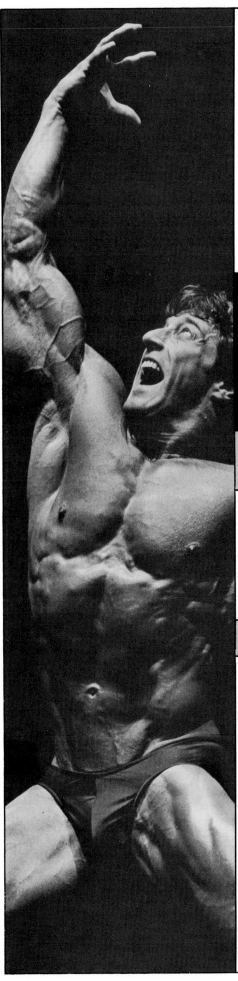

Frank Zane

Products

If you're looking for something special—from anatomy charts to workout records—check out this product list. For more complete addresses and information about a particular company, see the Companies section.

ANATOMY CHARTS

Nautilus Sports/Medical Industries, Inc.
DELAND, FL 32720

Viamonte Design, Inc.
CHERRY HILL, NJ 08034

Weider Health and Fitness, Inc.
WOODLAND HILLS, CA 91367

ART

Appian Way Sculpture Studio
JOHNSTON, RI 02919

American Studio Arts
ONEONTA, NY 13820

Jay Casagrande
NORWALK, CT 06851

D. S. Products
SACRAMENTO, CA 95823

GMV Gallery
SAN JOSE, CA 95154-4802

Orrin J. Heller
NORWALK, CT 90650

National Health Products
UTICA, NY 13502

Spong Studios
KIRKWOOD, NJ 08043

L. D. Stokes Studios
LONG BEACH, CA 90804

Work Out
BOONTON, NJ 07005

BODYBUILDING ADVICE AND CONSULTANTS*

*See "Fitness/Exercise Consultants" and "Personalized Training Programs"

Andreas Cahling Enterprises
VENICE, CA 90294

Clarence Bass RIPPED Enterprises
ALBUQUERQUE, NM 87108

Randy Morris
AKRON, OH 44350

Muscle Grams
READING, PA 19601

BOOKS, TRAINING COURSES AND ROUTINES, AND MAGAZINES*

*See Appendix

ARMS
FITCHBURG, MA 01420

Charles Atlas
NEW YORK, NY 10010

Samir Bannout
SANTA MONICA, CA 90406

Tim Belknap
SANTA MONICA, CA 90406

Mike Bridges Systems
ARLINGTON, TX 76022

Doug Brolus
DETROIT, MI 48224

A. Brooks
ROHNERT PARK, CA 94928

Andreas Cahling Enterprises
VENICE, CA 90294

R. Casey
LOS ANGELES, CA 90045

Charlton Publications, Inc.
DERBY, CT 06418

Bud Charniga
LIVONIA, MI 48150

K. K. Clark
NEW YORK, NY 10019

Boyer Coe
HUNTINGTON BEACH, CA 92646

Franco Columbu
SANTA MONICA, CA 90406

Crain Power-Plus
SHAWNEE, OK 74801

Darden Research Corp.
LAKE HELEN, FL 32744

Steve Davis Fitness Center
NEWHALL, CA 91321

DEM Publishing
MARINA DEL REY, CA 90291

Chris Dickerson, Inc.
VENICE, CA 90291

Discovery Publishing
TACOMA, WA 98401

Diversified Products Corp.
Opelika, AL 36802

D & L Publishing
MIDDLETOWN, OH 45042

Doc's Sports
COLLEGE PARK, GA 30349-0338

Dynakaz
AUBURN, AL 36830

Sam Easterwood
SAN ANTONIO, TX 78210

Lou Ferrigno
SANTA MONICA, CA 90406

1st Fitness International
OCEANSIDE, CA 92054

Fitness Consultants & Supply
WICHITA FALLS, TX 76302

Fitness King
MINNEAPOLIS, MN 55411

Tim Belknap

Fitness & Nutrition Center, Inc.
NORTH MIAMI BEACH, FL 33160

Getting Strong Book Series
LOS ANGELES, CA 90067

Vince Gironda
NORTH HOLLYWOOD, CA 91604

Ron J. Goodman
MONROVIA, CA 91016

Bill Grant Enterprises
SANTA MONICA, CA 90406

Fred Hatfield
VAN NUYS, CA 91406

Health Culture
ROCKAWAY, NJ 07866

Health-for-Life
LOS ANGELES, CA 90046

William F. Hinbern
FARMINGTON, MI 48024

Iron Man **Magazine**
ALLIANCE, NE 69301

Angelo Iuspa
NEWARK, NJ 07107

Laser Publications
MOGADORE, OH 44260

L. H.'s Art
NORWALK, CA 90650

The Library
VAN NUYS, CA 91406

J. F. Loccisano
LANCASTER, PA 17603

L & S Research
TOMS RIVER, NJ 08753-0550

Dan Lurie Barbell Co., Inc.
SPRINGFIELD GARDENS, NY 11413

MAGAZINES
HOLYOKE, MA 01040

Rachel McLish
SANTA MONICA, CA 90406

Mike Mentzer
DELAND, FL 32720

Mills Enterprises
MIDWAY CITY, CA 92655

Milton T. Moore, Jr.
DALLAS, TX 75214-0280

Mr. Universe Enterprises
OAK FOREST, IL 60452

Muscle-Up
JANESVILLE, WI 53547

Muscle World
CLAYTON, OK 74536

National Health Products
UTICA, NY 13502

Nautilus Sports/Medical Industries, Inc.
DELAND, FL 32720

O.E.M. Publishing
SANTA MONICA, CA 90405

Olympus Gym
WARRINGTON, PA 18976

Pacifico Enterprises
DAYTON, OH 45414

Danny Padilla
SANTA MONICA, CA 90406

Bill Pearl's Physical Fitness Architects
PASADENA, CA 91106

Tom Platz, Inc.
SANTA MONICA, CA 90406

Power By Cash
DAYTON, OH 45420

RayCo
NEW YORK, NY 10185

Steve Reeves
VALLEY CENTER, CA 92082

Robby Robinson
VENICE, CA 90291

San Carlos Exercise Equipment Co.
SAN CARLOS, CA 94070

Arnold Schwarzenegger
SANTA MONICA, CA 90406

Larry Scott
NORTH SALT LAKE, UT 84054

Shannon Publishing and Mail Order
DUBLIN, CA 94568

Sports Conditioning Services
VAN NUYS, CA 91406

Sports Science Consultants
NATICK, MA 01760

Steroids
ORANGE, CT 06477

Strong Barbell Co.
SACRAMENTO, CA 95838

Clarence Bass

Dennis Tinerino
NORTHRIDGE, CA 91328

Universal Fitness Products
PLAINVIEW, NY 11803

Universal Gym Equipment, Inc.
CEDAR RAPIDS, IA 52406

Vegebody
ST. PETERSBURG, FL 33733

Venus Food Supplements
Thousand Oaks, CA 91360

Casey Viator
NIWOT, CO 80544

Weider Health and Fitness, Inc.
WOODLAND HILLS, CA 91367

Claudia Cornell Wilbourn
SANTA MONICA, CA 90406

W.S.P.
HOHOKUS, NJ 07423

York Barbell Co., Inc.
YORK, PA 17405

Frank Zane
SANTA MONICA, CA 90406

BUMPER PLATES/ STICKERS

Crain Power-Plus
SHAWNEE, OK 74801

Expression
VAN NUYS, CA 91401

Power By Cash
DAYTON, OH 45420

CASSETTE TAPES*
*See "Videos (Beta/VHS) and Films"

Achievement Plus
MARINA DEL REY, CA 90291

Clarence Bass RIPPED Enterprises
ALBUQUERQUE, NM 87108

Andreas Cahling Enterprises
VENICE, CA 90294

Steve Davis Fitness Center
NEWHALL, CA 91321

Discovery Publishing
TACOMA, WA 98401

Lou Ferrigno
SANTA MONICA, CA 90406

Fitness
VENICE, CA 93001

Fitness Institute of Hypnosis
SANTA MONICA, CA 90403

Ernie and Diane Frantz Health Studio
AURORA, IL 60504

Mike Mentzer
DELAND, FL 32720

Casey Viator
NIWOT, CO 80544

Claudia Cornell Wilbourn
SANTA MONICA, CA 90406

Wysong Medical, Inc.
MIDLAND, MI 48640

CLOTHING AND EXERCISE WEAR*
*See "T-Shirts"

Aerobic Wear, Inc.
HUNTINGTON STATION, NY 11746

AMF Voit, Inc.
SANTA ANA, CA 92702

Karen Angelone
RIDGEWOOD, NY 11385

Apparel Warehouse
TARZANA, CA 91356

Athtex
GASTONIA, NC 28052

Samir Bannout
SANTA MONICA, CA 90406

Barbell Sportswear
JACKSONVILLE, FL 32205

Barely Legal
COSTA MESA, CA 92627

Big Boy Enterprises
LOS ANGELES, CA 90026

Fig. 1

Body Building Unlimited
MOORE, OK 73153

The Body Shop
SAN FRANCISCO, CA 94128

The Body Shoppe
JACKSONVILLE, FL 32205

Stevi Brooks
LOS ANGELES, CA 90055

Fig. 2

Builders Sportswear
ADDISON, TX 75001

California Shape
WESTWOOD VILLAGE, CA 90024

Chelsea Gym
NEW YORK, NY 10011

Clarence Bass RIPPED Enterprises
ALBUQUERQUE, NM 87108

Boyer Coe
HUNTINGTON BEACH, CA 92646

Crain Power-Plus
SHAWNEE, OK 74801

Chris Dickerson, Inc.
VENICE, CA 90291

Custom Built
JACKSONVILLE, AR 72076

C. W. Stapp Sportswear
MOORE, OK 73160

Dalon
TARZANA, CA 91356

Dance France
SANTA MONICA, CA 90405

Designer Sport, Inc.
CHATSWORTH, CA 91311

Doc's Sports
COLLEGE PARK, GA 30349-0338

Dolfin Corp.
SHILLINGTON, PA 19607

Ferrero Designs
DEPUE, IL 61322

Fireworks by Julie St. Anne
NASHVILLE, TN 37212

1st Fitness International
OCEANSIDE, CA 92054

Fitness Fashions
LOCUST VALLEY, NY 11560

Flextard
LOS ANGELES, CA 90064

Gateway Graphics
ST. LOUIS, MO 63118

General Nutrition Corp.
PITTSBURGH, PA 15222

Cathy George Designs
BURBANK, CA 91502

Vince Gironda
NORTH HOLLYWOOD, CA 91604

Nautilus Sports/Medical Industries, Inc.
DELAND, FL 32720

Danny Padilla
SANTA MONICA, CA 90406

Bob Paris Fashions
LOS ANGELES, CA 90046

Performance Plus Sports Products
ORANGE, CA 92667

Pitt Barbell & Healthfood Corp.
PITTSBURGH, PA 15235

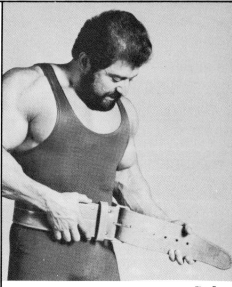

Fig. 5

Arnold Schwarzenegger
SANTA MONICA, CA 90406

Larry Scott
NORTH SALT LAKE, UT 84054

Scrub Duds
CHESHIRE, CT 05410

Sheritha Enterprises
BALTIMORE, MD 21214

Softouch Co., Inc.
HOLLYWOOD, FL 33021

Mandy Tanny
WOODLAND HILLS, CA 91365

Tickets of California
LOS ANGELES, CA 90007

Titan Bodybuilding, Inc.
JACKSONVILLE, FL 32205

Travolta by Carushka
NORTH HOLLYWOOD, CA 91605

Venus Bodywear Ltd.
JACKSONVILLE BEACH, FL 32250

Casey Viator
NIWOT, CO 80544

Viking Gym, Inc.
BROOKLYN CENTER, MN 55429

VIM
CUYAHOGA FALLS, OH 44223

Weider Health and Fitness, Inc.
WOODLAND HILLS, CA 91367

Weightlifter's Warehouse
LAKEWOOD, CA 90713

The Weight Room
LOS ANGELES, CA 90009

Woman to Woman
EDEN PRAIRIE, MN 55344

Work Out
BOONTON, NJ 07005

World Gym
SANTA MONICA, CA 90405

York Barbell Co., Inc.
YORK, PA 17405

Frank Zane
SANTA MONICA, CA 90406

Fig. 3

Gold's Gym
VENICE, CA 90291

Inzer Power Shirts
LONGVIEW, TX 75606

Iron Man's Gym
OCEANSIDE, CA 92054

Lisa Lyon
SANTA MONICA, CA 90406

Malepak
ATLANTA, GA 30349

Marathon Distributing Co.
PALOS VERDES ESTATES, CA 90274

McCain Productions
AUSTIN, TX 78704

Rachel McLish
SANTA MONICA, CA 90406

Mike Mentzer
DELAND, FL 32720

Jim Michaels Art Co.
PALM HARBOR, FL 33563

Mike Minor Enterprises
NACOGDOCHES, TX 75961

Mojo Manor Studios
SYRACUSE, NY 13224

Muscle Shorts
SANTA MONICA, CA 90405

National Sports Warehouse
BALTIMORE, MD 21221

Tom Platz, Inc.
SANTA MONICA, CA 90406

Nancy Pollak
NEW YORK, NY 10024

Powerhouse Gym
HIGHLAND PARK, MI 48203

Powers Gym
FT. WALTON BEACH, FL 32548

Pro Gym Fitness Center
ALBUQUERQUE, NM 87123

Rain Beau
SAN FRANCISCO, CA 94107

Ripley Custom Shirtmakers
NEW ORLEANS, LA 70119

Robby Robinson
VENICE, CA 90291

San Carlos Exercise Equipment Co.
SAN CARLOS, CA 94070

Fig. 4

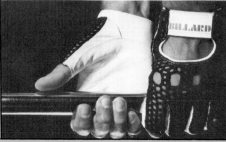

COMPUTERIZED NUTRITIONAL AND DIETARY ANALYSIS*

*See "Nutritional Guides and Consultants"

Mike Benton
AUSTIN, TX 78758

Nutri-Data, Inc.
MIAMI, FL 33116

COOKBOOKS*

*See "Foods"

Bodybuilder's Cookbook
QUINBY, SC 29501

Body Transformation
STOCKTON, CA 95209

Country Life Farm
NEWTON, NJ 07860

Healthy Ventures
ANCHORAGE, AK 99503

L & S Research
TOMS RIVER, NJ 08753-0550

V. Moon
OCEANSIDE, CA 92054

Simply Healthy Products
SEABROOK, TX 77586

DMSO*

*See "Muscle Creams and Rubs"

Arbol
ATLANTA, GA 30362

Crain Power-Plus
SHAWNEE, OK 74801

Doc's Sports
COLLEGE PARK, GA 30349-0338

Ernie and Diane Frantz Health Studio
AURORA, IL 60504

Mike MacDonald Systems
DULUTH, MN 55802

Nutri Biotics
SANTA CRUZ, CA 95062

Omni-Gym Products
PHOENIX, AZ 85069

V. V., Inc.
PORTLAND, OR 97232

Fig. 6

ENTERTAINMENT

Ken Passariello
ORANGE, CT 06477

SHE-BEAST by Pillow
VENICE, CA 90294

Russ Testo
TROY, NY 12180

Mike Torchia
HAWTHORNE, NY 10572

EQUIPMENT*

*The term *equipment* generally refers to the following:
abdominal boards, barbell plates, barbells and dumbbells, bars, benches, cables, collars, dipping and chinning bars, dumbbell racks, machines (abdominal, bicep curl, chest press, deadlift, deltoid, forearm, hack, hip flexor, lat, leg curl, leg extension, leg press, neck, pullover, shoulder press, standing and seated calf, thigh-knee, triceps), Olympic plates, pec decks, plate racks, power racks, pulleys, Roman chairs, slant boards, squat stands/racks, T-bar rowers.

BUILD YOUR OWN

Concepts Unlimited
WORCESTER, MA 01601

Design Products
BAKERSFIELD, CA 93389

Jabel Products
BEVERLY HILLS, CA 90210

L. E. Jacobson
SEDRO WOOLLEY, WA 98284

C. Miller
FT. LAUDERDALE, FL 33302-1234

Omnibod System
BISBEE, AZ 85603

T.A.F. Enterprises, Inc.
PALOS HEIGHTS, IL 60463

Vienna Health Products
VIENNA, OH 44473

MANUFACTURED

AMEREC CORP.
BELLEVUE, WA 98009

AMF American
JEFFERSON, IA 50129

Atlantic Fitness Products
GLEN BURNIE, MD 21061

Clarence Bass RIPPED Enterprises
ALBUQUERQUE, NM 87108

Fig. 8

Berry's Barbell and Equipment Co.
COLUMBUS, OH 43205

Billard Barbell Co.
READING, PA 19602

Body Culture Equipment Co.
ALLIANCE, NE 69301

Body Exercise Equipment
TOPEKA, KS 66611

Body Masters Sports Industry, Inc.
RAYNE, LA 70578

Fig. 7

Brad's Gym
ACUSHNET, MA 02743

Buckeye Barbell
POWELL, OH 43065

Dick Burke's Mail Order Co.
OKLAHOMA CITY, OK 73101

The Caines Co.
GREER, SC 29652

Frank Calta's Super Fitness
TAMPA, FL 33617

Campbell Enterprises
BURLINGTON, VT 05402

Carolina Fitness Equipment
CHARLOTTE, NC 28234

Champion Barbell Manufacturing Div.
ARLINGTON, TX 76010

Clarendex Corp.
CATAUMET, MA 02534

Corbin-Gentry, Inc.
SOMERSVILLE, CT 06072

Joe Corsi Fitness Equipment Co.
HAYWARD, CA 94541

Fig. 9

Crain Power-Plus
SHAWNEE, OK 74801

Custom Gym Equipment
SINKING SPRING, PA 19608

Cybex
RONKONKOMA, NY 11779

Dax Fitness Industries
PHOENIX, AZ 85009

Decathlon Exercise Equipment Co.
ST. PAUL, MN 55102

A. W. Diciolla, Jr., Co.
CLEVELAND, OH 44102

Diversified Products Corp.
OPELIKA, AL 36802

DLC Fabricating Co., Inc.
ST. LOUIS, MO 63110

Donkey Raise Machine
APOPKA, FL 32703

Fig. 10

Dynamics Health Equipment Manufacturing Co., Inc.
SOUTH HOUSTON, TX 77587

East Coast Body Building
FARMINGDALE, NY 11735

Edward, Gregory, Leigh
SEATTLE, WA 98124

Elmo's Exercise Equipment
EVERGREEN PARK, IL 60642

1st Fitness International
OCEANSIDE, CA 92054

Fitness America
COSTA MESA, CA 92627

Fitness Factory
EDISON, NJ 08818

Fitness Gym Systems, Inc.
SANTA PAULA, CA 93060

Fitness Industries, Inc.
PHOENIX, AZ 85069

Fitness & Nutrition Center, Inc.
NORTH MIAMI BEACH, FL 33160

Flex Gym Equipment
ORANGE, CA 92667

Fraco, Inc.
MIDDLETOWN, IN 47356

Free Weight Systems, Inc.
BUTTE, MT 59701

Future Equipment Co., Inc.
CLEARWATER, FL 33515

General Nutrition Corp.
PITTSBURGH, PA 15222

Johnny Gibson's Health and Gym Equipment
TUCSON, AZ 85701

Goliath Gym Equipment
SANTA ANA, CA 92703

Good Sports
PITTSBURGH, PA 15224

Green Valley Gym Equipment
CRESTON, IA 50801

Greenville Health Club
GREENVILLE, SC 29609

Hastings Barbell Co.
HASTINGS, MI 49058

High-Tech Fitness, Inc.
LOS ANGELES, CA 90069

High-Tech Tools, Inc.
COLUMBIA, MD 21045

Hoggan Health Equipment
SALT LAKE CITY, UT 84107

Howard's Equipment Co.
FOUNTAIN VALLEY, CA 92708

Huffy Corp.
MILWAUKEE, WI 53207

Hydra-Gym Athletics, Inc.
BELTON, TX 76513

Inertia Dynamics Corp.
PHOENIX, AZ 85012

Irmo Sports
COLUMBIA, SC 29210

Iron Co.
SAN DIEGO, CA 92110

Iron Man Magazine
ALLIANCE, NE 69301

Jubinville Weight Exercising Equipment
HOLYOKE, MA 01040

Keiser Sports Health Equipment
FRESNO, CA 93706

Kellogg, Inc.
DACUNO, CO 80514

K & K Arm Strong Fitness Equipment
VINELAND, NJ 08360

Kreis Sports, Inc.
NASHVILLE, TN 37212

Douglas James Leger
LEOMINSTER, MA 01453

Lifeline Production and Marketing, Inc.
MADISON, WI 53715

Bill Lopez Gym Equipment
CARSON, CA 90745

Dan Lurie Barbell Co., Inc.
SPRINGFIELD GARDENS, NY 11413

Fig. 11

Fig. 12

Lyons Health & Fitness
GLENDALE, CA 91203

Mac Barbell Equipment
GRAND PRAIRIE, TX 75050

Mike MacDonald Systems
DULUTH, MN 55802

Magnum Exercise Equipment, Inc.
AUSTIN, TX 78758

Malepak
ATLANTA, GA 30349

Joe Marino's Gym Equipment Co.
RIDGEWOOD, NJ 07451

Mav-Rik
LOS ANGELES, CA 90065

Jim Moore's World Gym
CHARLOTTE, NC 28210

Morden Weightlifting Products
LANSING, MI 48915

Steve Mott
COLUMBUS, OH 43214

Muscle Dynamics, Ltd.
CARSON, CA 90746

Fig. 13

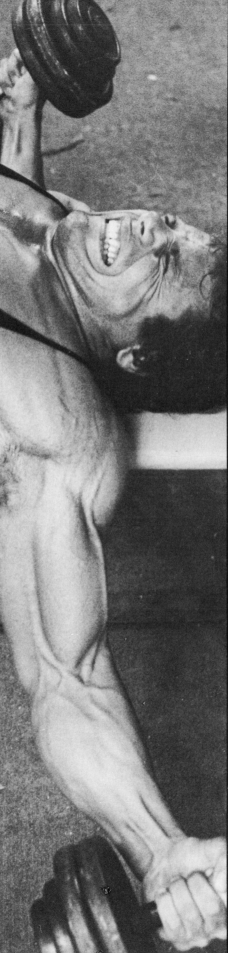

John Cardillo

Muscle Head
PITTSBURGH, PA 15205

MuscleMag International
BRAMPTON, ONTARIO, CANADA L6W 3M5

Muscle Mart
SAN DIEGO, CA 92111

Muscle World
CLAYTON, OK 74536

National Health Products
UTICA, NY 13502

National Sports Warehouse
BALTIMORE, MD 21221

Natural Health Foods and Barbell Center
YOUNGSTOWN, OH 44512

Natural Stuff, Inc.
ROCKAWAY, NJ 07866

Fig. 14

Nautilus Sports/Medical Industries, Inc.
DELAND, FL 32720

Northeast Power & Fitness
EASTON, PA 18042

Nu Life
ST. PETERSBURG, FL 33710

Nu-Life Fitness
FT. LAUDERDALE, FL 33329

Oakglade Industries
HOUSTON, TX 77071

O.E.M. Publishing
SANTA MONICA, CA 90405

Olympia Health & Exercise Products
LOS ANGELES, CA 90036

Olympic Health Equipment, Inc.
CINCINNATI, OH 45239

Nautilus

Mike Mentzer

Port-A-Gym Co.
LONGVIEW, WA 98632

PowerMax GymSystems
PHOENIX, AZ 85029

Power Place Products, Inc.
WEST LAFAYETTE, IN 47906

Power Plus
ARTESIA, MN 88210

Pow'r Body Building
MINNEAPOLIS, MN 55413

Pro-Line
PHOENIX, AZ 85969

Pro-tron
NEWPORT BEACH, CA 92660

Quality Designs
SUPERIOR, WI 54880

Queststar
SANTA MONICA, CA 90401

Rocky Mountain Gym Equipment Co., Inc.
COMMERCE CITY, CO 80022

Roseglen Ironworks
EL MONTE, CA 91732

Fig. 17

Omni-Gym Products
PHOENIX, AZ 85069

G. Pacillo Co., Inc.
BUFFALO, NY 14216

ParaBody, Inc.
Minneapolis, MN 55413

Paramount Fitness Equipment Corp.
LOS ANGELES, CA 90058

Tom Petro's Health Emporium
TRENTON, NJ 08611

Pitt Barbell & Healthfood Corp.
PITTSBURGH, PA 15235

Polaris
SAN DIEGO, CA 92110

Leonard Poole
APOPKA, FL 32703

Fig. 15

Standard Gym Equipment, Inc.
ROCHESTER, NY 14624

Stone Enterprises, Inc.
HANOVER, MA 02339

Streamline Gym & Fitness Equipment
EAST STROUDSBURG, PA 18301

Strength, Inc.
TWIN FALLS, ID 83301

Suncoast Exercise Equipment
PALM HARBOR, FL 33563

Superior Gym Equipment
IOWA CITY, IA 52240

TDS Barbell & Gym Equipment
BROOKLYN, NY 11222

Texas Imperial American, Inc.
TYLER, TX 75710

Fig. 19

Fig. 16

Royal House
OKLAHOMA CITY, OK 73101

R & R Industries
TARZANA, CA 91356

Saf-T-Gym
HEALDSBURG, CA 95448

Samco
NORTH RIDGEVILLE, OH 44039-0088

San Carlos Exercise Equipment Co.
SAN CARLOS, CA 94070

Shannon Publishing and Mail Order
DUBLIN, CA 94568

The Sharper Image
SAN FRANCISCO, CA 94111

Soloflex
HILLSBORO, OR 97123

Fig. 18

Fig. 20

T. K. Equipment
MT. VERNON, NY 10550

Total Gym, Inc.
SAN DIEGO, CA 92111

Train Right Fitness Center
HINGHAM, MA 02043

Ultimate Fitness Enterprises
BUENA VISTA, CO 81211

United Food & Fitness, Inc.
BRIARCLIFF MANOR, NY 19510

Universal Fitness Products
PLAINVIEW, NY 11803

Universal Gym Equipment, Inc.
CEDAR RAPIDS, IA 52406

Valley Machine Shop
FARMINGTON, NM 87401

Viking Barbell Co. & Health Club
BELLEVILLE, NJ 07109

Wallingford Barbell Co.
WALLINGFORD, CT 06492

Russ Warner Exercise Equipment Co.
SAN JOSE, CA 95126

Wate-Man Sales, Inc.
LIVONIA, MI 48152

Weider Health and Fitness, Inc.
WOODLAND HILLS, CA 91367

World Barbell & Healthfoods
UNIONTOWN, PA 15401

World of Health
ALHAMBRA, CA 91801

Worldwide Gym Equipment
PHOENIX, AZ 85069

York Barbell Co., Inc.
YORK, PA 17405

FITNESS/EXERCISE CONSULTANTS*

*See "Bodybuilding Advice and Consultants" and "Personalized Training Programs"

D. Ann Browne
RANDALLSTOWN, MD 21133

Execs, Inc.
NORTHRIDGE, CA 91326

Randy Morris
AKRON, OH 44320

Mike Torchia
HAWTHORNE, NY 10572

FLOORING

Atlantic Fitness Products
GLEN BURNIE, MD 21061

Muscle Mart
SAN DIEGO, CA 92111

Pawling Rubber
PAWLING, NY 12564

RCM
ANOKA, MN 55303

Rubber Products
TAMPA, FL 33614

Universal Fitness Products
PLAINVIEW, NY 11803

Universal Gym Equipment, Inc.
CEDAR RAPIDS, IA 52406

FLOTATION TANKS

Float to Relax, Inc.
LAKEWOOD, CO 80214

Oasis Relaxation Tank Co., Inc.
HOUSTON, TX 77098

Fig. 21

FOODS*
See "Cookbooks"

R. J.'s Kitchen
WORTH, IL 60482

Royal American Food Co.
BLUE SPRINGS, MO 64015

SAN
IRWIN, PA 15642

Stroud's Lifeline
CARLSBAD, CA 92008

Superior Health Studios for Men & Women
TAMPA, FL 33612

T & C Health Foods
TOPEKA, KS 66605

T. R. Enterprises
KATY, TX 77449

World Barbell & Healthfoods
UNIONTOWN, PA 15401

York Barbell Co., Inc.
YORK, PA 17405

Fig. 23

Fig. 22

GLANDULARS*
See "Steroid Substitutes"

Alt Enterprises
LOS ANGELES, CA 90049

Andy Alvardo
MODESTO, CA 95354

Body World Enterprises
LAUREL, MD 20708-0644

Bonilla
BEVERLY HILLS, CA 90211

Bricker Labs
VALLEY CENTER, CA 92082

Charles & Associates
PITTSBURGH, PA 15235

Colonna Health Products, Inc.
NORFOLK, VA 23523

Conan Research Corp.
MACEDONIA, OH 44056

Doug's Gym & Health Studio
BISMARCK, ND 58502

Dynakaz
AUBURN, AL 36830

1st Fitness International
OCEANSIDE, CA 92054

Mike MacDonald Systems
DULUTH, MN 55802

Marathon Nutrition, c/o Marathon Distributing Co.
PALOS VERDES ESTATES, CA 90274

National Health Products
UTICA, NY 13502

North American Competitions International
COLUMBUS, OH 43223

Nutri-Tech
AKRON, OH 44319

Nutritional Factors
CONCORD, CA 94524

Search Labs
NILES, IL 60648

Shannon Publishing and Mail Order
DUBLIN, CA 94568

Sterling Labs
VALLEY CENTER, CA 92082

Strength Source Unlimited
LOS ANGELES, CA 90041

Train Right Fitness Center
HINGHAM, MA 02043

Universal Supplements Corp.
LINDEN, NJ 07036

Venus Food Supplements
THOUSAND OAKS, CA 91360

Weider Health and Fitness, Inc.
WOODLAND HILLS, CA 91367

Weightlifter's Warehouse
LAKEWOOD, CA 90713

Wheeler's Fitness and Strength Enterprises
BAKERSFIELD, CA 93302

Fig. 24

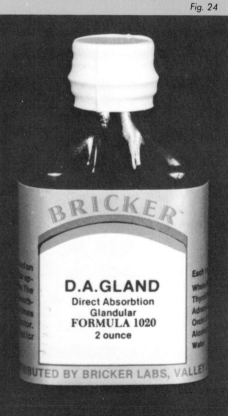

GYM FRANCHISES

Fitness & Nutrition Center, Inc.
NORTH MIAMI BEACH, FL 33160

Gold's Gym
VENICE, CA 90291

Superbodies Fitness Centers
COSTA MESA, CA 92627

Joe Gold

HEALTH-CLUB CONSULTANTS

D. Ann Browne
RANDALLSTOWN, MD 21133

Fitness Marketing Co.
COLUMBUS, OH 43215

Savage Enterprises
CASCADE, MD 21719

Fig. 25

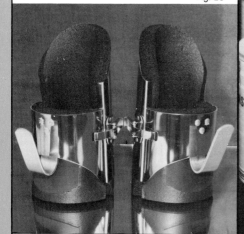

INVERSION EQUIPMENT

Doc's Sports
COLLEGE PARK, GA 30349-0338

D & S Manufacturing & Marketing, Inc.
LITITZ, PA 17543

1st Fitness International
OCEANSIDE, CA 92054

Fitness Factory
EDISON, NJ 08818

General Nutrition Corp.
PITTSBURGH, PA 15222

Gravity Research
DEL MAR, CA 92014

Gravity Sciences
LOS ANGELES, CA 90064

H. W. E., Inc.
LOS ANGELES, CA 90028

Inversion Therapy Equipment
FREMONT, CA 94539

Life Style Products
MOUNTAIN VIEW, CA 94043

Dan Lurie Barbell Co., Inc.
SPRINGFIELD GARDENS, NY 11413

Muscle Mart
SAN DIEGO, CA 92111

National Sports Warehouse
BALTIMORE, MD 21221

New Health Marketing
MINNEAPOLIS, MN 55423

Tom Petro's Health Emporium
TRENTON, NY 08611

San Carlos Exercise Equipment Co.
SAN CARLOS, CA 94070

Skyhook
ENGLEWOOD, CO 80155

SKY Products
GARDEN GROVE, CA 92643

Sky's the Limit
SUMNER, WA 98390

Spartacus Fitness Systems
LOS ANGELES, CA 90004

Suntron Corp.
FT. WAYNE, IN 46802

Universal Fitness Products
PLAINVIEW, NY 11803

JEWELRY*

*See "Patches, Decals, and Pins"

Gershon Jewelers
CEDARHURST, NY 11516

Golden Eagle Jewelry Co.
ALBUQUERQUE, NM 87108

Jewelry by Roger
WHITTIER, CA 90609

Masterworks
RENO, NV 89509

Ooh La La!, Inc.
MONTEREY PARK, CA 91754

P. J. Jewelry
SUNNYSIDE, NY 11104

Fig. 26

Pro Gym Fitness Center
ALBUQUERQUE, NM 87123

MILK PROTEIN

G & S Distributors
WASHINGTON, IN 47501

MusclePower International USA
AZUSA, CA 91702

MUSCLE CREAMS AND RUBS*

*See "DMSO"

Adria Labs, Inc.
COLUMBUS, OH 43215

Muscle Dynamics, Ltd.
CARSON, CA 90746

Muscle Mart
SAN DIEGO, CA 92111

National Sports Warehouse
BALTIMORE, MD 21221

Sports Research Corp.
SAN PEDRO, CA 90731

Weider Health and Fitness, Inc.
WOODLAND HILLS, CA 91367

York Barbell Co., Inc.
YORK, PA 17405

NUTRITIONAL GUIDES AND CONSULTANTS*

*See "Computerized Nutritional and Dietary Analysis"

Body Mechanics, Ltd.
RICHMOND, VA 23226

D. Ann Browne
RANDALLSTOWN, MD 21133

Crain Power-Plus
SHAWNEE, OK 74801

EARN Fitness
IMPERIAL, PA 15126

Fenton Products
SILVER SPRING, MD 20910

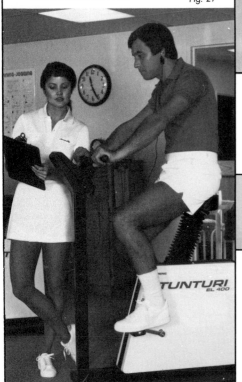

Fig. 27

Fitness and Physiology
AMHERST, MA 01004

Fitness Library
ST. ANN, MO 63074

Jeff King
SPRINGFIELD, MA 01108

Ron Kosloff
DETROIT, MI 48205

Natural Source Products, Inc.
CANOGA PARK, CA 91304

Nutritional Charts
PORTLAND, OR 97230

Triple L Enterprises
ROSEMEAD, CA 91770

Vita Chart
SOUTHAMPTON, PA 18966

Fig. 28

PATCHES, DECALS, AND PINS*

*See "Jewelry"

United States Weightlifting Federation, Inc.
COLORADO SPRINGS, CO 80909

Weider Health and Fitness, Inc.
WOODLAND HILLS, CA 91367

PERSONALIZED TRAINING PROGRAMS

Samir Bannout
SANTA MONICA, CA 90406

Ken Broussard
NEW IBERIA, LA 70560

D. Ann Browne
RANDALLSTOWN, MD 21133

Franco Columbu
SANTA MONICA, CA 90406

Steve Davis Fitness Center
NEWHALL, CA 91321

Vince Gironda
NORTH HOLLYWOOD, CA 91604

Bill Grant Enterprises
SANTA MONICA, CA 90406

Dave Groscup
BIRDSBORO, PA 19508

R. Hubbard
SCOTCH PLAINS, NJ 07076-0311

Iron Man's Gym
OCEANSIDE, CA 92054

Jeff King
SPRINGFIELD, MA 01108

J. F. Loccisano
LANCASTER, PA 17603

Lisa Lyon
SANTA MONICA, CA 90406

Joe Miller
COLLEGE PARK, MD 20783

Randy Morris
AKRON, OH 44320

Danny Padilla
SANTA MONICA, CA 90406

Robby Robinson
VENICE, CA 90291

Larry Scott
NORTH SALT LAKE, UT 84054

Strength Source Unlimited
LOS ANGELES, CA 90041

Dennis Tinerino
NORTHRIDGE, CA 91328

Mike Torchia
HAWTHORNE, NY 10572

Venus Food Supplements
THOUSAND OAKS, CA 91360

Casey Viator
NIWOT, CO 80544

Claudia Cornell Wilbourn
SANTA MONICA, CA 90406

PHOTOS

George Aiken Photography
DEL MAR, CA 92014

John Balik
SANTA MONICA, CA 90406

Samir Bannout
SANTA MONICA, CA 90406

Tim Belknap
SANTA MONICA, CA 90406

Andreas Cahling Enterprises
VENICE, CA 90294

K. K. Clark
NEW YORK, NY 10019

Boyer Coe
HUNTINGTON BEACH, CA 92646

Crain Power-Plus
SHAWNEE, OK 74801

Steve Davis Fitness Center
NEWHALL, CA 91321

Chris Dickerson, Inc.
VENICE, CA 90291

Lou Ferrigno
SANTA MONICA, CA 90406

**Ernie and Diane Frantz
Health Studio**
AURORA, IL 60505

Bill Grant Enterprises
SANTA MONICA, CA 90406

Orrin J. Heller
NORWALK, CA 90650

Jeff King
SPRINGFIELD, MA 01108

LIVE
FULLERTON, CA 92634

Lisa Lyon
SANTA MONICA, CA 90406

Rachel McLish
SANTA MONICA, CA 90406

Mike Mentzer
DELAND, FL 32720

William Moore
TUSCALOOSA, AL 35402-0732

Mr. Universe Enterprises
OAK FOREST, IL 60452

Miss Olympia
MT. HOLLY, NJ 08060

Danny Padilla
SANTA MONICA, CA 90406

Tom Platz, Inc.
SANTA MONICA, CA 90406

Power By Cash
DAYTON, OH 45420

Robby Robinson
VENICE, CA 90291

Arnold Schwarzenegger
SANTA MONICA, CA 90406

Larry Scott
NORTH SALT LAKE, UT 84054

SHE-BEAST by Pillow
VENICE, CA 90294

Mandy Tanny
WOODLAND HILLS, CA 91365

Dennis Tinerino
NORTHRIDGE, CA 91328

Alan Tuck Associates
UNION, NJ 07083

Casey Viator
NIWOT, CO 80544

Claudia Cornell Wilbourn
SANTA MONICA, CA 90406

W.S.P.
HOHOKUS, NJ 07423

Frank Zane
SANTA MONICA, CA 90406

PHYSIQUE PHOTOGRAPHY

Adonis Productions
JOPPA, MD 21085

Amelia Lavin
BALTIMORE, MD 21201

Matt
QUEENS, NY 11415

Richard Muldez
VIRGINIA BEACH, VA 23454

Kay King-Nealy
NEW YORK, NY 10010

Pro-Photo
MONTGOMERY, AL 36116

Paul Roberts
PLAINFIELD, NJ 07060

Kathy Tuite
CONCORD, CA 94524

POSING OIL/GEL

Hawaiian Resources
HONOLULU, HI 96816

Muscle Mart
SAN DIEGO, CA 92111

New Horizons
NEW YORK, NY 10016

POSING WEAR

Clarence Bass RIPPED Enterprises
ALBUQUERQUE, NM 87108

Andreas Cahling Enterprises
VENICE, CA 90294

Boyer Coe
HUNTINGTON BEACH, CA 92646

Steve Davis Fitness Center
NEWHALL, CA 91321

Chris Dickerson, Inc.
VENICE, CA 90291

Ferrero Designs
DEPUE, IL 61322

Lou Ferrigno
SANTA MONICA, CA 90406

LIVE
FULLERTON, CA 92634

Dan Lurie Barbell Co., Inc.
SPRINGFIELD GARDENS, NY 11413

Rachel McLish
SANTA MONICA, CA 90406

National Health Products
UTICA, NY 13502

Bill Pearl's Physical Fitness Architects
PASADENA, CA 91106

Physique Boutique
LAS VEGAS, NV 89112-1855

Tom Platz, Inc.
SANTA MONICA, CA 90406

Shannon Publishing and Mail Order
DUBLIN, CA 94568

Sheritha Enterprises
BALTIMORE, MD 21214

Dennis Tinerino
NORTHRIDGE, CA 91328

Titan Bodybuilding, Inc.
JACKSONVILLE, FL 32205

Ujena
LOS ANGELES, CA 90067

Weider Health and Fitness, Inc.
WOODLAND HILLS, CA 91367

York Barbell Co., Inc.
YORK, PA 17405

Danny Padilla

POSTERS

Achievement Plus
MARINA DEL REY, CA 90291

Andreas Cahling Enterprises
VENICE, CA 90294

K. K. Clark
NEW YORK, NY 10019

Franco Columbu
SANTA MONICA, CA 90406

Chris Dickerson, Inc.
VENICE, CA 90291

Lou Ferrigno
SANTA MONICA, CA 90406

K & D Co.
SALEM, MA 01971

Lisa Lyon
SANTA MONICA, CA 90406

Rachel McLish
SANTA MONICA, CA 90406

Mr. Universe Enterprises
OAK FOREST, IL 60452

Nautilus Sports/Medical Industries, Inc.
DELAND, FL 32720

Tom Platz, Inc.
SANTA MONICA, CA 90406

PS Products
MONUMENT, CO 80132

San Carlos Exercise Equipment Co.
SAN CARLOS, CA 94070

Arnold Schwarzenegger
SANTA MONICA, CA 90406

Larry Scott
NORTH SALT LAKE, UT 84054

George Butler

SHE-BEAST by Pillow
VENICE, CA 90294

Mandy Tanny
WOODLAND HILLS, CA 91367

The Voight Fitness Center
LOS ANGELES, CA 90069

Weider Health and Fitness, Inc.
WOODLAND HILLS, CA 91367

Claudia Cornell Wilbourn
SANTA MONICA, CA 90406

Frank Zane
SANTA MONICA, CA 90406

ROWING MACHINES

AMEREC Corp.
BELLEVUE, WA 98009

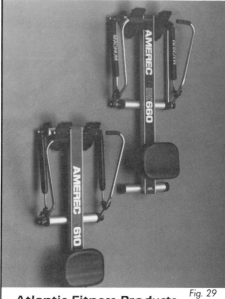

Fig. 29

Atlantic Fitness Products
GLEN BURNIE, MD 21061

Doc's Sports
COLLEGE PARK, GA 30349-0338

Edward, Gregory, Leigh
SEATTLE, WA 98124

General Nutrition Corp.
PITTSBURGH, PA 15222

Life Style Products
MOUNTAIN VIEW, CA 94043

National Sports Warehouse
BALTIMORE, MD 21221

Natural Health Foods and Barbell Center
YOUNGSTOWN, OH 44512

Pitt Barbell & Healthfood Corp.
PITTSBURGH, PA 15235

Rock & Row
CORRYTON, TN 37721

San Carlos Exercise Equipment Co.
SAN CARLOS, CA 94070

The Sharper Image
SAN FRANCISCO, CA 94111

Universal Fitness Products
PLAINVIEW, NY 11803

Weider Health and Fitness, Inc.
WOODLAND HILLS, CA 91367

SCHOOLS AND LEARNING CENTERS

Fitness Institute of Hypnosis
SANTA MONICA, CA 90403

Great Lakes Sports Academy
MARQUETTE, MI 49855

Pacific Western University
ENCINO, CA 91436

The School of Natural Bodybuilding
RICHMOND, VA 23231

United States Sports Academy
MOBILE, AL 36608

Frank Zane's Zane Haven
PALM SPRINGS, CA 92263

SEMINARS*

*Check to see if your favorite bodybuilder is listed here (see The Directory section in the Appendix). Most give seminars.

Samir Bannout
SANTA MONICA, CA 90406

Tim Belknap
SANTA MONICA, CA 90406

Roger Callard
SANTA MONICA, CA 90406

Dave Draper

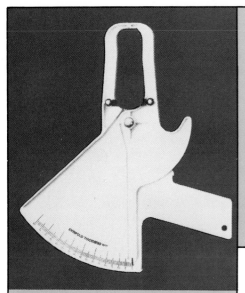

Fig. 30

Boyer Coe
HUNTINGTON BEACH, CA 92646

Rickey Dale Crain
SHAWNEE, OK 74801

Bill Grant Enterprises
SANTA MONICA, CA 90406

Jeff King
SPRINGFIELD, MA 01108

Lisa Lyon
SANTA MONICA, CA 90406

Danny Padilla
SANTA MONICA, CA 90406

Ken Passariello
ORANGE, CT 06477

Don Ross
VALLEJO, CA 94590

Dennis Tinerino
NORTHRIDGE, CA 91328

Casey Viator
NIWOT, CO 80544

Frank Zane
SANTA MONICA, CA 90406

SKIN CARE* AND HAIR CARE

*See "Tanning Equipment and Products"

Baxter of California
BEVERLY HILLS, CA 90211

Body Love Co.
PETALUMA, CA 94953

Derma-Research
HOUSTON, TX 77042

Peggy Guthridge
WICHITA, KS 67207

Ilona of Hungary
DENVER, CO 80206

Interface Products for Men
MARINA DEL REY, CA 90291

Gordon Lee Products
NEW YORK, NY 10021

Malepak
ATLANTA, GA 30349

Mill Creek Natural Products
ROLLING HILLS, CA 90274

Plus Products
IRVINE, CA 92714

Skin Control Systems, Inc.
BEVERLY HILLS, CA 90211

Jan Stuart Natural Skin Care Ltd.
NEW YORK, NY 10022

Weider Health and Fitness, Inc.
WOODLAND HILLS, CA 91367

Western Natural Products
SOUTH PASADENA, CA 91030

SKINFOLD CALIPERS

Creative Health Products
PLYMOUTH, MI 48170

Exercise Dynamics
BEMIDJI, MN 56601

Sweat, Inc.
CINCINNATI, OH 45201

STEROID SUBSTITUTES*

*See "Glandulars"

Conan Research Corp.
MACEDONIA, OH 44056

Fig. 31

J. A. Feliciano
FOUNTAIN VALLEY, CA 92708

Mike Hiebert
BETHANY, OK 73008

C. Miller
FT. LAUDERDALE, FL 33302-1234

National Health Products
UTICA, NY 13502

Nutri-Tech
AKRON, OH 44319

Nutritional Athletic Products
DAVIE, FL 33328

Samra Nutrition
SANTA MONICA, CA 90406

Universal Supplements Corp.
LINDEN, NJ 07036

Weider Health and Fitness, Inc.
WOODLAND HILLS, CA 91367

TANNING EQUIPMENT AND PRODUCTS

Bahama Tanning Products
FT. LAUDERDALE, FL 33301

Börlind of Germany
GRANTHAM, NH 03753

David Carter Products
VENICE, CA 90291

The Grow-Eery
PHILADELPHIA, PA 19151

Betty Kerr Enterprises
MARINA DEL REY, CA 90291

Mill Creek Natural Products
ROLLING HILLS, CA 90274

Nutrabiotics
CAPITOLA, CA 95010

Product Support
SAN DIEGO, CA 92122

S.C.A. Corp.
REDMOND, WA 98052

Silver Solarium
SAN FRANCISCO, CA 91403

Solana, Inc.
IRWINDALE, CA 91706

Sontegra
FT. LEE, NJ 07024

Suncorp.
SANTA CRUZ, NM 87567

Sunmaker, Inc.
FT. WAYNE, IN 46898

The SunTan People
ROCKVILLE, MD 20850

Tanning Hut, Inc.
ALBANY, NY 12205

Ultimate Aminos
SAN DIEGO, CA 92138-1886

York Barbell Co., Inc.
YORK, PA 17405

Fig. 32

TRAINING AIDS*

*The term *training aids* generally refers to the following:
ankle, vest, and wrist weights; arm blasters, backswings, barbell pads, bullworkers, cable springs, chalk, chest pulls, cycles, dipping belts, exercise charts, exercise wheels, gloves, hand grips, head straps, iron boots, iron claws, joggers, jump ropes, kettlebells, knee and wrist braces, lifting belts, lifting shoes, lifting suits, mats, power twisters, pulse meters, push-up bars, sports bags, strands, supporters, toning wheels, training straps, twist boards, waist trimmers, wraps, wrist rollers.

AMEREC Corp.
BELLEVUE, WA 98009

American Athletic Supply, Inc.
KNOXVILLE, TN 37901

American Exercise & Gym Equipment Co.
SOUTHFIELD, MI 48034

AMF American
JEFFERSON, IA 50129

AMF Voit, Inc.
SANTA ANA, CA 92702

A.R.P.-Rhombus
OAK FOREST, IL 60452

Athletic Fitness Co.
AUBURN, NY 13022

Atlantic Fitness Products
GLEN BURNIE, MD 21061

Clarence Bass RIPPED Enterprises
ALBUQUERQUE, NM 87108

Beacon Enterprises, Inc.
NEW YORK, NY 10001

Berry's Barbell and Equipment Co.
COLUMBUS, OH 43205

Billard Barbell Co.
READING, PA 19602

Blackmon Enterprises
WICHITA, KS 67213

Bob's Custom Lifting Belts
POMONA, CA 91766

Body Bar Systems
BRONX, NY 10460

Body Culture Equipment Co.
ALLIANCE, NE 69301

Bollinger Industries
IRVING, TX 75062

Mike Bridges Systems
ARLINGTON, TX 76011

Bristol Sports Corp.
BOHEMIA, NY 11716

Bill Bronk
CUSTER, WI 54423

D. Ann Browne
RANDALLSTOWN, MD 21133

David Campbell
NEW ROCHELLE, NY 10801

Ken Charles, Inc.
BROCKTON, MA 02403

Fig. 33

Charlton Publications, Inc.
DERBY, CT 06418

Franco Columbu
SANTA MONICA, CA 90406

Conejo Leathers
PT. HUENEME, CA 93014

CPC
MICHIGAN CITY, IN 46360

Crain Power-Plus
SHAWNEE, OK 74801

Cybex
RONKONKOMA, NY 11779

A. W. Diciolla, Jr., Co.
CLEVELAND, OH 44102

Chris Dickerson, Inc.
VENICE, CA 90291

The Di Mark Co.
MARINA DEL REY, CA 90295

Diversified Products Corp.
OPELIKA, AL 36802

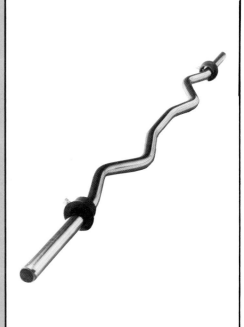

Fig. 34

Doc's Sports
COLLEGE PARK, GA 30349-0338

Dragonfly Enterprises
CLIMAX, MI 49034

Edward, Gregory, Leigh
SEATTLE, WA 98124

Elite Sales, Inc.
AUSTIN, TX 78764

Elmer's Weights, Inc.
LUBBOCK, TX 79490

Exercircle
GENEVA, IL 60134

Exercise Chart Series
BAKERSFIELD, CA 93304

Exerco, Inc.
PLEASANTVILLE, NY 10570

Lou Ferrigno
SANTA MONICA, CA 90406

Fig. 35

1st Fitness International
OCEANSIDE, CA 92054

Fitness Consultants & Supply
WICHITA FALLS, TX 76302

Fitness Factory
EDISON, NJ 08818

Fitness King
MINNEAPOLIS, MN 55411

Fitness & Nutrition Center, Inc.
NORTH MIAMI BEACH, FL 33160

Fitnus
BAKERSFIELD, CA 93304

Foothill Enterprises
SAN DIMAS, CA 91773

Fox Marketing
BLOOMINGTON, IL 61701

Ernie and Diane Frantz Health Studio
AURORA, IL 60504

Gainers
GARWOOD, NJ 07027

Fred Hatfield
VAN NUYS, CA 91406

Heavyhands
DES MOINES, IA 50306

Jim Hix
SPOKANE, WA 99213-3453

Hoggan Health Equipment
SALT LAKE CITY, UT 84107

Mark Horn
SOUTHFIELD, MI 48075

Improvement Products Corp.
NEW YORK, NY 10017

Irmo Sports
COLUMBIA, SC 29210

Iron Man **Magazine**
ALLIANCE, NE 69301

Jabel Products
BEVERLY HILLS, CA 90210

Jubinville Weight Exercising Equipment
HOLYOKE, MA 01040

Lifeline Production and Marketing, Inc.
MADISON, WI 53715

Life Style Products
MOUNTAIN VIEW, CA 94043

Little Grunt Productions
PORTLAND, OR 97205

Dan Lurie Barbell Co., Inc.
SPRINGFIELD GARDENS, NY 11413

MacLevy Products Corp.
ELMHURST, NY 11373

Marathon Distributing Co.
PALOS VERDES ESTATES, CA 90274

C. Miller
FT. LAUDERDALE, FL 33302-1234

Minitec Marketing, Inc.
CARSON, CA 90746

Muscle Mart
SAN DIEGO, CA 92111

The Muscle Shop
ARLINGTON, TX 76010

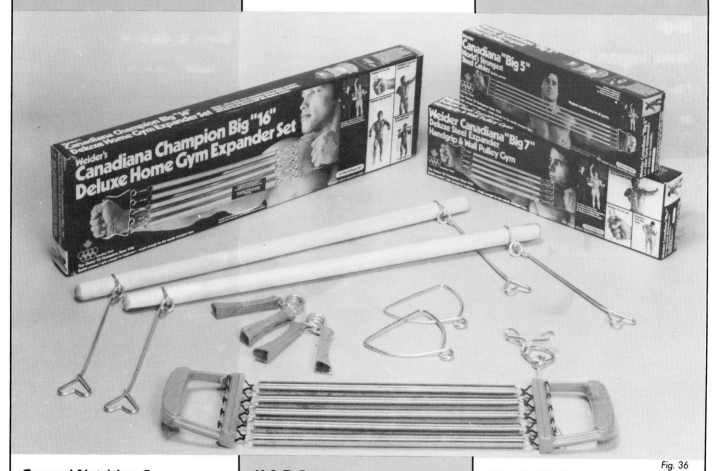

Fig. 36

General Nutrition Corp.
PITTSBURGH, PA 15222

Vince Gironda
NORTH HOLLYWOOD, CA 91604

Greenville Health Club
GREENVILLE, SC 29609

Hammel Training
EULESS, TX 76039

Hammer Fist
BELLMORE, NY 11710

K & D Co.
SALEM, MA 01971

Susan Koch
LITTLE SILVER, NJ 07739

Kuc's Total Fitness Systems
MOUNTAINTOP, PA 18707

Steve Lennard
MIAMI, FL 33129

Lifecycle, Inc.
IRVINE, CA 92714

Muscle World
CLAYTON, OK 74536

National Health Products
UTICA, NY 13502

National Sports Warehouse
BALTIMORE, MD 21221

Natural Health Foods and Barbell Center
YOUNGSTOWN, OH 44512

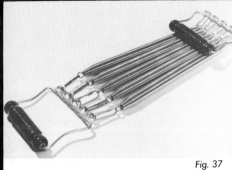

Fig. 37

Tom Petro's Health Emporium
TRENTON, NJ 08611

Pitt Barbell & Healthfood Corp.
PITTSBURGH, PA 15235

Power By Cash
DAYTON, OH 45420

Power Design
SEATTLE, WA 98111-1204

Eduardo Kuwak

Fig. 39

Natural Stuff, Inc.
ROCKAWAY, NJ 07866

Nutritional Athletic Products
DAVIE, FL 33328

Obertini Publishing Co.
EAST KANKAKEE, IL 60901

Olympia Health & Exercise Products
LOS ANGELES, CA 90036

Omni-Gym Products
PHOENIX, AZ 85069

Orion
ATLANTA, GA 30329

Ortho Support Wraps
NORCO, CA 91760

Pacifico Enterprises
DAYTON, OH 45414

Bill Pearl's Physical Fitness Architects
PASADENA, CA 91106

Fig. 38

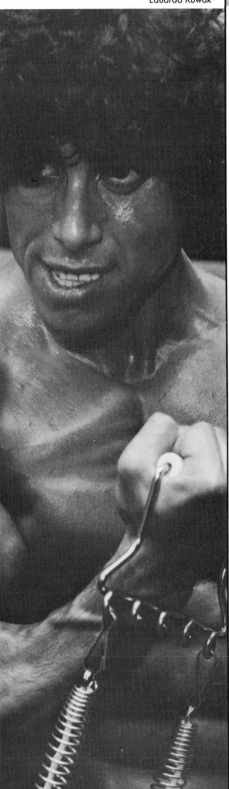

Power Place Products, Inc.
WEST LAFAYETTE, IN 47906

Product Support
SAN DIEGO, CA 92122

PS Co.
WELLESLEY, MA 02181

Quality Designs
SUPERIOR, WI 54880

Regal Enterprises
DALLAS, TX 75206-2908

Reid's Fitness Equipment
MARYSVILLE, MI 48040

Richards Medical Co.
MEMPHIS, TN 38116

L. Rolfe's Leather
NEWARK, DE 19711

Roseglen Ironworks
EL MONTE, CA 91732

San Carlos Exercise Equipment Co.
SAN CARLOS, CA 94070

Arnold Schwarzenegger
SANTA MONICA, CA 90406

Larry Scott
NORTH SALT LAKE, UT 84054

Shannon Publishing and Mail Order
DUBLIN, CA 94568

The Sharper Image
SAN FRANCISCO, CA 94111

Simmons Co.
CHATTANOOGA, TN 37404

Sports Conditioning Services
VAN NUYS, CA 91406

Sports Discount Center
SAN FRANCISCO, CA 94128

Strength Tech, Inc.
STILLWATER, OK 74076

Fig. 40

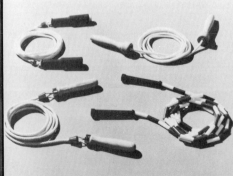

Strong-Lon of California
NORTHRIDGE, CA 91325

Sure Grips
DALLAS, TX 75235

Surgrip
MODESTO, CA 95354

Sweat, Inc.
CINCINNATI, OH 45201

Sword Enterprises
COLUMBUS, OH 43215

Mandy Tanny
WOODLAND HILLS, CA 91365

TDS Barbell & Gym Equipment
BROOKLYN, NY 11222

Titan Suits
CORPUS CHRISTI, TX 78412

Total Living Communications, Inc.
ISLE OF PALMS, SC 29451

Train Right Fitness Center
HINGHAM, MA 02043

United States Weightlifting Federation, Inc.
COLORADO SPRINGS, CO 80909

Universal Fitness Products
PLAINVIEW, NY 11803

Universal Gym Equipment, Inc.
CEDAR RAPIDS, IA 52406

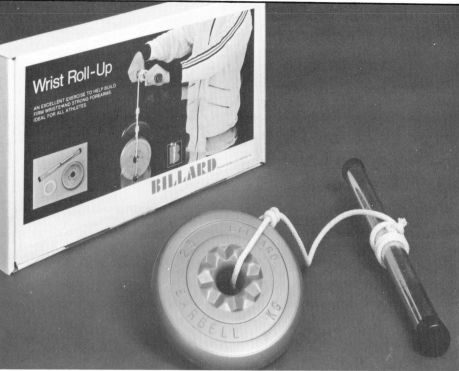

Fig. 42

Fig. 41

Venus Food Supplements
THOUSAND OAKS, CA 91360

Weider Health and Fitness, Inc.
WOODLAND HILLS, CA 91367

Weightlifter's Warehouse
LAKEWOOD, CA 90713

The Weight Room Co.
POCATELLO, ID 83201

Werling
VENICE, CA 90291

Betty Williams
CARTERSVILLE, GA 30120

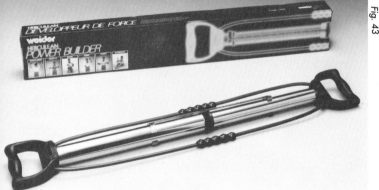

Fig. 43

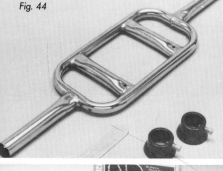

Fig. 44

Fig. 45

World of Health
ALHAMBRA, CA 91801

Wysong Medical, Inc.
MIDLAND, MI 48640

Fig. 46

York Barbell Co., Inc.
YORK, PA 17405

T-SHIRTS*

*See "Clothing"

Achievement Plus
MARINA DEL REY, CA 90291

Samir Bannout
SANTA MONICA, CA 90406

Clarence Bass RIPPED Enterprises
ALBUQUERQUE, NM 87108

Black's Health World
CLEVELAND, OH 44111

Body Building Unlimited
MOORE, OK 73153

Body Mechanics, Ltd.
RICHMOND, VA 23226

K. K. Clark
NEW YORK, NY 10019

Boyer Coe
HUNTINGTON BEACH, CA 92646

Colonna's Gym
CHESAPEAKE, VA 23323

Franco Columbu
SANTA MONICA, CA 90406

Crain Power-Plus
SHAWNEE, OK 74801

Custom Built
JACKSONVILLE, AR 72076

Steve Davis Fitness Center
NEWHALL, CA 91321

Dayton Unlimited, Inc.
CONCORD, CA 94524

Chris Dickerson, Inc.
VENICE, CA 90291

Dynakaz
AUBURN, AL 36830

Ferrero Designs
DEPUE, IL 61322

Fitness Consultants & Supply
WICHITA FALLS, TX 76302

Fitness Fashions
LOCUST VALLEY, NY 11560

General Nutrition Corp.
PITTSBURGH, PA 15222

Vince Gironda
NORTH HOLLYWOOD, CA 91604

The Good News Shirt Shop
REIDSVILLE, NC 27320

Bill Grant Enterprises
SANTA MONICA, CA 90406

Inzer Power Shirts
LONGVIEW, TX 75606

Jubinville Weight Exercising Equipment
HOLYOKE, MA 01040

K & D Co.
SALEM, MA 01971

Jeff King
SPRINGFIELD, MA 01108

Bob Krech-Art
WILLINGBORO, NJ 08046

LIVE
FULLERTON, CA 92634

Lisa Lyon
SANTA MONICA, CA 90406

Rachel McLish
SANTA MONICA, CA 90406

Mike Mentzer
DELAND, FL 32720

Jim Michaels Art Co.
PALM HARBOR, FL 33563

Mid-West T-Shirt Art
ARNOLD, MO 63010

Mojo Manar Studios
SYRACUSE, NY 13224

Mr. Universe Enterprises
OAK FOREST, IL 60452

MuscleMag International
BRAMPTON, ONTARIO, CANADA L6W 3M5

Muscle World
CLAYTON, OK 74536

National Health Products
UTICA, NY 13502

North American Competitions International
COLUMBUS, OH 43223

The North Light
BURBANK, CA 91505

Olympic Trophy and Awards Co.
CHICAGO, IL 60630

Omni-Gym Products
PHOENIX, AZ 85069

Danny Padilla
SANTA MONICA, CA 90406

Bill Pearl's Physical Fitness Architects
PASADENA, CA 91106

Tom Platz, Inc.
SANTA MONICA, CA 90406

C. L. Pohlmar
LEXINGTON PARK, MD 20653

Power By Cash
DAYTON, OH 45420

Powerhouse Gym
HIGHLAND PARK, MI 48203

The Power Pit
AIEA, HI 96701

Pro Gym Fitness Center
ALBUQUERQUE, NM 87123

Arnold Schwarzenegger
SANTA MONICA, CA 90406

Larry Scott
NORTH SALT LAKE, UT 84054

SHE-BEAST by Pillow
VENICE, CA 90294

S & J Studios
LATHRUP VILLAGE, MI 48076

Sportscreen
WHITELAND, IN 46184

Dennis Tinerino
NORTHRIDGE, CA 91328

Titan Bodybuilding, Inc.
JACKSONVILLE, FL 32205

United States Weightlifting Federation, Inc.
COLORADO SPRINGS, CO 80909

Vegebody
ST. PETERSBURG, FL 33733

Venus Food Supplements
THOUSAND OAKS, CA 91360

Casey Viator
NIWOT, CO 80544

The Weight Room
LOS ANGELES, CA 90009

World Gym
SANTA MONICA, CA 90405

York Barbell Co., Inc.
YORK, PA 17405

Frank Zane
SANTA MONICA, CA 90406

Bertil Fox

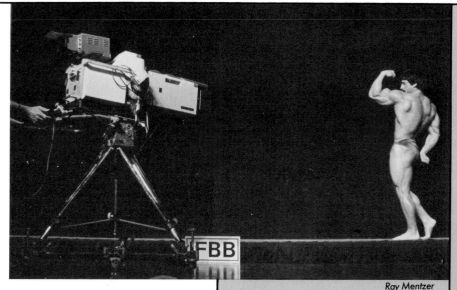

Ray Mentzer

VIDEOS (BETA/ VHS) AND FILMS*
*See "Cassette Tapes"

AB Video
NEW YORK, NY 10019

Mike Bridges Systems
ARLINGTON, TX 76011

Classic Films
LOS ANGELES, CA 90045

Franco Columbu
SANTA MONICA, CA 90406

Crain Power-Plus
SHAWNEE, OK 74801

Get Fit Video Series
MOUNTAIN VIEW, CA 94043

Orrin J. Heller
NORWALK, CA 90650

William F. Hinbern
FARMINGTON, MI 48024

Kreis Sports, Inc.
NASHVILLE, TN 37212

Mike Mentzer
DELAND, FL 32720

Omni-Gym Products
PHOENIX, AZ 85069

Pacifico Enterprises
DAYTON, OH 45414

Quantum Productions
ROMEO, MI 48065

Universal Fitness Products
PLAINVIEW, NY 11803

Universal Gym Equipment, Inc.
CEDAR RAPIDS, IA 52406

V.B.M.
NEW YORK, NY 10019

Video Action
JERSEY CITY, NJ 07307

Video Associates
LOS ANGELES, CA 90006

Video 4 Productions
WOODLAND HILLS, CA 91367

Weider Health and Fitness, Inc.
WOODLAND HILLS, CA 91367

W.S.P.
HOHOKUS, NJ 07423

VITAMINS, MINERALS, SUPPLEMENTS

Advanced Nutrition
HACIENDA HEIGHTS, CA 91745

All American Products
BEVERLY HILLS, CA 90210

Associated Products
COLD SPRING HARBOR, NY 11724

Ballena Valley Natural Food Supplements
RAMONA, CA 92065

Clarence Bass RIPPED Enterprises
ALBUQUERQUE, NM 87108

Bee Pollen from England
NEWTON LOWER FALLS, MA 02161

Jeffrey Bernard
NEW YORK, NY 10024

Beverly International
LAGUNA HILLS, CA 92653

Body Dynamics, Inc.
INDIANAPOLIS, IN 46201

Body World Enterprises
LAUREL, MD 20708-0644

Bonilla
BEVERLY HILLS, CA 90211

Bricker Labs
VALLEY CENTER, CA 92082

Mike Bridges Systems
ARLINGTON, TX 76011

Charlton Publications, Inc.
DERBY, CT 06418

Charles & Associates
PITTSBURGH, PA 15235

Clean Water Systems
EAU CLAIRE, WI 54701

Colonna Health Products, Inc.
NORFOLK, VA 23523

Conan Research Corp.
MACEDONIA, OH 44056

Bob Cornelius
VILLA RICA, GA 30180

Crain Power-Plus
SHAWNEE, OK 74801

Custom Gym Equipment
SINKING SPRING, PA 19608

Dayton Unlimited, Inc.
CONCORD, CA 94524

Chris Dickerson, Inc.
VENICE, CA 90291

Diet-Labs, Inc.
CLIMAX, NC 27233

Doc's Sports
COLLEGE PARK, GA 30349-0338

Doug's Gym & Health Studio
BISMARCK, ND 58502

Dynakaz
AUBURN, AL 36830

Earthrise Spirulina
BOULDER, CO 80306

Edgewood Enterprises
GROVE CITY, PA 16127

ELF Research
PAUILLO, HI 96776

Lou Ferrigno
SANTA MONICA, CA 90406

Fillmore Foods, Inc.
HAYWARD, CA 94545

1st Fitness International
OCEANSIDE, CA 92054

Fig. 47

Fitness & Nutrition Center, Inc.
NORTH MIAMI BEACH, FL 33160

FP Products
SADDLE BROOK, NJ 07662

Ernie and Diane Frantz Health Studio
AURORA, IL 60504

Futurebiotics, Inc.
W. CHESTERFIELD, NH 03466

Gainers
GARWOOD, NJ 07027

General Nutrition Corp.
PITTSBURGH, PA 15222

Vince Gironda
NORTH HOLLYWOOD, CA 91604 •

Golden Pro, Inc.
BIRMINGHAM, AL 35235

Gold's Gym
VENICE, CA 90291

Great Earth International, Inc.
SANTA ANA, CA 92702

Peggy Guthridge
WICHITA, KS 67207

Health from the Sun Products, Inc.
DOVER, MA 02030

Healthy 'N Fit
BRONX, NY 10461

High-Performance Products
LAWRENCEBURG, IN 47025

hiTech Sports & Fitness Products
SUNNYVALE, CA 94089

R. Hughes
ADA, OK 74820

Irmo Sports
COLUMBIA, SC 29210

Iron Man's Gym
OCEANSIDE, CA 92054

Betty Kerr Enterprises
MARINA DEL REY, CA 90291

Lancon's Vitamins
BETHLEHEM, PA 18016

Lederle Labs
WAYNE, NJ 07170

John LeGear
CHICAGO, IL 60606

Life Cycle Vitamin Co.
VAN NUYS, CA 91401

Light Force Spirulina Co.
BOULDER CREEK, CA 95006

Linquist
DAVIS, CA 95616

L & J Enterprises
CASPER, WY 82602

L & S Research
TOMS RIVER, NJ 08733-0550

Dan Lurie Barbell Co., Inc.
SPRINGFIELD GARDENS, NY 11413

Mike MacDonald Systems
DULUTH, MN 55802

Magenst Publications
NEW YORK, NY 10028

Marathon Nutrition, c/o Marathon Distributing Co.
PALOS VERDES ESTATES, CA 90274

E. H. McDowell
CHICAGO, IL 60606

C. Miller
FT. LAUDERDALE, FL 33302-1234

Mills Enterprises
MIDWAY CITY, CA 92655

Mr. Universe Enterprises
OAK FOREST, IL 60452

Muscle Factory
ROWAYTON, CT 06853

MuscleMag International
BRAMPTON, ONTARIO, CANADA L6W 3M5

MusclePower International USA
AZUSA, CA 91702

Natural Peak
SACRAMENTO, CA 95813

Natural Source Products, Inc.
CANOGA PARK, CA 91304

Natures Best
FT. WALTON BEACH, FL 32548

North American Competitions International
COLUMBUS, OH 43223

Nutrabiotics
CAPITOLA, CA 95010

Nutri-Foods
CANOGA PARK, CA 91303

Nutri-Research
FT. LAUDERDALE, FL 33307

Nutri-Source Nutritional Products
ORANGE, CA 92667

Nutri-Tech
AKRON, OH 44319

Fig. 48

Muscle-Up
JANESVILLE, WI 53547

Muscle World
CLAYTON, OK 74536

National Health Products
UTICA, NY 13502

Natural
MCMINNVILLE, OR 97128

Natural Health Foods and Barbell Center
YOUNGSTOWN, OH 44512

Naturally Vitamin Supplements, Inc.
SCOTTSDALE, AZ 85254

Nutritional Athletic Products
DAVIE, FL 33328

Omni-Gym Products
PHOENIX, AZ 85069

Ortho Molecular Nutrition International
MANCHESTER, NH 03108

Performance Plus Sports Products
ORANGE, CA 92667

Tom Petro's Health Emporium
TRENTON, NJ 08611

Plus Products
IRVINE, CA 92714

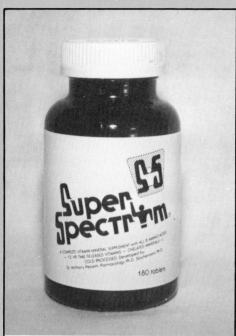

Fig. 49

Sports Medical Nutrition
CONCORD, CA 94518

Strength Source Unlimited
LOS ANGELES, CA 90041

Trace Minerals
CEDAR CITY, UT 84720

Train Right Fitness Center
HINGHAM, MA 02043

Ultimate Aminos
SAN DIEGO, CA 92138-1886

Unicorn Press
RESEDA, CA 91335

United Food & Fitness, Inc.
BRIARCLIFF MANOR, NY 19510

Universal Supplements Corp.
LINDEN, NJ 07036

Venus Food Supplements
THOUSAND OAKS, CA 91360

Viking Barbell Co. & Health Club
BELLEVILLE, NJ 07109

Fig. 51

Boyer Coe

Pro-Power Supplements
QUEENS VILLAGE, NY 11428

Rejuvenators
SANTA FE, NM 87501

Tim Roberts
KATY, TX 77449

Samra Nutrition
SANTA MONICA, CA 90406

San Carlos Exercise Equipment Co.
SAN CARLOS, CA 94070

Search Labs
NILES, IL 60648

S.G.S. Enterprises
RAMONA, CA 92065

Shake Recipes
CINCINNATI, OH 45275

Shannon Publishing and Mail Order
DUBLIN, CA 94568

Smith's
PHILADELPHIA, PA 19132

Sportscience Laboratories
ESSEX JUNCTION, VT 05452

VIOBIN Corp.
MONTICELLO, IL 61856

Vitacrown, Inc.
HICKSVILLE, NY 11801

Vita-Fresh Vitamin Co.
GARDEN GROVE, CA 92642

Vita-Life Products
STATEN ISLAND, NY 10314

Vita Pro Products Co.
DALLAS, TX 75228

Weider Health and Fitness, Inc.
WOODLAND HILLS, CA 91367

Western Natural Products
SOUTH PASADENA, CA 91030

Wheeler's Fitness and Strength Enterprises
BAKERSFIELD, CA 93302

Wilson Sports Vitamins
GARDEN GROVE, CA 92641

World Gym Supplements
REGO PARK, NY 11374

World of Health
ALHAMBRA, CA 91801

Wysong Medical, Inc.
MIDLAND, MI 48640

York Barbell Co., Inc.
YORK, PA 17405

Frank Zane
SANTA MONICA, CA 90406

WORKOUT RECORDS

P. C. House
ROCKAWAY, NJ 07866

Universal Fitness Products
PLAINVIEW, NY 11803

Universal Gym Equipment, Inc.
CEDAR RAPIDS, IA 52406

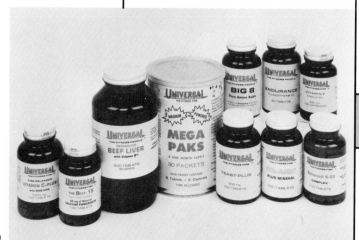

Fig. 50

MISCELLANEOUS

ADVERTISING/MODELING AGENCY

Body Dynamics, Inc.
INDIANAPOLIS, IN 46201

AEROBIC FITNESS MONITOR

BioTechnology, Inc.
MIAMI, FL 33166

AIR-IONIZATION EQUIPMENT

Zestron, Inc.
CAMPBELL, CA 95008

BELT BUCKLES

Collector's Casting
MORA, MN 55051

BICEP BOOSTER

Bicep Booster
TULSA, OK 74155

BLOOD-PRESSURE MONITOR

Sunshine Express
MARINA DEL REY, CA 90296

BODYBUILDING HOROSCOPE

BIO-SPORT
DOUGLAS, WY, 82633

BODY COMPOSITION KIT

J & B Albrights
ELKHORN, NE 68033

BODY FAT CALCULATORS AND TESTING

Katch's-FAT
ANN ARBOR, MI 48106

G. Potter
PACIFIC, MO 63069

CALENDARS

Ingenuts Enterprises
LOS ANGELES, CA 90049

Sterling Publishing Co.
NEW YORK, NY 10016

COMPUTERIZED FITNESS EVALUATION

Sport Medical Technology Corp.
CENTER MORICHES, NY 11934

Susie Green

COMPUTERIZED TRAINING PROGRAM

Bio Fitness
GUTTENBERG, NJ 07093

COMPUTERIZED WEIGHTLIFTING SCHEDULE

C. W. S.
SYLVESTER, GA 31791

ELECTRO-RELAXER HEALTH MASSAGER

Diamant Trading Co.
BROOKLYN, NY 11219

FAN CLUB

William Moore
TUSCALOOSA, AL 35402-0732

FITNESS DIARY

ORG Products
SEATTLE, WA 98168

Fig. 52

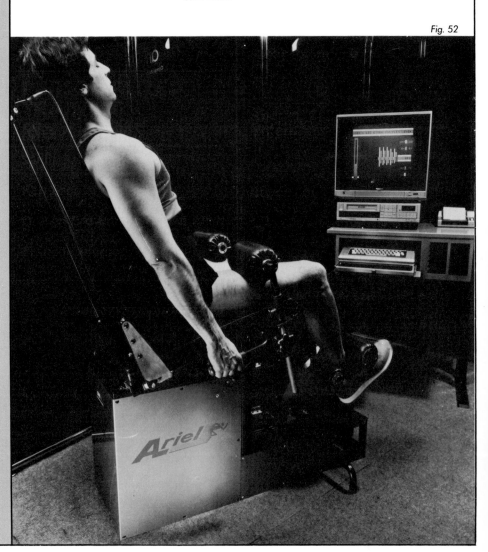

FITNESS MANAGEMENT SERVICE

Fitness Management Service
SNYDER, TX 79549

FITNESS PROGRAMS

Stroud's Lifeline
CARLSBAD, CA 92008

GYM MANUAL

Joe Mullen
DELAND, FL 32720

GYM PLANNING SERVICE

Polaris
SAN DIEGO, CA 92110

HEALTH-CLUB INSURANCE

Baldinger Insurance Group, Inc.
FT. LEE, NJ 07024

HEART-RATE MONITOR

Sunshine Express
MARINA DEL REY, CA 90296

HERBAL DIURETIC

Andy Alvarado
MODESTO, CA 95354

HYPNOTHERAPIST

Achievement Plus
MARINA DEL REY, CA 90291

INSPIRATIONAL LETTERS AND TAPES

K & D Co.
SALEM, MA 01971

Cindy Martin
NORTHBROOK, IL 60062

IRON MAN INDEX

Joe Roark's Musclesearch
ST. JOSEPH, IL 61873

MAILING LISTS

Alan Tuck Associates
UNION, NJ 07083

MIND-CONTROL COURSE

Dayton Unlimited, Inc.
CONCORD, CA 94524

MUSCLE GRAMS

Muscle-Gram
NEW YORK, NY 10128

Fig. 53

NEWSLETTER

John Balik
SANTA MONICA, CA 90406

NOVELTIES

McCain Productions
AUSTIN, TX 78704

Mighty Muscle Mugs
DETROIT, MI 48208

Pat's Mugs
ROSENHAYN, NJ 08352

United States Weightlifting Federation, Inc.
COLORADO SPRINGS, CO 80909

PLASTIC TRAVEL WEIGHTS

R. J. Bauer
DALLAS, TX 75220

POWERLIFTING ARTICLES

Tom McLaughlin
AUBURN, AL 36830

PROFESSIONAL SERVICES

United World Bodybuilders, Inc.
LOS ANGELES, CA 90069

PSYCHOLOGIST

David L. Albin, M.D., Inc.
LA HABRA HEIGHTS, CA 90631

SPORTS VACATIONS

Gartrell Travel Services
NEW ORLEANS, LA 70130

SQUAT-DEPTH INDICATOR

West Coast Fitness Center
SAN FRANCISCO, CA 94116

TESTOSTERONE

Adonis Herbs
LAWRENCE, KS 66044

TRAINING LOG

Personal Training
HAZELWOOD, MO 63042

TROPHIES/AWARDS/PLAQUES

Olympic Trophy and Awards Co.
CHICAGO, IL 60630

VITAMIN CHART

Vita Chart
SOUTHAMPTON, PA 18966

WATER FILTER/IONIZER

Body World Enterprises
LAUREL, MD 20708-0644

WILD HERBS & SPECIALTIES

Wild Herbs & Specialties
SALT LAKE CITY, UT 84110

WORKOUT MUSIC

Songgram
MERCERVILLE, NJ 08618

YEAST

Research Specialties
GREEN BAY, WI 54308

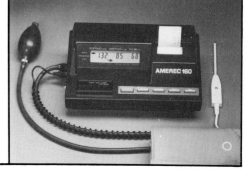

Fig. 54

Pete Grymkowski

Companies

There are hundreds of companies all over the United States that specialize in selling bodybuilding and weight-training items. Whatever you are looking for, the chances are good that there exists a company that sells it.

The following is an alphabetical listing of American companies and the products they sell. (A listing of foreign companies and their products starts on page 76.) Most would be quite willing to provide you with a free catalog, pamphlet, or price list upon request. More importantly, many companies have a toll-free number for your convenience, or at least a number you can call if letter writing is not convenient.

This is not an all-inclusive listing. With so many companies starting up or going out of business all of the time, it is practically impossible to present a completely up-to-date registry.

AB Video
355 W. 52ND ST., NEW YORK, NY 10019
212-246-2937/1-800-223-7930
videos of the 1982 and 1983 Miss Olympia contest

Achievement Plus
444 LINCOLN BLVD., SUITE 308, MARINA DEL REY, CA 90291
213-399-1963
motivational tapes (ultra-success series, motivation series, intensity series, women's physique-training series) by registered hypnotherapist Peter C. Siegel; posters, T-shirts—endorsed by Samir Bannout, Candy Csencsits, and David and Peter Paul (the Barbarians)

Adonis Herbs
PO BOX 174, LAWRENCE, KS 66044
testosterone

Adonis Productions, c/o Jim Wilmer
204 CHELL RD., JOPPA, MD 21085
301-679-7604
physique photography

Adria Labs, Inc.
PO BOX 2450, COLUMBUS, OH 43215
Myoflex—analgesic cream for aching muscles and joints

Advanced Nutrition
15865-B GALE AVE., SUITE 711, HACIENDA HEIGHTS, CA 91745
vitamins and supplements

Aerobic Wear, Inc.
25 DEPOT RD., HUNTINGTON STATION, NY 11746
516-673-1084/1-800-645-1001
exercise wear for women

George Aiken Photography
14029 MIRA MONTANA DR., DEL MAR, CA 92014
photo sets of the 1983 American Women's Bodybuilding Championships

David L. Albin, M.D., Inc.
2500 E. SKYLINE DR., LA HABRA HEIGHTS, CA 90631
treatment (in person and by mail) of emotional problems related to bodybuilding

All American Products
336 N. FOOTHILL RD., SUITE 2, BEVERLY HILLS, CA 90210
vitamins and supplements

Alt Enterprises
612 N. SEPULVEDA BLVD., SUITE 9, LOS ANGELES, CA 90049
glandular supplements

Andy Alvarado
419 THRASHER, MODESTO, CA 95354
herbs with hormones (testosterone, estrogen, and progesterone)

AMEREC Corp.
PO BOX 3825, BELLEVUE, WA 98009
206-643-1000/1-800-426-0858
ergometers, exercise bars, home cycles, joggers, pulse meters, rowing machines, saunas, steamers, vital-sign monitors, other health/leisure products—a supplier to Edward, Gregory, Leigh

American Athletic Supply, Inc.
PO BOX 15003, KNOXVILLE, TN 37901
615-521-1984
training aids

American Exercise & Gym Equipment Co.
29191 NORTHWESTERN HWY., SOUTHFIELD, MI 48034
313-358-0550
bar pads, lifting gloves

American Studio Arts
PO BOX 354, ONEONTA, NY 13820
body portraiture—original works of art produced from photos

AMF American, American Athletic Equipment Div.
200 AMERICAN AVE., JEFFERSON, IA 50129
515-386-3125/1-800-247-3978
equipment, Spectrum 2000 (a complete physical-fitness system which uses hydraulic cylinders), Computrum 900 (ergometric exerciser), chalk holders, floor plates, running harnesses, running cones, stopwatches, stretch mats, training manuals

AMF Voit, Inc.

PO BOX 958, SANTA ANA, CA 92702

3-, 5-, and 6-way home gyms; Jaguar 2000 (total body conditioner), chest pulls, conditioning belts and shorts, dumbbells, exercise bikes, exercise mats, exercise suits, gym bars, hand grips, lace weights, muscle exercisers, physical-fitness products, shoe weights, skip ropes, stretch-row body exercisers, striking-bag swivels, thigh conditioners, tone wheels; wrist, ankle, and hip weights

Karen Angelone

58-02 CENTRE ST., PO BOX 3211, RIDGEWOOD, NY 11385

clothes

Apparel Warehouse

18318 OXNARD ST., #1, TARZANA, CA 91356
213-344-3224

exercise wear for women

Appian Way Sculpture Studio

10 APPIAN WAY, JOHNSTON, RI 02919

sculpture

Arbol

PO BOX 47786-1, ATLANTA, GA 30362

DMSO liquid and cream

ARMS

PO BOX 873, FITCHBURG, MA 01420

training courses for arms

A.R.P.-Rhombus

15053 MISSION, OAK FOREST, IL 60452

training aids

Associated Products

PO BOX 484, COLD SPRING HARBOR, NY 11724

Albumix—100 percent egg-albumin protein

Athletes Additions

PO BOX 23, WOODMERE, NY 11598

jewelry

Fig. 55

Athletic Fitness Co.

PO BOX 7191, AUBURN, NY 13022
315-252-8190

training gloves with removable weights

Athtex

PO BOX 1886, 2922 REALTY CT., GASTONIA, NC 28052
1-800-438-8369

exercise wear for women

Atlantic Fitness Products

170-A PENROD CT., GLEN BURNIE, MD 21061
301-761-6246/301-261-2097

ankle straps, barrel rollers, bars and handles, belt vibrators, belts, cycles, equipment, gloves, gym tights, health walkers, joggers, lockers, rowing machines, saunas, scales, selector keys, steam cabinets, training manuals, treadmills, whirlpools, workout cards

Charles Atlas

49 W. 23RD ST., NEW YORK, NY 10010

dynamic-tension course

Bahama Tanning Products

201 NE 2ND ST., FT. LAUDERDALE, FL 33301

suntan pills (to use without or with sun), tanning lotions and oils

Baldinger Insurance Group, Inc.

PO BOX 1343, FT. LEE, NJ 07024
212-772-0212/201-944-3201/1-800-526-4688

insurance specialists for the health-club industry

John Balik

PO BOX 777, SANTA MONICA, CA 90406

newsletters, photos

Ballena Valley Natural Food Supplements

18616 LITTLEPAGE RD., RAMONA, CA 92065/619-789-7679

supplements

Samir Bannout

PO BOX 244, SANTA MONICA, CA 90406

personalized training programs, photos, seminars, tank tops, T-shirts

Barbell Sportswear

PO BOX 27097, JACKSONVILLE, FL 32205

clothing

Barely Legal

1012 BRIOSO DR., SUITE 105, COSTA MESA, CA 92627
714/645-3359

exercise wear for women

Clarence Bass RIPPED Enterprises

528 CHAMA NE, ALBUQUERQUE, NM 87108
505-266-5858

books, cassette tapes, gym equipment, lifting belts, personal advice, photos, posing trunks and suits, shorts, supplements, tank tops, towels, T-shirts

R. J. Bauer

2933 LADYBIRD LANE, DALLAS, TX 75220
214-353-9333

free weights, plastic travel weights

Baxter of California

345 S. ROBERTSON BLVD., BEVERLY HILLS, CA 90211

skin-care products

Baystar

110 PAINTERS MILL RD., OWINGS MILLS, MD 21117
301-363-4304

fingertip pulse monitors

Beacon Enterprises, Inc.

NEW YORK, NY 10001

sit-up bars

Bee Pollen from England

PO BOX 636, NEWTON LOWER FALLS, MA 02161

bee pollen (pods and cream), bekunis, efavit, energy drink, evening primrose oil, LSO-1 (skin ointment), nordisk, selenium-ACE

Tim Belknap

PO BOX 944, SANTA MONICA, CA 90406

exhibitions, seminars, training courses

Mike Benton

COLLEGE OF LIFE SCIENCE, AUSTIN, TX 78758

computerized dietary analysis

Fig. 56

Jeffrey Bernard
331 W. 89TH ST., #1B, NEW YORK, NY 10024
vitamins, minerals, supplements

Berry's Barbell and Equipment Co.
2995 E. LIVINGSTON AVE., COLUMBUS, OH 43205
614-236-8080
equipment, EZ-on collars, gloves, knee wraps, lifting belts, squat pads, training shoes

Beverly International
24991 CAROL LANE, LAGUNA HILLS, CA 92653
vitamins, minerals, supplements—endorsed by John Powers and Pam Meister

Bicep Booster
PO BOX 54861, TULSA, OK 74155
equipment

Big Boy Enterprises
PO BOX 26222, LOS ANGELES, CA 90026
tank tops

Billard Barbell Co.
208 CHESTNUT ST., READING, PA 19602
215-375-4333
ankle weights, chest expanders, equipment, gloves, hand grips, horseshoe sets, iron boots, pitching quoits, power twisters, sauna suits, shot puts, skip ropes, spat weights, triceps exercisers, wrist rollers, wrist weights

Bio Fitness
7004 BOULEVARD EAST, SUITE 15-K, GUTTENBERG, NJ 07093
computerized and individualized physical-training system for men called COSMOS, which includes: a 200-page manual, test analysis, four personal programs, and updates for three months

BIO SPORT
145 WINDRIVER DR., DOUGLAS, WY 82633
bodybuilding horoscopes

BioTechnology, Inc.
6924 NORTHWEST 46TH ST., MIAMI, FL 33166
305-592-6069/1-800-327-1033
computerized exercise equipment: The Coach (microcomputer that monitors heart rate during exercise)

Blackmon Enterprises
PO BOX 13311, WICHITA, KS 67213
316-263-0240
total fitness machine called Rug Rat for over 40 isotonic, isometric, and stretching exercises

Black's Health World
11934 LORAIN AVE., CLEVELAND, OH 44111
T-shirts

Fig. 57

Bob's Custom Lifting Belts
1605 E. MISSION, SUITE A, POMONA, CA 91766
714-620-8957
lifting belts

Body Bar Systems
1454 COMMONWEALTH AVE., BRONX, NY 10460
body bars

Bodybuilder's Cookbook
PO BOX 15086, QUINBY, SC 29501
cookbook for bodybuilders

Body Building Unlimited
PO BOX 6475, MOORE, OK 73153
tank tops, T-shirts

Fig. 58

Body Culture Equipment Co.
808 W. 5TH, PO BOX 10, ALLIANCE, NE 69301
biceps blasters, head straps, hip belts, lifting belts, magic circles, super grippers, triceps bars, and other equipment

Body Dynamics, Inc.
PO BOX 11063, INDIANAPOLIS, IN 46201
317-631-8718/317-631-7227/1-800-428-2352
advertising/modeling agency, biological stimulants, diet aids, vitamins

Body Exercise Equipment
2910 KANSAS AVE., TOPEKA, KS 66611
1-800-255-2302
equipment

Body Love Co.
PO BOX 2711, PETALUMA, CA 94953
707-795-8174
natural skin-care products

Body Masters Sports Industry, Inc.
PO BOX 259, RAYNE, LA 70578
318-984-0319/318-334-9829
equipment

Body Mechanics, Ltd.
C/O BARRY NEWMYER, 7025 (REAR) THREE CHOPT RD., VILLAGE SHOPPING CENTER, RICHMOND, VA 23226
804-282-1472
equipment, nutritional guidance, personalized training programs, T-shirts

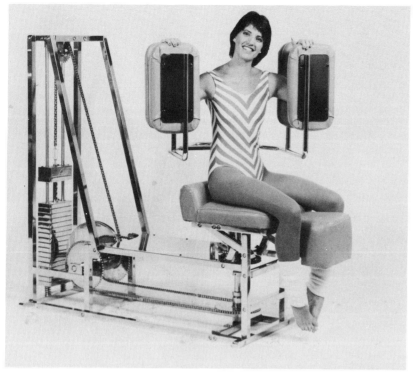

Fig. 59

The Body Shop
PO BOX 8418, SAN FRANCISCO, CA 94128
exercise wear for women

The Body Shoppe
1034 S. EDGEWOOD AVE., JACKSONVILLE, FL 32205
904-388-9534
shirts, sweaters, T-shirts, ties (personalized monograms available)

Body Transformation
3627 CUMBERLAND CT., STOCKTON, CA 95209
cookbooks (recipes of female bodybuilding stars)

Body World Enterprises
PO BOX 2614, LAUREL, MD 20708-0644
amino acids, glandulars, water filter ionizers

Bollinger Industries
222 W. AIRPORT FREEWAY, IRVING, TX 75062
lifting belts, waist trimmers

Bonilla
8306 WILSHIRE BLVD., SUITE 286, BEVERLY HILLS, CA 90211
Samra products: amino-acid capsules, beef liver grains, Naturol, multi-glandular capsules

Börlind of Germany
PO BOX 307, GRANTHAM, NH 03753
603-863-5966
all-natural herbal skin-care cosmetics and products, sunless bronzes

Brad's Gym
PO BOX 22, ACUSHNET, MA 02743
two-station dip machines

Bricker Labs
18722 SANTEE LANE, VALLEY CENTER, CA 92082
619-749-8609/1-800-952-9568
protein (Recover), natural steroid (Growth), direct absorption glandulars (DAG)

Mike Bridges Systems
PO BOX 5801, ARLINGTON, TX 76011
817-860-3099
deadlifting straps, elbow warmers, performance shoes, powerlifting training aids: bars, belts, books, suits; protein powders, vitamins, minerals, supplements, videos (beta/VHS), waist trimmers, wraps

Doug Brolus
4842 BISHOP, DETROIT, MI 48224
book on abdominal development

Bristol Sports Corp.
481 JOHNSON AVE., BOHEMIA, NY 11716
dumbbells, plates, power twisters

Bill Bronk
PO BOX 85, CUSTER, WI 54423
gloves, training straps

A. Brooks
140 SANTA ALICIA DR., #48, ROHNERT PARK, CA 94928
book on body fat

Stevi Brooks
PO BOX 6120, LOS ANGELES, CA 90055
213-680-4100
exercise wear for women

Ken Broussard
RT. B, PO BOX 259, NEW IBERIA, LA 70560
personalized training service

D. Ann Browne
3430 CARRIAGE HILL CIRCLE, 203, RANDALLSTOWN, MD 21133
designer of custom-made lifting belts, health-club consultant, nutrition counselor, personal trainer, fitness consultant

Buckeye Barbell
PO BOX 90, POWELL, OH 43065
614-764-4549
equipment

Fig. 60

Builders Sportswear
PO BOX 850, ADDISON, TX 75001
214-620-9013
clothes

Dick Burke's Mail Order Co.
PO BOX 1211, OKLAHOMA CITY, OK 73101
405-942-5606
equipment (Universal, Champion, AMF, Mac, York, Sonata, Walton, RocMo)

Andreas Cahling Enterprises
PO BOX 929, VENICE, CA 90294
bodybuilding courses, photos, posing/swim suits for men and women (variety of colors available), posters, vegetarian bodybuilding tape cassettes

The Caines Co.
PO BOX 84, GREER, SC 29652
equipment

California Shape
1020 WESTWOOD BLVD., WESTWOOD
VILLAGE, CA 90024
exercise wear for women

Roger Callard
PO BOX 41, SANTA MONICA, CA 90406
213-306-3957
seminars

Frank Calta's Super Fitness
4241 E. BUSCH BLVD., TAMPA, FL 33617
813-985-0580
equipment

David Campbell
NEW ROCHELLE FITNESS CENTER
585 NORTH AVE., NEW ROCHELLE, NY 10801
training aids

Campbell Enterprises
PO BOX 972, BURLINGTON, VT 05402
exercise devices designed for arms

Carolina Fitness Equipment
1215 THOMAS AVE., CHARLOTTE, NC 28234
704-3.'5-8607
equipment

David Carter Products
PO BOX 972, VENICE, CA 90291
213-899-8393
"Easy Tan" (tablet form)

Jay Casagrande
20 KAREN DR., NORWALK, CT 06851
personalized drawings

R. Casey
5818 W. 78 PLACE, LOS ANGELES, CA
90045
books and magazines

Champion Barbell Manufacturing Div.
PO BOX 1507, ARLINGTON, TX 76010
817-261-1139
equipment

Champion Sports Nutrition
110 GAY ST., PO BOX 1507, ARLINGTON, TX
76010
817-261-1139
electrolyte tablets

Ken Charles, Inc.
PO BOX 470, BROCKTON, MA 02403
lifting belts

Fig. 62

Charlton Publications, Inc.
CHARLTON BLDG., DERBY, CT 06418
books, E-Z curl bars, hand grips, head harnesses, juicers, jump ropes, lifting belts, magazines, supplements, triceps bombers, vitamins, waist trimmers

Charles & Associates
PO BOX 10676, PITTSBURGH, PA 15235
glandulars, supplements, vitamins

Bud Charniga
11024 DENNE, LIVONIA, MI 48150
books on weightlifting

Chelsea Gym
267 W. 17TH ST., NEW YORK, NY 10011
clothes

Clarendex Corp.
PO BOX 659, CATAUMET, MA 02534
home gym

K. K. Clark
PO BOX 1490, RADIO CITY STATION, NEW
YORK, NY 10019
book (Staying Hard), photos and posters of Bill Grant, T-shirts

Classic Films
PO BOX 45653, LOS ANGELES, CA 90045
films of bodybuilders

Fig. 61

Clean Water Systems
4025 HOUSE RD., EAU CLAIRE, WI 54701
distilled water, vitamins

Boyer Coe
PO BOX 5877, HUNTINGTON BEACH, CA 92646
books, "Legg" shoes, photos, posing trunks, seminars, sports bags, tank tops, training courses, T-shirts

Collector's Casting
RT. 3, PO BOX 283, MORA, MN 55051
belt buckles

Colonna's Gym
831 ST. LAURENCE DR., CHESAPEAKE, VA 23323
804-545-6417
T-shirts

Colonna Health Products, Inc.
400 E. INDIAN RIVER RD., PO BOX 4688, NORFOLK, VA 23523
804-545-2300
bee pollen, beef-liver extract, chelated minerals, energy oils, enzymes, fat burners, glandulars, health foods, lipotropics, liquid collagen, protein, vitamins, supplements

Fig. 63

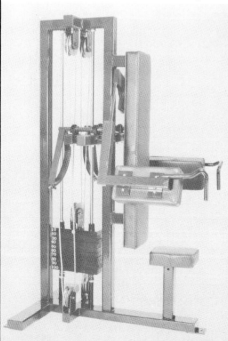

Franco Columbu
PO BOX 415, SANTA MONICA, CA 90406
213-474-8089
criss-cross belts, elbow, wrist, knee, and ankle supports; personalized training programs, posing films, training films, posters, training courses, T-shirts

Conan Research Corp.
PO BOX 174, MACEDONIA, OH 44056
natural anabolic formula in capsule form called "the steroid alternative," which contains: plant sterols, growth-hormone releasers, glandulars, fat emulsifiers, herbal extracts, dynamic energy builders

Concepts Unlimited
PO BOX 1568, FEDERAL STATION, WORCESTER, MA 01601
build-your-own equipment

Conejo Leathers
PO BOX 814, PT. HUENEME, CA 93014
lifting belts, dip belts

Corbin-Gentry, Inc.
40 MAPLE ST., SOMERSVILLE, CT 06072
203-749-2238
equipment

Bob Cornelius
PO BOX 837, VILLA RICA, GA 30180
405-492-0455
vitamins (Super Spectrum), nutrients

Joe Corsi Fitness Equipment Co.
22570 FOOTHILL BLVD., HAYWARD, CA 94541
equipment

Country Life Farm
R.D. 4, PO BOX 57, NEWTON, NJ 07860
201-579-1060
cookbook for fruits, nuts, and whole grains called Country Life Natural Foods Something Better Nutritional Seminar Cookbook

CPC
206 LOUISIANA, MICHIGAN CITY, IN 46360
training aids

Crain Power-Plus
726 N. HARRISON, PO BOX 1322, SHAWNEE, OK 74801
405-275-3689
belts, books, bumper stickers, chalk, DMSO, equipment, floor mats, health foods, magazines, nutrition consultants, photos, protein powders, seminars, smelling salts, sports bags, supplements, training straps, T-shirts, video tapes of powerlifting meets, vitamins, waist trimmers, warm-up suits, weight-training shoes, wraps

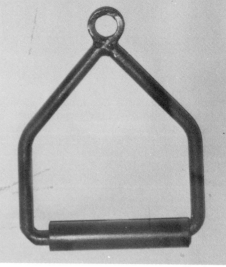

Fig. 64

Creative Health Products
5148 SADDLE RIDGE RD., PLYMOUTH, MI 48170
313-453-5309/313-453-0177/1-800-742-4478
skin calipers

Custom Built
PO BOX 701, JACKSONVILLE, AR 72076
custom-made sport shirts, tank tops, and T-shirts

Custom Gym Equipment
PO BOX 2073, SINKING SPRING, PA 19608
215-670-0103
weightlifting and bodybuilding equipment, food supplements

C.W.S.
RT. 1, PO BOX 69, PINEKNOLL RD., SYLVESTER, GA 31791
computerized weightlifting schedule

C. W. Stapp Sportswear
625 SW 26TH ST., MOORE, OK 73160
405-794-4267/1-800-654-2801
women's sportswear: bikini shorts, cover-ups (short & long), leotards (T-back & plain), unitard (T-back & plain), T-back shirt (short & long), wrap shorts—endorsed by Mary Roberts

CYBEX

Cybex, Div. of Lumex, Inc.
2100 SMITHTOWN AVE., RONKONKOMA, NY 11779
516-585-9000
free-weight equipment, isokinetic systems for testing and exercise, upper-body ergometer, variable-resistance exercise machines (Eagle Performance Systems)

Dalon
18324 OXNARD ST., TARZANA, CA 91356
exercise wear for women

Dance France
2503 MAIN ST., SANTA MONICA, CA 90405
213-392-9786/213-396-1665/
1-800-421-1543
exercise wear for women

Darden Research Corp.
DR. ELLINGTON DARDEN, PO BOX 1016,
LAKE HELEN, FL 32744
*books on bodybuilding, conditioning,
nutrition, strength training, and vitamins*

Steve Davis Fitness Center
23115 LYONS AVE., NEWHALL, CA 91321
805-255-7373
*cassettes, personalized training courses,
photos, posing trunks, T-shirts*

Fig. 65

Design Products
PO BOX 10583, BAKERSFIELD, CA 93389
805-831-6262 (OR CONTACT GARY LACK,
3905 CELINE CT., BAKERSFIELD, CA 93309)
*build-your-own equipment called The
Spartan Fitness Center (made from
polyvinyl chloride pipe; lightweight
materials can be bought for $100 and
made in four hours), build-your-own
weight benches and incline sit-up boards*

Designer Sport, Inc.
9960 CANOGA AVE., D-7, CHATSWORTH, CA
91311
213-700-1040
exercise wear for women

Diamant Trading Co.
947 46TH ST., BROOKLYN, NY 11219
212-871-7539
*elbow and knee supporters, electronic
acupuncture, electro-relaxer health
massager; magnetized acupuncture
insoles, bracelets, cushions, necklaces;
waist belts*

A. W. Diciolla, Jr., Co.
3460 W. 47TH ST., CLEVELAND, OH 44102
*close-grip chinning and rowing bars;
thick-handle dumbbells, wrist rollers,
cambered curl bars, deadlift bars*

Steve Davis

Dax Fitness Industries, Inc.
4101 W. VAN BUREN, SUITE 2, PHOENIX, AZ
85009
1-800-622-BODY
equipment

Dayton Unlimited, Inc.
PO BOX 6410, CONCORD, CA 94524
415-827-5654/415-680-6524
*mind-control courses, T-shirts, vitamins,
supplements*

Decathlon Exercise Equipment Co.
1044 W. 74TH ST., ST. PAUL, MN 55102
612-228-0818
equipment

Carlos DeJesus, The School of Natural Bodybuilding
1822 WILLIAMSBURG RD., SUITE 10,
RICHMOND, VA 23231
*a school of natural bodybuilding based
on the instinctive training of Dr. Carlos
DeJesus*

DEM Publishing
1716 MAIN ST., SUITE 193, MARINA DEL REY,
CA 90291
books

Derma-Research
RICHMOND GREEN BLDG., 9940
RICHMOND, #1021, HOUSTON, TX 77042
natural shaving aid

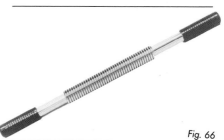

Fig. 66

Chris Dickerson, Inc.
GOLD'S GYM, 360 HAMPTON DR., VENICE, CA 90291
213-399-2972

gloves, jogging suits, knee wraps, photos, posing trunks, posters, protein powders, supplements, tank tops, T-shirts, training courses, vitamins, wrist straps

SUPPLYING WHAT
THE BODY NEEDS

Diet-Labs, Inc.
PO BOX 69, CLIMAX, NC 27233
919-674-7903

appetite suppressants, diet products, spirulina, stimulant capsules, vitamins

Di Mark Co.
PO BOX 11382, MARINA DEL REY, CA 90295
high-tech lever-action weightlifting belts

Discovery Publishing
PO BOX 983, TACOMA, WA 98401
206-383-4070

self-help and metaphysical tapes (BodyPsych), albums, books

Diversified Products Corp.
309 WILLIAMSON AVE., PO BOX 100, OPELIKA, AL 36802
205-749-9001

ankle and wrist weights, barbells, basketball equipment, books, boxing equipment, chest pulls, DP 650 USA Fitness Gym, DP Gympac 1000 and 1500, dumbbells, exercise benches, exercise bikes, exercise mats, exercise shoes, exercise wands, exercise wheels, fitness bars, games (darts, table tennis, etc.), hand grips, joggers, jump ropes, push-up stands, racquetball equipment, sit-up straps, slant boards, smart belles, sports bags, squat racks, super trimmers, triceps exercisers, weighted jump ropes, weightlifting belts

DLC Fabricating Co., Inc.
4809 MIAMI ST., ST. LOUIS, MO 63110
314-351-9778

Anterion equipment

D & L PUBLISHING
PO BOX 8513-P, MIDDLETOWN, OH 45042
training books

Doc's Sports
PO BOX 490338, COLLEGE PARK, GA 30349-0338
404-996-3627

bands (knee, elbow, and waist), books, DMSO, dip-stand gloves, equipment, ergometers, gravity boots, head straps, inversion racks, jump ropes, lifting belts and suits, physique accessories, push bars, rowing machines, supplements, trampolines, vitamins

Dolfin Corp.
PO BOX 98, SHILLINGTON, PA 19607
exercise wear

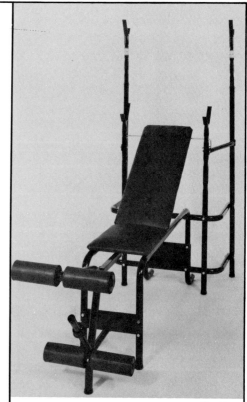

Fig. 68

Donkey Raise Machine
C/O LEONARD POOLE, PO BOX 161, APOPKA, FL 32703
donkey raise machine

Doug's Gym & Health Studio
PO BOX 2486, BISMARCK, ND 58502
digestive aids, glandulars, supplements

Dragonfly Enterprises
PO BOX 237, CLIMAX, MI 49034
lifting belts

D & S Manufacturing & Marketing, Inc., Health Products Div.
PO BOX 171, LITITZ, PA 17543
717-627-1128
body inverters

D. S. Products
PO BOX 9694, SACRAMENTO, CA 95823
drawings of feminine women of huge muscularity and superhuman strength (8-in × 10-in. at $10 each)

Dynakaz
PO BOX 1974A, AUBURN, AL 36830
raw glandulars, supplements, training courses, T-shirts, vitamins

Dynamics Health Equipment Manufacturing Co., Inc.
1538 COLLEGE AVE., SOUTH HOUSTON, TX 77587
713-946-5734/1-800-231-4245
equipment

Fig. 67

EARN Fitness
PO BOX 14, IMPERIAL, PA 15126
> *nutritionally balanced daily menus for weight loss or weight gain*

Earthrise Spirulina
PO BOX 33, BOULDER, CO 80306
> *spirulina*

East Coast Body Building
3 WILLOW PARK CENTER, FARMINGDALE, NY 11735
516-752-9518
> *equipment*

Sam Easterwood
370 RIVERSIDE DR., SAN ANTONIO, TX 78210
> *magazines and books*

Edgewood Enterprises
524 OAKLAND AVE., GROVE CITY, PA 16127
412-458-5975
> *amino acids, beef-liver extract, glandulars, minerals, proteins, supplements, vitamins*

Edward, Gregory, Leigh
2455 3RD SOUTH, PO BOX 24348, SEATTLE, WA 98124
1-800-227-1617, EXT. 617
> *AMEREC Health Care Products: ergometers, exercise bars, home cycles, joggers, pulse meters, rowing machines, saunas, steamers, vital-signs monitors*

ELF Research
PO BOX 33M, PAUILLO, HI 96776
> *vitamins*

Elite Sales, Inc.
PO BOX 3742, AUSTIN, TX 78764
512-441-7993
> *lifting belts*

Elmer's Weights, Inc.
PO BOX 16326, LUBBOCK, TX 79490
1-800-858-4568
> *ankle, hand, leg, therapeutic, vest, and wrist weights; waist trimmers, weightlifting belts*

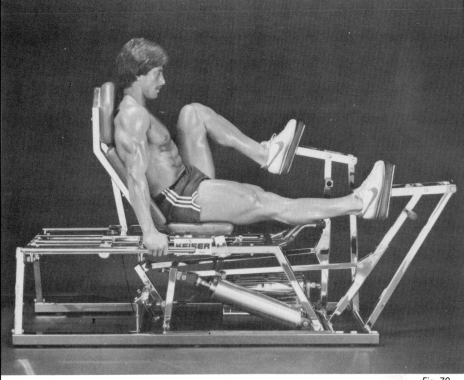

Fig. 70

Elmo's Exercise Equipment
9570 S. UTICA, EVERGREEN PARK, IL 60642
312-423-5559
> *equipment*

Execs, Inc., c/o Jeff Everson, Samson and Delilah Enterprises
19001 MERION DR., NORTHRIDGE, CA 91326
> *exercise consulting service*

Exercircle
PO BOX 414, GENEVA, IL 60134
1-800-554-3000
> *exercircle—a device for building and maintaining upper-body musculature*

Fig. 69

Exercise Chart Series
1513 EL SERENO DR., BAKERSFIELD, CA 93304
805-832-7317
> *exercise charts*

Exercise Dynamics
HIGHWAY 71N, BEMIDJI, MN 56601
> *skinfold calipers*

Exerco, Inc.
436 MANVILLE RD., PLEASANTVILLE, NY 10570
914-238-8802
> *ankle and wrist weights*

Expression
14157 CALIFA ST., VAN NUYS, CA 91401
> *bumper plates, key chains, T-shirts*

Fig. 71

J. A. Feliciano, Howard's Sports Training
17435 NEWHOPE, FOUNTAIN VALLEY, CA 92708
714-751-1674

steroid products

Fenton Products
8200-A FENTON ST., SILVER SPRING, MD 20910

nutritional guides

Ferrero Designs
PO BOX 448, DEPUE, IL 61322

custom-made men's sportswear: athletic and casual shirts, lounging pants, posing and sunning briefs, swimwear shorts, T-shirts

Lou Ferrigno
PO BOX 1671, SANTA MONICA, CA 90406

books, photos, posing trunks, posters, seminar tapes, shorts, tank tops, T-shirts, weightlifting belts, and a new product called State of the Art which includes: Gain Weight, Nutritional Bar, Supreme Protein, Mega-Pak, Weight Loss

Fillmore Foods, Inc.
3138 DEPOT RD., HAYWARD, CA 94545
415-783-5855

gain-weight supplements, M-L-O products, Mus-l-on, protein products, snack bars, yogurt drink mix

Fireworks by Julie St. Anne
1201 16TH AVE. SOUTH, NASHVILLE, TN 37212
615-327-4729

exercise wear for women

1st Fitness International
2933 OCEANSIDE BLVD., OCEANSIDE, CA 92054
1-800-852-2020/1-800-334-3030

ankle and wrist weights, arm blasters, athletic shoes, barbell pads, books, bullworkers, dip stands, dipping belts, equipment, exercise bikes, exercise clothing, exercise wheels, figure trimmers, football jerseys, gloves, handwraps, head straps, heel cushions, inversion boots, jogmeters, jump ropes, knee and wrist braces, maxercise creams, minerals, multi-glandulars, pedometers, power twisters, push-up bars, socks, supplements, treadmills, triceps bars, vitamins, weightlifting belts

Fitness
PO BOX 1153, VENICE, CA 93001

mind tapes

Fitness America
1807-1/2 NEWPORT BLVD., COSTA MESA, CA 92627
714-642-0989

equipment

Fitness and Physiology
PO BOX 431, AMHERST, MA 01004

listing of the nutritive value of over 350 common foods, including specialty and fast-food items

Fitness Consultants & Supply
1610 CHRISTINE ST., WICHITA FALLS, TX, 76302

books, lifting belts, T-shirts, wraps

Fitness Factory
PO BOX 1351, EDISON, NJ 08818
201-287-0616

barbells, barbell pads, bars, duffle bags, gloves, gravity boots, lifting belts, powder, T-shirts, wraps

Fitness Fashions
PO BOX 229 LV, LOCUST VALLEY, NY 11560

custom-fitted apparel for bodybuilders

Fitness Gym Systems, Inc.
603 E. MAIN ST., PO BOX 561, SANTA PAULA, CA 93060
805-933-2133

The Fitness Gym—the ultimate home-gym machine—a combination of 30 barbell and machine-type exercises

Fitness Industries, Inc.
PO BOX 39696, PHOENIX, AZ 85069
602-942-6791/1-800-821-4223

equipment

Fitness Institute of Hypnosis
2210 WILSHIRE BLVD., SUITE 753, SANTA MONICA, CA 90403

cassette tapes

Fitness King
PO BOX 11314, MINNEAPOLIS, MN 55411

Sit-eze (equipment for performing sit-ups), training course entitled The World's Famous Secrets to a Tight Stomach

Fitness Library
PO BOX 1443 M, ST. ANN, MO 63074

nutrition almanac

Fitness Management Service
PO BOX 1071, SNYDER, TX 79549

management service for prospective gym owners

Fitness Marketing Co.
80 S. SIXTH ST., COLUMBUS, OH 43215
614-464-3261

consultants for planning gym/health clubs

Fitness & Nutrition Center, Inc.
2250 NE 163RD ST., NORTH MIAMI BEACH, FL 33160
1-800-344-GYMS

equipment, bodybuilding accessories, boxing equipment, fitness books, protein and food supplements, vitamins, sports aids, weightlifting equipment, Weider retail dealership

Fig. 72

Fig. 73

Fitnus
1513 EL SERENO DR., BAKERSFIELD, CA 93304
805-832-7317

exercise charts for health and fitness facilities

Flex Gym Equipment
1100 W. KATELLA, #J, ORANGE, CA 92667
714-633-6340

equipment

Flextard
11755 EXPOSITION BLVD., LOS ANGELES, CA 90064

exercise wear for women

Float to Relax, Inc.
5835 W. 6TH AVE., SUITE A, LAKEWOOD, CO 80214
303-232-9545

flotation tanks

Foothill Enterprises
724 E. FOOTHILL BLVD., PO BOX 655, SAN DIMAS, CA 91773
714-592-5050

bar pads, gloves, lifting straps

Fox Marketing
611 N. MCLEAN, BLOOMINGTON, IL 61701
1-800-447-4170

weighted gloves

FP Products
PO BOX 6666, SADDLE BROOK, NJ 07662

vitamins

Fraco, Inc.
RT. 1, PO BOX 73-C, MIDDLETOWN, IN 47356
317-779-4601/317-646-8978

equipment

Ernie and Diane Frantz Health Studio
21 N. BROADWAY, AURORA, IL 60504
312-892-1491/312-554-1805

cassettes, chalk, deadlift shoes and straps, DMSO, gloves, lifting belts, patches (U.S. Powerlifting Federation), photos, protein drinks, squat suits, training routines, vitamins, waist trimmers, workout logbooks, wraps

Free Weight Systems, Inc.
835 MISSOULA AVE., BUTTE, MT 59701
406-782-6181

equipment

Futurebiotics, Inc.
W. CHESTERFIELD, NH 03466

vitamins, supplements

FUTURE

Future Equipment Co., Inc.
135 U.S. HIGHWAY 19 NORTH, CLEARWATER, FL 33515
813-797-0900/813-938-4617

equipment

Gainers
PO BOX 233, GARWOOD, NJ 07027

chalk

Gartrell Travel Service
433 GRAVIER ST., NEW ORLEANS, LA 70130
504-525-4040

sports vacations

Gateway Graphics
PO BOX 2814, ST. LOUIS, MO 63118

clothes

General Nutrition Corp.
418 WOOD ST., NUTRITION SQUARE, PITTSBURGH, PA 15222
1-800-457-2000

aerobic rebounders, ankle and wrist weights, barbells, bars, bee pollen, biceps builders, books, chest expanders, equipment, exercise cycles, exercise mats, hand grips, inversion systems, jump ropes, lifting gloves, magazines, plates, protein and mineral supplements, protein powders, rowing machines, slant boards, tank tops, T-shirts, vitamins, waist trimmers, weighted gloves

Cathy George Designs
152 W. CYPRESS AVE., BURBANK, CA 91502
213-846-6630

exercise wear for women

Gershon Jewelers
135 CEDARHURST AVE., CEDARHURST, NY 11516

gold pendants and rings

Get Fit Video Series
1400 STIERLIN RD., MOUNTAIN VIEW, CA 94043

fitness video cassettes for women

Getting Strong Book Series
10100 SANTA MONICA BLVD., SUITE 2065, LOS ANGELES, CA 90067

ten-volume series of strength-training books for women called Getting Strong: arms, back and shoulders, bodybuilding, body sculpturing, building bulk, buttocks, chest, legs, nutrition, waist

HEALTH AND GYM EQUIPMENT

Johnny Gibson's Health and Gym Equipment
52 N. 6TH AVE., TUCSON, AZ 85701
602-622-1275/602-622-8410

equipment

Vince Gironda, Vince's Gym
11262 VENTURA BLVD., NORTH HOLLYWOOD, CA 91604

articles, booklets, bulletins, gloves, grips, lifting belts, pants, programs, supplements, sweatshirts, tank tops, T-shirts, vitamins, wrist straps

GMV Gallery
PO BOX 24802, SAN JOSE, CA 95154-4802

reproductions of art by physique artist Gilbert III

Golden Eagle Jewelry Co.
3600 COPPER NE, ALBUQUERQUE, NM 87108
505-255-6523

body jewelry

Golden Pro, Inc.
935 ROCKINGHAM RD., BIRMINGHAM, AL 36235
205-853-9493

Super Spectrum food supplements

Gold's Gym
360 HAMPTON DR., VENICE, CA 90291
213-396-7426

gym franchise, sportswear, supplements, vitamins—located in 32 states and in Canada, England, France, Greece, Italy, the West Indies

Goliath Gym Equipment
4717 W. 1ST ST., SUITE A, SANTA ANA, CA 92703
714-839-3260

equipment

Ron J. Goodman
PO BOX 1596, MONROVIA, CA 91016

motivational books on powerlifting

The Good News Shirt Shop
RT. 7, PO BOX 612-A, REIDSVILLE, NC 27320

T-shirts for the Christian bodybuilder

Good Sports
610 S. MATHILDA ST., PITTSBURGH, PA 15224
412-621-6644

equipment

Bill Grant Enterprises
PO BOX 1493, SANTA MONICA, CA 90406

personalized training programs, photos, seminars, tank tops, T-shirts

Gravity Research
1237 CAMINO DEL MAR, SUITE C-131, DEL MAR, CA 92014
619-481-6665

anti-gravity bars and boots

Gravity Sciences
11844 W. PICO BLVD., LOS ANGELES, CA 90064
213-477-9041/1-800-235-7974

inversion equipment includes: gravity traction system, backswing

Great Earth International, Inc.
PO BOX 1993, SANTA ANA, CA 92702
1-800-638-6075/1-800-492-1171

vitamins, minerals, supplements, bee pollen, cosmetics, diet and digestive aids, minerals, protein herbs; exclusive products: Body Control (for energy, stamina, endurance, optimum mental performance), Earth Bloom (natural skin-care line), Greater Greens (for prevention of disease), Hem-Iron; Hunger-Free Diet Packs, Life Span I, II, III, Maintain (for weight control), Oxy E, PMS (for premenstrual syndrome), Stress Calm, Workout (aerobic enhancer)

Great Lakes Sports Academy
PEIF 101-A, MARQUETTE, MI 49855

training facility

Green Valley Gym Equipment, c/o Don Barnes
602 N. POPLAR, CRESTON, IA 50801
515-782-8143

Olympic sets

Greenville Health Club
221 WHITE OAK RD., GREENVILLE, SC 29609
803-268-5203/803-244-5531

chalk, equipment, exercise bikes, lifting and suits straps (distributors for Universal, Weider, Superior Health, Custom Exercise Equipment, York, and Hoffman)

Dave Groscup
RD. 1, BIRDSBORO, PA 19508

training consultant

The Grow-Eery
6526 LANSDOWNE AVE., PHILADELPHIA, PA 19151

canthaxanthin tablets

G & S Distributors
PO BOX 232, WASHINGTON, IN 47501

milk protein

Peggy Guthridge
VP-3, 8406 E. Harry, #221, WICHITA, KS 67207

food supplements, herbs, minerals, protein powders, skin-care products, vitamins

Dr. C. F. Smith

h

Hammel Training
804 KOEN LANE, EULESS, TX 76039
training aids—frontal-neck development system

Hammer Fist
PO BOX 1164, BELLMORE, NY 11710
training aids

Hastings Barbell Co.
2257 HEATH RD., HASTINGS, MI 49058
619-948-2462/619-765-5101
equipment

Fred Hatfield Fitness Systems
15343 VANOWEN ST., #235, VAN NUYS, CA 91406
power hook (takes the place of the dip belt), power training products and courses

Hawaiian Resources
PO BOX 10036, HONOLULU, HI 96816
French-Tahitian body oil called Monio Tahiti

Health Culture
PO BOX 125, ROCKAWAY, NJ 07866
pre-exhaustion schedule

Health-for-Life
8033 SUNSET BLVD., SUITE 483(F), LOS ANGELES, CA 90046
213-452-0707
SynerAbs—a program which tones the stomach muscles synergistically

Health from the Sun Products, Inc.
PO BOX 477, DOVER, MA 02030
617-449-1580
(see products under Bee Pollen from England)

Healthy 'N Fit
1617 STILLWELL AVE., BRONX, NY 10461
212-828-3616
protein mix, supplements, vitamins—endorsed by Richard Baldwin

Healthy Ventures
200 W. 34TH AVE., SUITE 270, ANCHORAGE, AK 99503
recipes for protein drinks

Heavyhands
PO BOX 10362, DES MOINES, IA 50306
1-800-247-8080
hand weights

Fig. 75

Orrin J. Heller
PO BOX 301, NORWALK, CA 90650
drawings, illustrated stories, movies, and photos of female bodybuilders (and rare footage of early muscle women), women wrestlers, powerlifters, and circus performers

Mike Hiebert
PO BOX 1598, BETHANY, OK 73008
a natural steroid from an exotic herb—a complete report of where to buy it and how to extract it

High-Performance Products
PO BOX 362, LAWRENCEBURG, IN 47025
L-ornithine and L-arginine

High-Tech Fitness, Inc.
617 N. LA CIENEGA BLVD., LOS ANGELES, CA 90069
213-854-7744
equipment

High-Tech Tools, Inc.
8570 TAMAR DR., COLUMBIA, MD 21045
301-997-8577
bull builder—a weightlifting system

William F. Hinbern
32430 CLOVERDALE, FARMINGTON, MI 48024
313-477-2739
rare and back-dated albums, books, booklets, courses, films, magazines (Hinbern buys, sells, and trades.)

hiTech Sports & Fitness Products
1289 FORGEWOOD AVE., SUNNYVALE, CA 94089
408-734-3840/1-800-621-6070
Unipro amino acids and peak performance Carboplex

Jim Hix
PO BOX 13453
SPOKANE, WA 99213-3453
muscle charts

Hoggan Health Equipment
6651 S. STATE ST., SALT LAKE CITY, UT 84107
801-266-5337
equipment (CamStar): barbells, benches, dumbbells, exercise bikes, figure bars, massagers

Mark Horn
19525 MELROSE
SOUTHFIELD, MI 48075
wrist supports

Howard's Equipment Co.
SPORTS TRAINING RESEARCH CENTER, 17435 NEWHOPE, FOUNTAIN VALLEY, CA 92708
equipment

R. Hubbard
PO BOX 311, SCOTCH PLAINS, NJ 07076-0311
conditioning programs

Fig. 76

Fig. 77

Huffy Corp.
2018 S. FIRST ST., PO BOX 07493,
MILWAUKEE, WI 53207
equipment, sporting goods

R. Hughes
800 E. 10TH ST., SUITE 1, ADA, OK 74802
bee pollen, vitamins

Hydra-Gym Athletics, Inc.
2121 INDUSTRIAL PARK RD., PO BOX 599,
BELTON, TX 76513
817-939-1831/1-800-792-3013
*Hydra-Fitness Omnikinetic exercise
equipment*

H. W. E., Inc.
1638 N. LA BREA AVE., LOS ANGELES, CA
90028
213-466-8400
multi-functional inversion gym

I. Gym
PO BOX 288, RIDGEFIELD, NJ 07657
201-288-8363
tuck and roll gym bags

Ilona of Hungary
3201 E. 2ND AVE., DENVER, CO 80206
303-322-4212
skin-care products for men

Improvement Products Corp.
535 FIFTH AVE., NEW YORK, NY 10017
*speed shaper for the abdomen, hips,
waist—endorsed by Olympic
weightlifting champion Ike Berger*

Inertia Dynamics Corp.
3550 N. CENTRAL AVE., PHOENIX, AZ 85012
602-264-7009/1-800-821-7143
*the Lean Machine—a single-unit, 45-
exercise machine (resistance through
high-quality, tandem-mounted, counter-
force springs)*

Ingenuts Enterprises
PO BOX 491141, LOS ANGELES, CA 90049
color calendar of female bodybuilders

Interface Products for Men
2321 WASHINGTON BLVD., MARINA DEL REY,
CA 90291
213-822-8855/1-800-227-1617, ext. 242
*fragrance-free, all-natural skin-care
products for men (work-out kit, deep
cleanser, toner, moisturizer, mask, herbal
scrub, elastin-collagen night replenisher,
EC-17 close-shave formula)*

Inversion Therapy Equipment
PO BOX 4325, FREMONT, CA 94539
inversion equipment

Inzer Power Shirts
PO BOX 2981, LONGVIEW, TX 75606
214-236-4012
*custom-made T-shirts for powerlifting
officially approved by the International
Powerlifting Federation*

Irmo Sports
6169 ST. ANDREWS RD.
COLUMBIA, SC
29210
*equipment, lifting belts, minerals, protein,
vitamins*

Iron Co.
5334 BANKS ST., SAN DIEGO, CA 92110
619-297-4349
Polaris equipment

Iron Man's Gym
404 MISSION AVE., PO BOX 30, OCEANSIDE,
CA 92054
*personalized training program by Charles
Bradshaw, protein and mineral
supplements, shorts, tank tops, T-shirts,
vitamins*

Iron Man Magazine
PO BOX 10, ALLIANCE, NE 69301
*books, courses, equipment, program
sheets, training aids*

Angelo Iuspa
474 N. 8TH ST.
NEWARK, NJ 07107
*old and new magazines and books
(bought, sold, and traded) on strength,
bodybuilding, weight-training, strong
men, etc.*

Jabel Products
9309 BEVERLY CREST, BEVERLY HILLS, CA
90210
grips

L. E. Jacobson
2098-44 GRIP RD., SEDRO WOOLLEY, WA
98284
*heavy-duty cable lat machine (build your
own)*

Jay's Gym
153 S. GALLATIN, LIBERTY, MO 64068
T-shirts

J & B Albrights
PO BOX 368-M
ELKHORN, NE 68033
*body-composition kit to determine your
percentage of muscle mass*

Jewelry by Roger
PO BOX 1011, WHITTIER, CA 90609
jewelry

Jogbra, Inc.
1 MILL ST., BURLINGTON, VT 05401
1-800-343-2020
*exercise wear and aids for women:
sports bra, sports brief, jogmit (gloves),
leotard with built-in breast support, leg
warmers, thermals, sportskins*

Jubinville Weight Exercising Equipment
PO BOX 662, HOLYOKE, MA 01040
413-534-0582
equipment, gloves, T-shirts

K & D Co.
PO BOX 8354, SALEM, MA 01971
404-252-5734
*Bill Kazmaier's products: books
(photographic history of Kazmaier),
inspirational tapes, posters, power hooks,
T-shirts*

Steve Karas Enterprises
103-27 114 ST., SUITE C1, RICHMOND HILL,
NY 11419
*original pen-and-ink drawings of
bodybuilders*

Katch's-FAT
PO BOX 2630, ANN ARBOR, MI 48106
information on body-fat testing

Keiser Sports Health Equipment
411 S. WEST AVE., FRESNO, CA 93706
209-266-2715
*pneumatic-resistance equipment—CAM II
series*

Kellogg, Inc.
PO BOX 220, DACUNO, CO 80514
303-833-3199
equipment

Kelso
RT. 1, PO BOX 272, BULLARD, TX 75757
*Kelso shrug techniques and other
courses*

Betty Kerr Enterprises
2554 LINCOLN BLVD., SUITE 1111, MARINA
DEL REY, CA 90291
213-367-5021
*natural health products: Alta 15, Alta sil-x
silica, B complex, Can-gest, cold and flu
formula, cycle herbs formula, Easy Tan,
herbal tea, herbal skin salve, Hi-lo
balance, Imu-gen, Instant Tan, Liv-99,
magnesium chloride, potassium chloride*

Jeff King
PO BOX 80306, FOREST PARK STATION,
SPRINGFIELD, MA 01108
*individual training programs, nutrition
counseling, photos, seminars, T-shirts*

Kisha Fitness System
PO BOX 592, DUQUESNE, PA 15110
simple bodybuilding system (12 min/day)

K & K Arm Strong Fitness Equipment
1537 S. DELSEA DR., VINELAND, NJ 08360
609-691-5373
equipment

Susan Koch
1 SYCAMORE AVE., LITTLE SILVER, NJ 07739
training aids for women

Ron Kosloff
RESEARCH NUTRITION, 14474 E. 7 MILE RD.,
DETROIT, MI 48205
nutrition advice

Lancon's Vitamins
PO BOX 680, BETHLEHEM, PA 18016
215-866-2229/1-800-523-9698
vitamins

Laser Publications
PO BOX 274, MOGADORE, OH 44260
handbook of bodybuilding drugs

Amelia Lavin
700 PARK AVE., #6B, BALTIMORE, MD 21201
301-225-7763
physique photography

Fig. 78

Bob Krech-Art
PO BOX 306, WILLINGBORO, NJ 08046
T-shirts

Kreis Sports Inc.
PO BOX 120158, NASHVILLE, TN 37212
equipment, video tapes

Kuc's Total Fitness Systems
PO BOX 215, MOUNTAINTOP, PA 18707
717-474-6914
*powerlifting training aids: bars, lifting
belts, wraps*

Lederle Labs
1 CYANAMID PLAZA,
WAYNE, NJ 07470
201-831-3250
*supplements, vitamins (packaged under
the names Spartacus, Centrum, and
Stresstabs)*

Gordon Lee Products
320 E. 65TH ST., SUITE 116
NEW YORK, NY
10021
212-570-1870/212-570-1871
skin-care products

Fig. 79

John LeGear, Clinton E. Frank, Inc.
120 S. RIVERSIDE, CHICAGO, IL 60606
312-454-5580
energy drinks

Douglas James Leger
181 EXCHANGE ST.
LEOMINSTER, MA 01453
equipment

Steve Lennard
430 SW 18TH TR, MIAMI, FL 33129
training aids

L. H.'s Art, Comics & Magazines
PO BOX 301, NORWALK, CT 90650
magazines

The Library
15343 VANOWEN, #235
VAN NUYS, CA
91406
books

Lifecycle, Inc.
10 THOMAS RD., IRVINE, CA 92714
714-859-1011
The Aerobic Trainer cycle

Life Cycle Vitamin Co.
6354 VAN NUYS BLVD., VAN NUYS, CA 91401
minerals, protein, supplements, vitamins and vitamin packs (female, male, professional, athletic, geriatric diet)

Lifeline Production and Marketing, Inc.
1421 S. PARK ST., MADISON, WI 53715
608-251-4778/1-800-356-9607
Lifeline gym (portable, variable-resistance exercise unit that combines total fitness and convenience): digital-counter jump rope, sit-up bar, waistliner, weighted training rope—endorsed by Fred Hatfield, Sylvester Stallone, Walter Payton, Dan Gable, Matthew Guidry

Life Style Products
1400 STIERLIN RD., MOUNTAIN VIEW, CA 94043
1-800-227-8318/1-800-982-6133
anti-gravity bars and boots, athletic footwear, chrome dumbbells, heavyhands aerobic weight set, jump ropes, lifeline gym, rowing machines

Light Force Spirulina Co., A Div. of Microalgae International Sales Corp.
BOX N., BOULDER CREEK, CA 95006
minerals, spirulina supplements, vitamins

Linquist
PO BOX 1524, DAVIS, CA 95616
diet information

Little Grunt Productions
1101 SW 18TH AVE., PORTLAND, OR 97205
503-223-0768
exercise illustrations

LIVE
PO BOX 6096, FULLERTON, CA 92634
photos, posing trunks, T-shirts

L & J Enterprises
PO BOX 792, CASPER, WY 82602
instant protein and multi-vitamins

J. F. Loccisano, Editor
1487-B ATKINS AVE., LANCASTER, PA 17603
instructional posing service, magazine

Bill Lopez Gym Equipment
22723 DELFORD, CARSON, CA 90745
213-835-0670
equipment

L & S Research
PO BOX 1577, TOMS RIVER, NJ 08753-0550
books on diet programs, recipes, and steroids

Dan Lurie Barbell Co., Inc.
219-10 S. CONDUIT AVE., SPRINGFIELD GARDENS, NY 11413
212-978-4200
arm blasters, bicycles, body bars, body weights, books, boxing gloves, bullworkers, cable springs, courses, energy-stamina packs, equipment, exerwheels, E-Z curl bars, gloves, hand springs, head harnesses, head straps, heavy bag and gloves, inversion equipment, iron boots, iron shoes, joggers, jump ropes, lifting belts, lifting suits, magazines, medicine balls, minerals, mini-trampolines, posing trunks, power bracelets, power coils, grips, shoes; protein powders, sauna suits, slimming suits, supports (ankle, elbow, knee, thigh, wrist), tiger suits, triceps bombers, twist 'n' tones, twisters, vitamins, waist trimmers, weight vests, weight-gain formulas, weight-loss packs, wrist rollers

Fig. 80

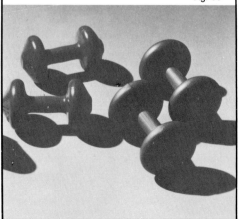

Lisa Lyon
PO BOX 585, SANTA MONICA, CA 90406
personalized training programs, photo albums, posters, seminars, tank tops, T-shirts

Lyons Health & Fitness
213 N. ORANGE ST.
GLENDALE, CA 91203
213-242-6730
equipment

Mac Barbell Equipment
1601 NW DALLAS
GRAND PRAIRIE, TX 75050
214-263-4828
equipment

Mike MacDonald Systems
15 N. LAKE AVE.
DULUTH, MN 55802
218-727-8847
amino acids, anabolic glandulars, DMSO, lipovites, powerlifting equipment and accessories, protein powder, supplements, vitamins

MacLevy Products Corp.
43-23 91ST PLACE, ELMHURST, NY 11373
1-800-221-0277
Omni fitness aids: exercise bikes, joggers, rowing machines, slant boards

MAGAZINES, c/o Ronald T. Choquette
161 S. HAMPTON RD., HOLYOKE, MA 01040
413-533-3527
magazines dated from 1954 to 1981

Magenst Publications
PO BOX 669, NEW YORK, NY 10028
vitamins

Magnum Exercise Equipment, Inc.
8222 JAMESTOWN DR., AUSTIN, TX 78758
512-454-6711
equipment

Malepak
PO BOX 490145, ATLANTA, GA 30349
404-996-3627/1-800-241-4975
equipment, men's apparel, skin-care products

Marathon Distributing Co.
1229 VIA LANDETS, PALOS VERDES ESTATES, CA 90274
213-519-7111/213-375-3802
powerlifting aids: lifting belts, straps, suits (Supersuit/Supersuit II)—products also sold under the name of Marathon Nutrition (vitamins, supplements, glandulars, etc.)

Fig. 81

Joe Marino's Gym Equipment Co.
PO BOX 144, RIDGEWOOD, NJ 07451
equipment

Cindy Martin
PO BOX 2444, NORTHBROOK, IL 60062
inspirational letters to bodybuilders who need motivation

Masterworks
502 W. MOANA, PO BOX 39, RENO, NV 89509
jewelry by Ronald Van Robinson

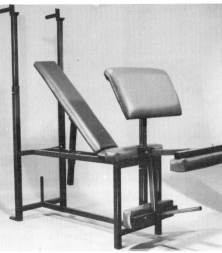

Fig. 82

Matt Physique Photography
PO BOX 25, QUEENS, NY 11415
212-847-0763
physique photography

Mav-Rik
3916 EAGLE ROCK BLVD., LOS ANGELES, CA 90065
equipment (the "one-piece sleeve")

McCain Productions
3100 S. LAMAR, SUITE 203, AUSTIN, TX 78704
powerlifting apparel and novelties

E. H. McDowell
323 FRANKLIN BLDG. SOUTH, SUITE 804, CHICAGO, IL 60606
vitamins

Tom McLaughlin
PO BOX 507, AUBURN, AL 36830
articles on the biomechanics of powerlifting

Rachel McLish, Flex Appeal
PO BOX 111
SANTA MONICA, CA 90406
competition guides and suits, courses, photos, posters, sleeveless T-shirts, tank tops, thigh-high shorts

Mike Mentzer
PO BOX 3825, DELAND, FL 32720
cassettes (video and audio), courses, photos, tank tops, T-shirts

Jim Michaels Art Co.
PO BOX 793, PALM HARBOR, FL 33563
tank tops, T-shirts

Mid-West T-Shirt Art
PO BOX 495, ARNOLD, MO 63010
T-shirts

Mighty Muscle Mugs
5914 12TH ST., DETROIT, MI 48208
313-871-8180
novelty bookends, dumbbell piggy banks, mugs, pencil holders, etc.

Mill Creek Natural Products
DEEP VALLEY DR., ROLLING HILLS, CA 90274
natural hair and skin-care products: cleansing bars, lotions, scrubs, shampoos and conditioners, tanning lotions

C. Miller
PO BOX 1234, FT. LAUDERDALE, FL 33302-1234
build-your-own gym equipment, grips, primo gland (natural steroid substitute), vitamins

Joe Miller
PO BOX 2A2, COLLEGE PARK, MD 20783
individualized training programs

Mills Enterprises
PO BOX 567, MIDWAY CITY, CA 92655
acupressure book entitled The Ultimate Bodybuilder/Powerlifter, *supplements, vitamins*

Minitec Marketing, Inc.
20710 S. LEAPWOOD, CARSON, CA 90746
heart-rate computer

Mike Minor Enterprises
PO BOX 2364, NACOGDOCHES, TX 75961
409-564-5054
custom-designed sportswear

Mojo Manor Studios
3000 ERIE BLVD. EAST, SYRACUSE, NY 13224
muscle T-shirts, chemises, tank tops

V. Moon
1443 S. PACIFIC ST., OCEANSIDE, CA 92054
recipes for natural desserts

Milton T. Moore, Jr.
PO BOX 140280, DALLAS, TX 75214-0280
books

Fig. 84

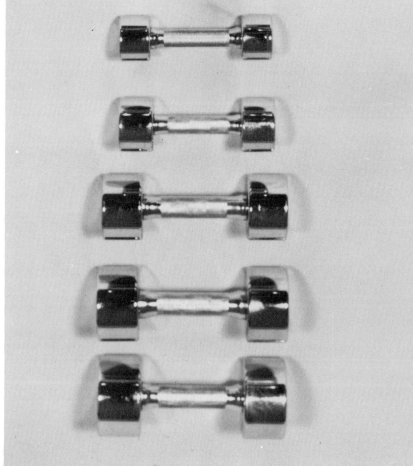

Fig. 10

William Moore, Joe Weider Fan Club
PO BOX 732, TUSCALOOSA, AL 35402-0732
fitness labels, newsletters, photos, rare physical culture items dating back to the late 1800s

Jim Moore's World Gym
5215 SOUTH BLVD., CHARLOTTE, NC 28210
704-527-0034
equipment

Morden Weightlifting Products
1712 N. GENESEE DR., LANSING, MI 48915
517-372-1776
equipment

Randy Morris
2035 COLLIER RD., AKRON, OH 44320
fitness consultant, individualized training programs

Steve Mott
4643 MOSS CT., COLUMBUS, OH 43214
614-451-6292
equipment

Mr. Universe Enterprises, c/o Lance Dreher
PO BOX 5, OAK FOREST, IL 60452
personalized courses, photos, posters, training programs, T-shirts, vitamins, minerals

Miss Olympia
703 SMITH LANE, MT. HOLLY, NJ 08060
photos of the Miss Olympia contest

Richard Muldez
PO BOX 4244, VIRGINIA BEACH, VA 23454
804-486-0755
physique photography

Joe Mullen
PO BOX 84, DELAND, FL 32720
gym manual

Muscle Dynamics, Ltd.
17022 MONTANERO, #5, CARSON, CA
90746
213-637-9500
*equipment (Maxicam and Maxitron),
maxercise cream, myo-cream*

Muscle Factory
8 WOODBINE RD., ROWAYTON, CT 06853
*beef-liver extract, protein, supplements,
vitamins*

Muscle-Gram, Inc.
1735 SECOND AVE., #5S, NEW YORK, NY
10128
212-534-2350
*bodybuilding service for complete party
entertainments*

Muscle Grams
414 BLAIR AVE., READING, PA 19601
bodybuilding consultant

Muscle Head
PO BOX 4555, PITTSBURGH, PA 15205
home gyms

MuscleMag International
UNIT 2, 52 BRAMSTEELE RD., BRAMPTON,
ONTARIO, CANADA L6W 3M5
equipment, magazines, training aids

Muscle Mart
7876 CONVOY CT., SAN DIEGO, CA 92111
619-277-LIFT
*ankle cuffs, ankle weights, bar pads,
chalk, deadlift slippers, dip belts,
equipment, gravity boots, hand grips,
head harnesses, iron shoes, jump ropes,
knee and wrist wraps, lifting gloves,
lifting suits, muscle rub, posing oil,
powerlifting belts, rubber matting*

MusclePower International USA
133 W. FOOTHILL BLVD., PO BOX 805,
AZUSA, CA 91702
213-334-8717
*pure (93.5%), natural, high-quality milk
protein made from fresh Dutch cow milk
available in two flavors: neutral and
Dutch chocolate; vitamins, minerals*

The Muscle Shop
806 E. ABRAM, SUITE 247, ARLINGTON, TX
76010
training aids

Muscle Shorts
2216 MAIN ST., PO BOX A, SANTA MONICA,
CA 90405
clothing

Muscle-Up
PO BOX 1935, JANESVILLE, WI 53547
muscle-building courses, drinks

Muscle World
PO DRAWER 700, CLAYTON, OK 74536
918-560-4105
*custom-made lifting belts, equipment
(hydraulic press and squat stands),
magazines, T-shirts, supplements, vitamins*

National Health Products
1924 GENESEE ST., UTICA, NY 13502
315-797-4191
*amino acids, belt buckles, courses,
equipment, fat burners, glandulars,
herbals, lifting belts, lifting gloves,
minerals, natural stimulants, posing trunks,
power twisters, protein powders,
sculpture, steroidlike substances
(Exsterol), sterols, supplements, T-shirts,
vitamins*

National Sports Warehouse
6 RIVERSIDE DR., BALTIMORE, MD 21221
301-687-8181/301-687-1336
*ankle and wrist weights, apparel, athletic
tape, caps, chest expanders, chinning
bars, cycles, dumbbells, equipment,
gloves, gravity bars and boots, hats, heat
sticks, heavy-hands equipment, heel
cushions, jump ropes, racquets, rowing
machines, shoes, socks, sports bags,
sports gear, warm-up suits, wraps*

Natural
PO BOX 73, MCMINNVILLE, OR 97128
vitamins

Fig. 85

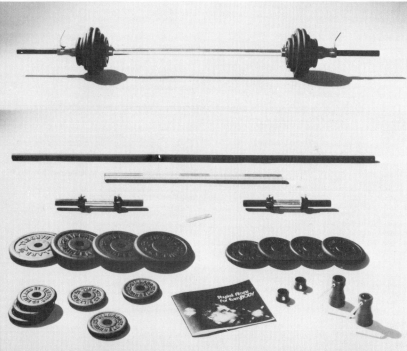

Natural Health Foods and Barbell Center
6981 MARKET ST., YOUNGSTOWN, OH 44512
216-758-0111/216-788-7295

ankle and wrist weights, backswings, biceps and triceps bombers, chest expanders, chinning bars, collars, equipment, exer-cycles, gloves, hand grips, iron shoes, kettlebell handles, knee pads, lifting belts, neck pads, rowing machines, supplements, vitamins, waist trimmers, weighted belts and vests, wrist developers

Naturally Vitamin Supplements, Inc.
14851 N. SCOTTSDALE RD., SCOTTSDALE, AZ 85254
602-991-0200

bio-strath, diet products, digestive aids, herbal formulas, minerals, supplements, vitamins

Natural Peak
PO BOX 13672, SACRAMENTO, CA 95813
minerals, supplements, vitamins

Natural Source Products, Inc.
PO BOX 1285, CANOGA PARK, CA 91304
213-998-5005

enzymes, minerals, nutritional analysis, protein, supplements, vitamins—endorsed by Scott Wilson and Serge Nubret

Natural Stuff, Inc.
165 RT. 46, ROCKAWAY, NJ 07866
201-627-7788

bar plates, equipment

Natures Best
169 MIRACLE STRIP, FT. WALTON BEACH, FL 32548
904-243-9044

protein drinks with all the essential amino acids in 11 flavors—weight gain (340 calories) and weight loss (146 calories)

Nautilus Sports/Medical Industries, Inc.
PO BOX 1783, DELAND, FL 32720
902-228-2884/1-800-874-8941

books, charts, clothing, equipment, magazines, posters

Fig. 86

Kay King-Nealy
12 E. 22ND ST., APT. PHD, NEW YORK, NY 10010
212-475-9172

physique photography

New Health Marketing
7630 LYNDALE AVE. SOUTH, MINNEAPOLIS, MN 55423
612-866-2549

anti-gravity bars and boots, portable back-ease system

New Horizons
245 FIFTH AVE., NEW YORK, NY 10016
posing oil

North American Competitions International
PO BOX 23153, POINT STATION, COLUMBUS, OH 43223

amino acids, enzymes, glandulars, high-protein mix, T-shirts

Northeast Power & Fitness
1937 WASHINGTON BLVD., EASTON, PA 18042
215-258-1023

equipment

The North Light
4219 W. OLIVE, SUITE 200, BURBANK, CA 91505

T-shirts

Nu Life
3401 71ST ST. NORTH, ST. PETERSBURG, FL 33710

triceps blasters

Nu-Life Fitness
PO BOX 290815, FT. LAUDERDALE, FL 33329
305-941-4521

equipment

Nutrabiotics
PO BOX 1247, CAPITOLA, CA 95010
408-425-1080

natural amino acids, cosmetics, digestive aids, herbal formulas, minerals, supplements, tanning products, vitamins, weight-loss formulas

Nutri Biotics
PO BOX 2836, SANTA CRUZ, CA 95062
DMSO, protein, spirulina, supplements, vitamins, zinc

Nutri-Data, Inc.
PO BOX 160267, MIAMI, FL 33116
computerized nutritional analysis

Nutri-Foods
7131 OWENSMOUTH AVE., SUITE 32A, CANOGA PARK, CA 91303
bee pollen

Nutri-Research
PO BOX 24342, FT. LAUDERDALE, FL 33307
Stamina Formula 1000, a power tablet which contains B-complex, octacosanol, kelp, herbs, minerals, RNA/DNA, fat metabolizers, and ATP-related nutrients

Nutri-Source Nutritional Products
PO BOX 5010, ORANGE, CA 92667
supplements, vitamins

Nutri-Tech
5008 WILL DR., AKRON, OH 44319
egg protein, high-potency, all-natural glandular tablets—endorsed by Bob Gallucci

Fig. 87

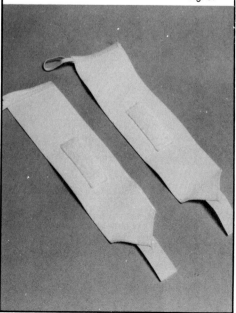

Nutritional Athletic Products
4627 UNIVERSITY DR., DAVIE, FL 33328
305-434-7200
*primo gland (a natural steroid substitute),
minerals, power-assist claw, vitamins*

Nutritional Charts
PO BOX 30265, PORTLAND, OR 97230
nutritional charts

Nutritional Factors
CONCORD, CA 94524
415-676-7201
glandulars

Oakglade Industries
7707 BANKSIDE DR., HOUSTON, TX 77071
equipment

Oasis Relaxation Tank Co., Inc.
1737 W. ALAMBA, HOUSTON, TX 77098
713-529-7210
flotation tanks

Obertini Publishing Co.
755 S. NELSON, SUITE 4, EAST KANKAKEE, IL
60901
training aids

O.E.M. Publishing
2801B OCEAN PARK, SUITE 25, SANTA
MONICA, CA 90405
213-452-5491
*books (Underground Steroid Handbook,
Ultimate Dieting Handbook, USH
Update), equipment*

Olympia Health & Exercise Products
5407 WILSHIRE BLVD., LOS ANGELES, CA
90036
213-938-1144
equipment, training aids

Olympic Health Equipment, Inc.
1717 W. GALBRAITH RD., CINCINNATI, OH
45239
513-522-7537
equipment

Olympic Trophy and Awards Co.
4408 N. MILWAUKEE AVE., CHICAGO, IL
60630
312-545-0449
*awards, certificates, medals, plaques,
ribbons—custom engraving available*

Olympus Gym
RT. 611, WARRINGTON, PA 18976
215-343-9191
*books on bodybuilding by George
Snyder, Lorraine Snyder, and Rick Wayne*

Omnibod System
PO BOX 226, BISBEE, AZ 85603
build-your-own equipment

Omni-Gym Products
PO BOX 37486, PHOENIX, AZ 85069
602-843-2403
*barbell pads, bee pollen, DMSO,
equipment, protein, sure-grip straps, T-
shirts, video training films, wraps*

Ooh La La!, Inc.
31 CUPANIA CIRCLE, PO BOX 2029,
MONTEREY PARK, CA 91754
1-800-527-3592, ext. 450
jewelry

ORG Products
PO BOX 68066, SEATTLE, WA 98168
fitness diaries

Orion
1462 LIVELY RIDGE DR., ATLANTA, GA 30329
gloves

Ortho Molecular Nutrition International
PO BOX 5036, MANCHESTER, NH 03108
603-434-6254
minerals, vitamins

Ortho Support Wraps
PO BOX 816, NORCO, CA 91760
714-737-5649
neoprene support wraps

Pacifico Enterprises
PO BOX 14152 N.R. BR., DAYTON, OH 45414
513-898-7245
*belts, books, courses, lifting straps,
powerlifting seminars and shoes, super
wraps, training aids, videos, waist
waisters*

G. Pacillo Co., Inc.
PO BOX 43, BUFFALO, NY 14216
equipment

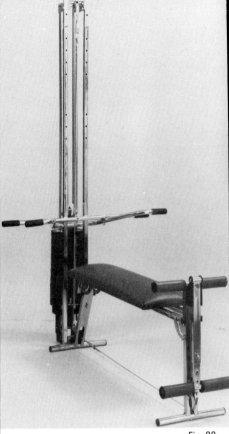

Fig. 88

Danny Padilla
PO BOX 1840, SANTA MONICA, CA 90406
*courses, personalized training programs,
seminars, photos, tank tops, T-shirts*

ParaBody, Inc.
1101 STINSON BLVD., SUITE 8, MINNEAPOLIS,
MN 55413
612-379-7675
Isotone—a home exercising unit

Paramount Fitness Equipment Corp.
3000 S. SANTA FE AVE., LOS ANGELES, CA
90058
213-583-2424
equipment

Bob Paris Fashions
8033 SUNSET BLVD., SUITE 238, LOS
ANGELES, CA 90046
clothing

Ken Passariello
PO BOX 761, ORANGE, CT 06477
*"The Demon" bodybuilding posing act,
seminars*

Pat's Mug
PO BOX 367, ROSENHAYN, NJ 08352
mugs

Pawling Rubber
157 MAPLE BLVD., PAWLING, NY 12564
*interlocking rubber floor systems for
weight equipment*

Fig. 89

P. C. House
PO BOX 125, ROCKAWAY, NJ 07866
workout record book

Bill Pearl's Physical Fitness Architects
100 S. MICHIGAN AVE., PASADENA, CA 91106
bars, books (Keys to the Inner Universe), elbow and knee protectors, lifting belts, posing briefs, training courses, T-shirts, trimmers

Performance Plus Sports Products
438 E. KATELLA AVE., SUITE 226, ORANGE, CA 92667
fitness accessories, food supplements

Personal Training
PO BOX 474, HAZELWOOD, MO 63042
training logs

Tom Petro's Health Emporium
808 S. BROAD ST., TRENTON, NJ 08611
609-396-7735
equipment (York and Weider), gloves, gravity boots, knee wraps, lifting belts, supplements

Physique Boutique
PO BOX 13855, LAS VEGAS, NV 89112-1855
custom-made posing suits for men and women

Pitt Barbell & Healthfood Corp.
126 PENN HILLS MALL, RODI RD. & FRANKSTOWN, PITTSBURGH, PA 15235
412-371-4366
bikes, equipment, gloves, karate bags, lifting belts, power belts, rowing machines, shoes, straps, sweat suits, training suits, treadmills

P. J. Jewelry
PO BOX 4126, SUNNYSIDE, NY 11104
212-937-9623
jewelry

Tom Platz, Inc.
PO BOX 1262, SANTA MONICA, CA 90406
photos, posing trunks, posters, sweat shirts, tank tops

Plus Products
2681 KELVIN AVE., IRVINE, CA 92714
714-556-8600
minerals, nutritional boosters, protein powders, skin- and hair-care products, stress supplements, vitamins

C. L. Pohlmar
PO BOX 797, LEXINGTON PARK, MD 20653
T-shirts for female bodybuilders and weightlifters

Polaris
5334 BANKS ST., SAN DIEGO, CA 92110
619-297-4349
equipment—endorsed by Mae Mollica and Jesse Lujan

Nancy Pollak
165 W. 83RD. ST., NEW YORK, NY 10024
212-874-0713
exercise wear for women

Leonard Poole
PO BOX 161, APOPKA, FL 32703
donkey raise machines

Port-A-Gym Co.
PO BOX 1051, LONGVIEW, WA 98632
equipment

G. Potter
24 CEDAR DR., PACIFIC, MO 63069
body-fat calculators

Power By Cash
1240 NORTON AVE., DAYTON, OH 45420
513-254-9337
belts, books, bumper plates, deadlifting slippers, gloves, photos, powerlifting suits, T-shirts, training routines, wraps

Power Design
PO BOX 1204, SEATTLE, WA 98111-1204
1-800-227-3800, ext. 223/1-800-792-0990, ext. 223
weightlifting racks

Power Grip
PO BOX 1, CATASAUQUA, PA 18032
power grips

Powerhouse Gym
16251 WOODWARD AVE., HIGHLAND PARK, MI 48203
313-868-3412
duffle bags, hats, shorts, sweat shirts, tank tops, training suits, T-shirts, visor caps

PowerMax GymSystems
11028 N. 22ND AVE., PHOENIX, AZ 85029
602-264-7009/1-800-821-7143
equipment (full-body isotonic-conditioning system)

Power Place Products, Inc.
124 E. STATE ST., WEST LAFAYETTE, IN 47906
317-743-3481
ankle weights, arm blasters, belts, chalk, chest expanders, deadlift shoes, equipment, exerbikes, exercise wheels, gloves, hand and scissor grips, joggers, jump ropes, lifting suits, power twisters, straps, trimmer exercisers, wraps

The Power Pit
98-820 MOANALUA RD., AIEA, HI 96701
808-487-6500
T-shirts

Power Plus
2702 MENEFEE, ARTESIA, MN 88210
505-746-6535
equipment

Powers Gym
169 MIRACLE STRIP, FT. WALTON BEACH, FL 32548
904-243-9044
sportswear: gym shorts, jackets, muscle shirts, nylon shorts, tank tops, T-shirts, warm-up suits—designed by John Powers and Pam Meister

Pow'r Body Building
1101 STINSON BLVD., SUITE 8, MINNEAPOLIS, MN 55413
1-800-328-9714
Hercules 12-station multi-gym

Product Support
8969 MONTROSE WAY, SAN DIEGO, CA 92122
619-453-4755/619-563-1709
abdominal racks, aerobic mats, exercycles, free weights, life cycles, lockers, saunas, suntan beds, twisters, whirlpools

Fig. 91

Pro Gym Fitness Center
322 MURIEL NE, ALBUQUERQUE, NM 87123
505-294-1221
jewelry, tank tops, T-shirts

Pro-Line
PO BOX 39696, PHOENIX, AZ 85069
equipment

Pro-Photo
PO BOX 6804, BRIAR GATE CT., MONTGOMERY, AL 36116
physique photography

Pro-Power Supplements
PO BOX 28092, QUEENS VILLAGE, NY 11428
212-526-5316
supplements

Pro-tron
840 NEWPORT CENTER DR., NEWPORT BEACH, CA 92660
714-720-0678/1-800-338-4338
equipment

PS Co.
PO BOX 91, WELLESLEY, MA 02181
athletic socks, bandanna kerchiefs, jock-straps, supporters (pro duke, the duke, duke swimmer)

PS Products
PO BOX 1, MONUMENT, CO 80132
posters, charts

Qualiform, Inc.
350 STATE ST., PO BOX 28, WADSWORTH, OH 44281
216-336-6777
colored (black, red, blue) bumpers for Olympic weights, solid rubber

Quality Designs
1302 N. 8TH ST., SUPERIOR, WI 54880
715-392-7200
benches, cambered bench press bars (endorsed by Mike MacDonald), lat machines, Olympic bars, plate racks, Roman chairs, safety stands

Quantum Productions
PO BOX 149, ROMEO, MI 48065
video on women's weight training and bodybuilding

Queststar
233 WILSHIRE BLVD., CALIFORNIA FEDERAL BLDG., SANTA MONICA, CA 90401
213-395-6102
equipment (called Water Machines)

Fig. 90

Rain Beau
55 STILLMAN, SAN FRANCISCO, CA 94107
415-777-5629
exercise wear for women

RayCo
PO BOX 2656, ROCKEFELLER CENTER STATION, NEW YORK, NY 10185
books on bodybuilding and nutrition

RCM
PO BOX 604, ANOKA, MN 55303
612-421-0129/1-800-328-9203
gym matting, weight-room matting

Steve Reeves, Classic Image Enterprises
PO BOX 807, VALLEY CENTER, CA 92082
books

Regal Enterprises, Sports Div.
5409 GREENVILLE AVE., S-229, DALLAS, TX 75206-2908
grips

Reid's Fitness Equipment
PO BOX 353, MARYSVILLE, MI 48040
neck harnesses, wrist and forearm developers

Rejuvenators, Studs, Ltd.
PO BOX 763, SANTA FE, NM 87501
vitamin-mineral-herb complex

Research Specialties
PO BOX 8266, GREEN BAY, WI 54308
liquid yeast product

Fig. 92

Don Ross
11 C ST., VALLEJO, CA 94590
seminars

Royal American Food Co.
PO BOX 1000, BLUE SPRINGS, MO 64015
816-229-1000
bakery goods, beverages, meatless meals made of soy products (high protein, low fat, low calories), tofu

Royal House
PO BOX 1211, OKLAHOMA CITY, OK 73101
405-942-5606
equipment (Mac, York, Sonata, Walton, Champion, Universal, AMF, Rocky Mountain)

R and R Brass
15 WOODBINE RD., ROWAYTON, CT 06853
miniature (4-1/2-in. × 1-1/2-in.-high) Olympic barbell set with stand

R & R Industries
PO BOX 651, TARZANA, CA 91356
213-710-8026
barbell pads, belts, chin and lat attachments, gloves, sit-up racks, sports wraps, sure-grip powder, sure-grip straps

Rubber Products, A Div. of Frankland Enterprises, Inc.
4521 W. CREST AVE., TAMPA, FL 33614
813-870-0390/813-870-0463
Tuflex live-rubber tile flooring for weightlifting

Richards Medical Co.
1450 BROOKS RD., MEMPHIS, TN 38116
thermal-action neoprene supports

Ripley Custom Shirtmakers
4153 CANAL ST., NEW ORLEANS, LA 70119
custom-made shirts

R. J.'s Kitchen
7326 W. 110TH ST., WORTH, IL 60482
food

Joe Roark's Musclesearch
PO BOX J., ST. JOSEPH, IL 61873
index to Iron Man magazine articles (from 1959 to the present)

Paul Roberts
PO BOX 2403, PLAINFIELD, NJ 07060
201-755-8525
physique portraiture

Tim Roberts
23843 TAYLOE HOUSE LANE, KATY, TX 77449
713-391-9816
blue-green manna products (has vitamins, minerals, amino acids, chlorophyll, lipids): mannacol, mannamist, mannapep, mannastat, mannazen, pro-t-col, t-col

Robby Robinson
PO BOX 982
VENICE, CA 90291
personalized dieting and training programs, photos, T-shirts (for men and women), vest tops (for women)

Rock & Row
PO BOX 169
CORRYTON, TN 37721
615-992-0370
rowing machines

Rocky Mountain Gym Equipment Co., Inc.
5745 MONACO ST.
COMMERCE CITY, CO 80022
303-287-8095/1-800-525-0708
equipment

L. Rolfe's Leather
PO BOX 4707, NEWARK, DE 19711
302-738-0444
10-cm power lifting belts, weight belts (4 inch and 6 inch), 2-inch wrist straps

Roseglen Ironworks
11632 E. ROSEGLEN
EL MONTE, CA 91732
213-446-7048/213-448-8981
equipment, wraps, suits

S

Saf-T-Gym
815 ALEXANDER VALLEY RD., HEALDSBURG, CA 95448
707-433-7661
conditioning machines

Samco
PO BOX 088, NORTH RIDGEVILLE, OH 44039-0088
216-327-5447
equipment

Samra Nutrition
PO BOX 1052, SANTA MONICA, CA 90406
213-396-2615
beef-liver extract, enzymes, diet-pack amino acids, minerals, protein powder, steroid substitute—"Naturol," spirulina, vitamins

SAN
PO BOX 168, IRWIN, PA 15642
food

San Carlos Exercise Equipment Co.
1600 EL CAMINO RD., SAN CARLOS, CA 94070
415-591-7115
books, equipment, exercycles, lifting belts, magazines, martial arts supplies, massage rollers, rowing machines, supplements, trampolines, vitamins, women's workout clothing (leg warmers, leotards, tights, tote bags, posing suits)

Savage Enterprises
PO BOX 854, CASCADE, MD 21719
health-club consultant

S.C.A. Corp., Wolff System
2795 152ND AVE., NE, REDMOND, WA 98052
206-881-6065/telex: 152144
suntanning equipment

Arnold Schwarzenegger
PO BOX 1234, SANTA MONICA, CA 90406
Arnold album, conditioning and training courses, Mr. Olympia tank tops and T-shirts, posters, training bags and belts, weight-training guide for women

Larry Scott
PO BOX 162, NORTH SALT LAKE, UT 84054
chinning straps, personalized workout routines, photos, posters, tank tops, T-shirts

Fig. 93

Scrub Duds
100 SUNSET RD., CHESHIRE, CT 05410
sportswear

Search Labs, A Div. of Nutri-Dyn Products, Inc.
5705 W. HOWARD ST., NILES, IL 60648
312-647-0350/1-800-323-4901
hypoallergenic products, milk and egg protein, minerals, raw glandular concentrates: adrenol, cardionol, heptinol, intrinsinol, lymphinol, mastinol, multinol, neurinol, nutridenum, orchinol, ostinol, ovinol, pancrinol, pangest, prolinol, splenol, thymusol, uterol; rehab exercise kits

S.G.S. Enterprises
PO BOX 1171, RAMONA, CA 92065
vitamins

Shake Recipes
PO BOX 75115, CINCINNATI, OH 45275
shake drinks

Shannon Publishing and Mail Order
6444 SIERRA CT., DUBLIN, CA 94568
415-828-1290
amino acids, books, energy wafers, equipment, health foods, liver tablets, minerals, posing trunks, protein, spirulina, supplements, weight gain glandulars, training accessories and courses, vitamins

The Sharper Image
1 MARITIME PLAZA, SUITE 745, SAN FRANCISCO, CA 94111
415-788-1111
multi-purpose home gym, rowing-weight machine, free weights, rowing machine, exercise bike

SHE-BEAST by Pillow
PO BOX 1076
VENICE, CA 90294
photos (color and B&W), posters, products by female bodybuilder Pillow: "SHE-BEAST" bodybuilding posing act, T-shirts

Sheritha Enterprises
2202 PINEWOOD AVE., #3C, BALTIMORE, MD 21214
301-254-0446
body stockings, custom-made posing suits (for men and women)

Silver Solarium
2 KANSAS ST., SUITE 450, SAN FRANCISCO, CA 94103
415-552-9916/1-800-828-2882
tanning equipment—endorsed by Samir Bannout and Inger Zetterqvist

Simmons Co.
54 SHALLOWFORD RD. CHATTANOOGA, TN 37404
ankle and wrist weights

Simply Healthy Products
PO BOX 894, SEABROOK, TX 77586
collection of low-fat, no-sugar, low-sodium yet high-protein, enzyme-rich natural-food recipes

S & J Studios
PO BOX 54, LATHRUP VILLAGE, MI 48076
T-shirts

Skin Control Systems, Inc.
8901 WILSHIRE BLVD., BEVERLY HILLS, CA 90211
1-800-453-6900
skin-control system: workout gel, vitalizing shave cream, protective gel, skin nutritive vitamins, revitalizing facial scrub, and restorative formula

Skyhook
PO BOX 5319, ENGLEWOOD, CO 80155
inversion gear

SKY Products
11611 SALINAS DR., GARDEN GROVE, CA 92643
inversion boots

Sky's the Limit
4106 SNAG ISLAND DR. SUMNER, WA 98390
206-863-0454
chinning bars, health boots, inversion rack

Smith's
2047 W. INDIANA AVE., PHILADELPHIA, PA 19132
vitamins

Softouch Co., Inc.
PO BOX 7351 HOLLYWOOD, FL 33021
305-962-9631/1-800-432-3633/ 1-800-327-1539
exercise wear for women

Solana, Inc.
5112 AZUSA CANYON RD., IRWINDALE, CA 91706
213-960-3885/1-800-TANNING/telefax: 213-359-8094
Swedish-manufactured tanning bed which utilizes UVA light

Soloflex
HAWTHORN FARM INDUSTRIAL PARK, HILLSBORO, OR 97123
1-800-453-9000
equipment

Songgram
109 LANSING AVE., MERCERVILLE, NJ 08619
workout music

Sontegra
222 BRIDGE PLAZA SOUTH, FT. LEE, NJ 07024
suntan spas (European suntanning salons and clubs)

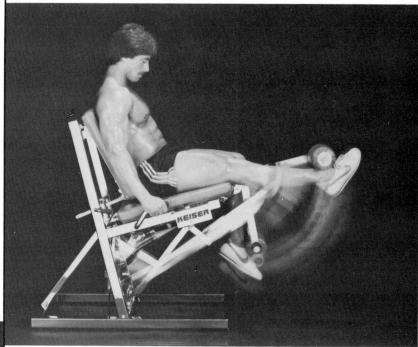

Fig. 95

Fig. 94

Spartacus Fitness Systems
135 N. COMMONWEALTH AVE., LOS ANGELES, CA 90004
gravity boots

Spong Studios
PO BOX 39, KIRKWOOD, NJ 08043
humorous color prints of powerlifting

Sport Medical Technology Corp.
PO BOX 656, CENTER MORICHES, NY 11934
516-878-0101
computerized fitness-evaluation systems

Sports Science Consultants
PO BOX 633, NATICK, MA 01760
books on anabolic steroids by James Wright

Sportscience Laboratories
PO BOX 390, ESSEX JUNCTION, VT 05452/802-878-5508/1-800-451-5190
nutrients, vitamins

Sports Conditioning Services
15343 VANOWEN, #235, VAN NUYS, CA 91406
books, lifting belts, power hooks, training courses

Sports Discount Center
PO BOX 8418, SAN FRANCISCO, CA 94128
heavyhands equipment

Sports Medical Nutrition
1061-B SHARY CIRCLE, CONCORD, CA 94518
415-827-2636
nutritional supplements for peak performance

Sports Research Corp
761 BASIN ST., PO BOX 1471, SAN PEDRO, CA 90731
213-519-1484
BBF maxercise crème

Sportsscreen
RT. 1, PO BOX 54, WHITELAND, IN 46184
T-shirts (custom imprinting available)

Standard Gym Equipment, Inc.
675 TRABOLD RD., PO BOX 24853, ROCHESTER, NY 14624
716-247-5174
equipment

Sterling Labs
18722 SANTEE, VALLEY CENTER, CA 92082
619-749-8609/1-800-952-9568
glandulars

Sterling Publishing Co., Inc.
TWO PARK AVE., NEW YORK, NY 10016
books, calendars

Steroids
PO BOX 761, ORANGE, CT 06477
books on steroids by Stanley W. Morey and Ken Passariello

L. D. Stokes Studios
1719 SHERMAN PLACE, STUDIO 7, LONG BEACH, CA 90804
213-433-2096
sculpture

Stone Enterprises, Inc.
14 HANOVER ST., PO BOX 2024, HANOVER, MA 02339
617-826-4668/617-826-9511
equipment—endorsed by Ken Passariello

Streamline Gym & Fitness Equipment
430 WILLOW ST., EAST STROUDSBURG, PA 18301
717-424-6488
equipment

Strength, Inc.
432 HIGHLAND AVE.
TWIN FALLS, ID 83301
208-734-6883
equipment

Strength Source Unlimited
2100 FAIR PARK AVE., #115, LOS ANGELES, CA 90041
213-257-5212
amino acids, glandulars, liver tablets, personalized training programs, protein powder, training aids, vitamins

Strength Tech, Inc.
PO BOX 1381, STILLWATER, OK 74076
405-377-7100
Okie grips for weights

Strong Barbell Co., c/o C. Teegarden
2225 DOWNAR WAY, SACRAMENTO, CA 95838
magazines (buy, sell, and trade)

Strong-Lon of California
17511 ROSCOE BLVD., NORTHRIDGE, CA 91325
213-343-4821
powerlifting suits

Stroud's Lifeline, Augie & Connie Digrazia, Distributors
2401 GRANADA WAY
CARLSBAD, CA 92008
619-729-5818
healthy gourmet foods and fitness programs

Jan Stuart Natural Skin Care Ltd.
663 FIFTH AVE., NEW YORK, NY 10022
1-800-323-1717
natural skin-care products for men with dry, normal, or oily skin: shaving-cleansing cream, aftershave/toner, aftershave/astringent, night cream/beard softener, firming masque, abrasive scrub, rejuvenating cream, moisturizer

Suncoast Exercise Equipment
134 LAKESHORE DR. NORTH, PALM HARBOR, FL 33563
813-938-4617
equipment

Suncorp
PO BOX 700, SANTA CRUZ, NM 87567
canthaxanthin tablets

Sunmaker, Inc.
PO BOX 8389, FT. WAYNE, IN 46898
219-483-1589
tanning equipment (sun beds)

Fig. 96

Sunshine Express
PO BOX 11266, MARINA DEL REY, CA 90296
213-822-7236
blood-pressure monitor, heart-rate monitor (for the wrist)

The SunTan People
PO BOX 1515, ROCKVILLE, MD 20850
1-800-531-5731
aloe vera-based suntan products (oil, lotions, moisturizers, lip balm)

Suntron Corp.
222 W. SUPERIOR ST., FT. WAYNE, IN 46802
219-426-4950
inversion boots and bars

Superbodies Fitness Centers
119 E. 18TH ST., COSTA MESA, CA 92627
714-646-0283
gym franchises

Superior Gym Equipment
426 UPLAND AVE., IOWA CITY, IA 52240
319-351-4522
equipment

Superior Health Studios for Men & Women
10024 N. 30TH ST., TAMPA, FL 33612
813-977-6297
health foods

Sure Grips, c/o T. Jolley
6721 ARTFUL DR., DALLAS, TX 75235
grips

Surgrip
909 15TH ST., SUITE 2A, MODESTO, CA 95354
grips

Sweat, Inc.
PO BOX 567, 3219 CLOSE CT., CINCINNATI, OH 45201
skinfold calipers

Sword Enterprises
821 NEIL AVE., D-2, COLUMBUS, OH 43215
belt squats, knee wraps

T.A.F. Enterprises, Inc.
PO BOX 463, PALOS HEIGHTS, IL 60463
build-your-own equipment

Tanning Hut, Inc.
116 WOLF RD., ALBANY, NY 12205
518-459-5115
suntanning units and beds

Mandy Tanny
PO BOX 3150, WOODLAND HILLS, CA 91365
*clothing, photos, posters, training
courses*

T & C Health Foods
420 SE 29TH, TOPEKA, KS 66605
913-235-0723
health foods

TDS Barbell & Gym Equipment
139 BANKER ST., BROOKLYN, NY 11222
212-388-2527
*equipment, accessories: dipping belts,
weightlifting gloves, iron boots,
horseshoe handles, triceps bars, triangle
bombers*

Russ Testo
3 OXFORD RD., TROY, NY 12180
518-274-0952
*pantomime/robot bodybuilding posing
act*

Texas Imperial American, Inc.
PO BOX 878, TYLER, TX 75710
equipment

Tickets of California
341 W. 31ST ST., LOS ANGELES, CA 90007
213-747-8466
dance wear/exercise wear for women

Dennis Tinerino
PO BOX 299, NORTHRIDGE, CA 91328
*photos, posing trunks, seminars, shorts,
tank tops, training courses*

Fig. 97

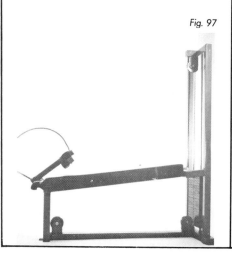

Fig. 98

Titan Bodybuilding, Inc.
314 N. 14TH AVE., JACKSONVILLE, FL 32205
904-246-2818/1-800-874-7742
*bodybuilding apparel: gym bags, head-
bands, knee wraps, lifting belts, posing
suits, shirts, tank tops, T-shirts—endorsed
by Shelley Gruwell and Boyer Coe*

Titan Suits
921 RICKEY, CORPUS CHRISTI, TX 78412
*quality, custom-designed powerlifting
suits in three sizes: regular fit, meet fit,
competition fit*

T. K. Equipment
4 FRANKLIN AVE., MT. VERNON, NY 10550
914-667-5959
equipment

Mike Torchia
13 BRADHURST AVE., HAWTHORNE, NY
10572
914-592-8761
*bodybuilding posing shows for discos,
fitness consultant, individualized training
programs*

Total Gym, Inc.
7161 ENGINEER RD., SAN DIEGO, CA 92111
1-800-854-1017
conditioning machines

Total Living Communications, Inc.
PO BOX 465, ISLE OF PALMS, SC 29451
training aids

Trace Minerals
PO BOX 628, CEDAR CITY, UT 84720
minerals

Train Right Fitness Center
25 CENTRAL ST., HINGHAM, MA 02043
617-749-8968
*amino acids, equipment (York),
glandulars, gloves, lifting suits, natural
growth-factor stimulants*

Travolta by Carushka
7376 GREENBUSH AVE., NORTH
HOLLYWOOD, CA 91605
men's action wear

T. R. Enterprises
23843 TAYLOE HOUSE LANE, KATY, TX
77449
food

Triple L Enterprises
PO BOX 1399, ROSEMEAD, CA 91770
scientific nutritional course

Alan Tuck Associates
PO BOX 1532, UNION, NJ 07083
201-241-7376
*mailing lists of: bodybuilders, gyms,
product advertisers, promoters; photos*

Kathy Tuite
PO BOX 5075, CONCORD, CA 94524
physique photography

Ujena

10100 SANTA MONICA BLVD., SUITE 2065, LOS ANGELES, CA 90067

women's competition suits

Ultimate Aminos

PO BOX 81886, SAN DIEGO, CA 92138-1886

powdered, free-form amino acids (L-ornithine, L-arginine, and lysine), canthaxanthin—endorsed by Mae Mollica

Ultimate Fitness Enterprises

PO BOX 686, BUENA VISTA, CO 81211
303-395-2845

shoulder bombers (free-weight deltoid training)

Unicorn Press

PO BOX 1092, RESEDA, CA 91335

vitamins

United Food & Fitness, Inc.

531 N. STATE RD., BRIARCLIFF MANOR, NY 19510
914-941-2145/1-800-638-3800

elliptical dumbbells, Multi-power Formula 70 (protein/vitamin/mineral mix)—endorsed by Mike Torchia, official supplier of the International Weightlifting Federation

United States Weightlifting Federation, Inc.

1750 E. BOULDER ST., COLORADO SPRINGS, CO 80909
303-578-4508/telex: 452424

bumper stickers, decals, lapel pins, lifting shoes, mugs, patches, T-shirts

United World Bodybuilders, Inc.

PO BOX 691578, LOS ANGELES, CA 90069

professional services to bodybuilders and promotion of bodybuilding on national and international levels (membership fee of $25/year buys membership card, monthly newsletter, additional information, all services, and free legal advice)

Universal Fitness Products

20 TERMINAL DR. SOUTH, PLAINVIEW, NY 11803
516-349-8600/telex: 5102211827

abdominal boards, ballet bars, benches, bike accessories, books, Centurion single- and multistation systems, electronic pulsemeters, exercise bikes, exercise charts, flooring, free-weight systems, Gladiator single- and multi-station gyms, gravity-guiding systems, joggers, powerpack systems, pulley-weight machines, rowing machines, scales, training films, treadmills, workout records

Universal Gym Equipment Inc.

PO BOX 1270, CEDAR RAPIDS, IA 52406
319-365-7561/1-800-553-7901

ankle straps, ballet bars, books, double twisters, electronic pulsemeters, equipment, ergometers, exercise bars, exercise bikes, exercise charts, head harnesses, joggers, pace clocks, pamphlets, physicians' scales, rubber flooring, shot puts, stirrup handles, training films, treadmills, weight adapters, workout records

Universal Supplements Corp.

1826 E. ELIZABETH AVE., LINDEN, NJ 07036
201-486-2322/1-800-221-0890

amino acids, digestive aids, lipo plus, liquid glandular extracts, mega-vitamins, muscle builders, protein powders, raw orchic, supplements, trimmers, vitamins, weight-gain formulas

Valley Machine Shop

PO BOX 2699, FARMINGTON, NM 87401
505-327-6071

arm machines

V.B.M.

355 W. 52ND ST., NEW YORK, NY 10019
1-800-223-7930

video cassettes of Miss Olympia contests

Vegebody

PO BOX 14509, ST. PETERSBURG, FL 33733

books for the vegetarian bodybuilder and athlete, T-shirts

Venus Bodywear Ltd.

314 N. 14TH AVE., JACKSONVILLE BEACH, FL 32250
904-246-2818/1-800-874-7742

exercise wear for women

Venus Food Supplements

2666 CALLE MANZANO, THOUSAND OAKS, CA 91360
805-492-0455

amino acids, bee pollen, books, bran tabs, desiccated liver, electrolyte powders, gain-on, glandulars, herbs, no-carb, nutritional wheels, protein powders, seminars, Super Spectrum (a complete vitamin-mineral supplement with 8 amino acids and 12-hour time-released chelated minerals), supplements (time-released), training belts, training programs, tri-min, T-shirts, vitamins, weight-loss packs, yeast flakes

Viamonte Design, Inc.

PO BOX 1880, CHERRY HILL, NJ 08034

anatomy charts

Casey Viator

PO BOX 314, NIWOT, CO 80544

cassettes, personalized training programs, photos, seminars, tank tops, training courses

Video Action

237 OGDEN AVE., JERSEY CITY, NJ 07307

video

Video Associates

5306 BEETHOVEN ST., LOS ANGELES, CA 90006
1-800-528-6050, ext. 6160

home video fitness program (with booklet), complete workout including Arnold Schwarzenegger and Rachel McLish

Video 4 Productions

PO BOX 864
WOODLAND HILLS, CA 91367
1-800-423-5713

video of Mr. Olympia contests

Vienna Health Products, Kit Div.

5121 WILLIAMS DR., VIENNA, OH 44473
216-394-1306

build-your-own equipment

Viking Barbell Co. & Health Club

334 BELLEVILLE AVE.
BELLEVILLE, NJ 07109
210-751-0099

equipment, protein, vitamins

Viking Gym, Inc.

PO BOX 29181, BROOKLYN CENTER, MN 55429

tank tops

VIM

2592 23RD ST., #1, CUYAHOGA FALLS, OH 44223

clothes

Fig. 99

VIOBIN Corp., a Subsidiary of A. H. Robins Co.
MONTICELLO, IL 61856
217-762-2561
nutrients, octacosanol products

Vita Chart
PO BOX 969, SOUTHAMPTON, PA 18966
diet and nutrition charts

Vitacrown, Inc.
6 COMMERCIAL ST., HICKSVILLE, NY 11801
vitamin-mineral program called "The Formula"

Vita-Fresh Vitamin Co.
PO BOX 3185, GARDEN GROVE, CA 92642
1-800-854-6427
sports/vitamin programs (eight choices available with one especially for the bodybuilder)

Vita-Life Products
PO BOX C, STATEN ISLAND, NY 10314
amino acids, glandulars, protein, supplements, vitamins

Vita Pro Products Co.
PO BOX 28802, DALLAS, TX 75228
1-800-527-1273
vitamins

The Voight Fitness Center
980 N. LA CIENEGA, LOS ANGELES, CA 90069
213-854-0741
posters

V. V., Inc.
1618 NE SIXTH AVE., PORTLAND, OR 97232
1-800-547-7004
DMSO

Wallingford Barbell Co.
176 N. COLONY RD., WALLINGFORD, CT 06492
equipment

Wammer International Delivery
14239 8TH AVE., SW, SEATTLE, WA 98166
Hurley Town and Country pure water system

Russ Warner's Exercise Equipment Co.
1223 THE ALAMEDA, SAN JOSE, CA 95126
408-293-9966
equipment

Fig. 100

Wate-Man Sales, Inc.
29123 W. EIGHT MIKE RD., LIVONIA, MI 48152
313-477-7245
professional bodybuilding equipment

W. C. Leathers
4948 REFORMA RD., WOODLAND HILLS, CA 91364
213-874-6249
custom-made weightlifting belts available in a variety of colors and styles— endorsed by Vince Gironda

Weider Health and Fitness, Inc.
21100 ERWIN ST.
WOODLAND HILLS, CA 91367
213-884-6800/1-800-423-5713/
1-800-382-3399
anabolic mega packs, anatomy charts, ankle and wrist weights, arm blasters, barbells, body shapers, books, boxing equipment, calf-burner benches, cambered curl bars, chinning bars, competition suits, enzymes, equipment, exercise bikes, exercise boards, E-Z collars, fat burners, figure twisters, foods, glandulars, gloves, grippers, head straps, home gyms, iron boots, joggers, jump ropes, kettlebells, liquid collagen, long-line slimmers, magazines (Flex, Muscle & Fitness, Shape), minerals, multi-power Olympic equipment, muscle builders, muscle rubs, pins, plates, pocket exercisers, posing trunks, posters, power belts and bracelets, power builders, power twisters, power-boot bars, protein powders, pulse meters, rowing machines, sauna suits, skin-care formulas, slimming bells, sports bags, swing bells, tank tops, ties, torso leans, training belts, training courses, training manuals, trampolines, treadmills, triceps bombers, T-shirts, videos, vitamins, waist shapers, weight-gain formulas, workout mats

Weightlifter's Warehouse
5542 SOUTH ST.
LAKEWOOD, CA 90713
213-531-3731
bar pads, chalk, gloves, knee wraps, natural nontoxic SEARCH gland concentrates, tank tops, training straps, wrist wraps

The Weight Room
PO BOX 92921, LOS ANGELES, CA 90009
T-shirts

The Weight Room Co.
PO BOX 2938, POCATELLO, ID 83201
208-234-0699
weight vest (24 lbs.)

Werling
24 17TH AVE., #207, VENICE, CA 90291
grips

West Coast Fitness Center
2149 TARAVAL ST., SAN FRANCISCO, CA 94116
415-566-7086
electrical depth indicator for squats

Western Natural Products
511 MISSION ST., PO BOX 284, SOUTH PASADENA, CA 91030
bee pollen, bioflavinoids, brewer's yeast, digestive aids, folic acid, hair-care products, minerals, PABA, pantothenic acid, protein, spirulina, supplements, vitamins

Wheeler's Fitness and Strength Enterprises
PO BOX 1483, BAKERSFIELD, CA 93302
805-871-3925
raw glandulars, supplements

Claudia Cornell Wilbourn
PO BOX 167, SANTA MONICA, CA 90406
illustrated bodybuilding courses, motivational/informative tapes, personal consultations, photos, posters

Wild Herbs & Specialties
PO BOX 88, SALT LAKE CITY, UT 84110
801-533-0167
herbs, specialties

Betty Williams
PO BOX 219, CARTERSVILLE, GA 30120
mats for weightlifting

Wilson Sports Vitamins, Sports Nutrition Co.
7366 ORANGEWOOD AVE., GARDEN GROVE, CA 92641
714-898-9936/1-800-854-6427
diet, energy, and protein powders, vitamin program for bodybuilders

Woman to Woman
7525 MITCHELL RD., EDEN PRAIRIE, MN 55344
fashions

Work Out
PO BOX 510, BOONTON, NJ 07005
artwork, fashions

World Barbell & Healthfoods
46 MORGANTOWN ST., UNIONTOWN, PA 15401
412-43-TRAIN
equipment, health foods

World Gym
2210 MAIN ST.
SANTA MONICA, CA 90405
213-399-9888
sportswear: gym hats, shorts, sweat shirts, tank tops, T-shirts

World Gym Supplements
6161 WOODHAVEN BLVD., REGO PARK, NY 11374
supplements, vitamins

World of Health
1234 S. GARFIELD AVE.
ALHAMBRA, CA
91801
213-727-5075
ankle and wrist weights, ankle straps, equipment, head gear, iron boots, lifting belts, minerals, proteins, supplements, vitamins, waist-trim belts

Worldwide Gym Equipment
PO BOX 39986, PHOENIX, AZ 85069
602-861-2169
equipment

Fig. 101

W.S.P.
PO BOX 443, HOHOKUS, NJ 07423
book (The Female Physique Athlete), monthly magazine for women bodybuilders, photos and super 8 films of women bodybuilders

Wysong Medical, Inc.
4925 N. JEFFERSON, MIDLAND, MI 48640
health and fitness items: herbal blends, hypnosis tapes, massagers, nutrients, power bands, pulse monitors, vitamins

York Barbell Co., Inc.
26-52 NORTH RIDGE AVE., PO BOX 1707, YORK, PA 17405
717-848-1541/717-767-6481
chest expanders, equipment, gloves, hand grips, head straps, health shoes, Hoffman food products, kettlebell handles, knee bands, lifting belts, magazines (Strength & Health, Muscular Development), minerals, muscle rubs, posing trunks, protein powders, shirts, speed ropes, stretching charts, suntan lotions, T-shirts, training suits, vitamins, weight belts, windbreakers, wrist rollers

Frank Zane
PO BOX 366, SANTA MONICA, CA 90406
books, minerals, photos, posing trunks, posters, seminars, shirts, shorts, supplements, tank tops, training courses, T-shirts, vitamins

Frank Zane's Zane Haven
PO BOX 2031, PALM SPRINGS, CA 92263
619-323-7486
weight-training and mind-body fitness learning center for men and women

Zestron, Inc.
1901 S. BASCOM AVE., CAMPBELL, CA 95008
408-371-1200/1-800-392-1200/
1-800-372-1200
air-ionization equipment

State-by-State Listings

ALABAMA

Diversified Products Corp.
OPELIKA, AL 36802

Dynakaz
AUBURN, AL 36830

Golden Pro, Inc.
BIRMINGHAM, AL 36235

Tom McLaughlin
AUBURN, AL 36830

William Moore
TUSCALOOSA, AL 35402-0732

Pro-Photo
MONTGOMERY, AL 36116

ALASKA

Healthy Ventures
ANCHORAGE, AK 99503

ARIZONA

Dax Fitness Industries, Inc.
PHOENIX, AZ 85009

Fitness Industries, Inc.
PHOENIX, AZ 85069

Johnny Gibson's Health and Gym Equipment
TUCSON, AZ 85701

Inertia Dynamics Corp.
PHOENIX, AZ 85012

Naturally Vitamin Supplements, Inc.
SCOTTSDALE, AZ 85254

Omnibod System
BISBEE, AZ 85603

Omni-Gym Products
PHOENIX, AZ 85069

PowerMax GymSystems
PHOENIX, AZ 85029

For more complete addresses, see the Companies Section.

Pro-Line
PHOENIX, AZ 85069

Worldwide Gym Equipment
PHOENIX, AZ 85069

ARKANSAS

Custom Built
JACKSONVILLE, AR 72076

CALIFORNIA

Achievement Plus
MARINA DEL REY, CA 90291

Advanced Nutrition
HACIENDA HEIGHTS, CA 91745

George Aiken Photography
DEL MAR, CA 92014

David L. Albin, M.D., Inc.
LA HABRA HEIGHTS, CA 90631

All American Products
BEVERLY HILLS, CA 90210

Alt Enterprises
LOS ANGELES, CA 90049

Andy Alvarado
MODESTO, CA 95354

Apparel Warehouse
TARZANA, CA 91356

John Balik
SANTA MONICA, CA 90406

Ballena Valley Natural Food Supplements
RAMONA, CA 92065

Samir Bannout
SANTA MONICA, CA 90406

Barely Legal
COSTA MESA, CA 92627

Baxter of California
BEVERLY HILLS, CA 90211

Tim Belknap
SANTA MONICA, CA 90406

Beverly International
LAGUNA HILLS, CA 92653

Big Boy Enterprises
LOS ANGELES, CA 90026

Bob's Custom Lifting Belts
POMONA, CA 91766

Body Love Co.
PETALUMA, CA 94953

The Body Shop
SAN FRANCISCO, CA 94128

Body Transformation
STOCKTON, CA 95209

Bonilla
BEVERLY HILLS, CA 90211

Bricker Labs
VALLEY CENTER, CA 92082

A. Brooks
ROHNERT PARK, CA 94928

Stevi Brooks
LOS ANGELES, CA 90055

Andreas Cahling Enterprises
VENICE, CA 90294

California Shape
WESTWOOD VILLAGE, CA 90024

Roger Callard
SANTA MONICA, CA 90406

David Carter Products
VENICE, CA 90291

R. Casey
LOS ANGELES, CA 90045

Classic Films
LOS ANGELES, CA 90045

Boyer Coe
HUNTINGTON BEACH, CA 92646

Franco Columbu
SANTA MONICA, CA 90406

Conejo Leathers
PT. HUENEME, CA 93014

Joe Corsi Fitness Equipment Co.
HAYWARD, CA 94541

Dalon
TARZANA, CA 91356

Dance France
SANTA MONICA, CA 90405

Steve Davis Fitness Center
NEWHALL, CA 91321

Dayton Unlimited, Inc.
CONCORD, CA 94524

DEM Publishing
MARINA DEL REY, CA 90291

Design Products
BAKERSFIELD, CA 93389

Designer Sport, Inc.
CHATSWORTH, CA 91311

Chris Dickerson, Inc.
VENICE, CA 90291

Di Mark Co.
MARINA DEL REY, CA 90295

D. S. Products
SACRAMENTO, CA 95823

Execs, Inc.
NORTHRIDGE, CA 91326

Exercise Chart Series
BAKERSFIELD, CA 93304

Expression
VAN NUYS, CA 91401

J. A. Feliciano
FOUNTAIN VALLEY, CA 92708

Lou Ferrigno
SANTA MONICA, CA 90406

Fillmore Foods, Inc.
HAYWARD, CA 94545

1st Fitness International
OCEANSIDE, CA 92054

Fitness
VENICE, CA 93001

Fitness America
COSTA MESA, CA 92627

Fitness Gym Systems, Inc.
SANTA PAULA, CA 93060

Fitness Institute of Hypnosis
SANTA MONICA, CA 90403

Fitnus
BAKERSFIELD, CA 93304

Flex Gym Equipment
ORANGE, CA 92667

Flextard
LOS ANGELES, CA 90064

Foothill Enterprises
SAN DIMAS, CA 91773

Cathy George Designs
BURBANK, CA 91502

Get Fit Video Series
MOUNTAIN VIEW, CA 94043

Getting Strong Book Series
LOS ANGELES, CA 90067

Vince Gironda
NORTH HOLLYWOOD, CA 91604

GMV Gallery
SAN JOSE, CA 95154-4802

Gold's Gym
VENICE, CA 90291

Goliath Gym Equipment
SANTA ANA, CA 92703

Ron J. Goodman
MONROVIA, CA 91016

Bill Grant Enterprises
SANTA MONICA, CA 90406

Gravity Research
DEL MAR, CA 92014

Gravity Sciences
LOS ANGELES, CA 90064

Great Earth International, Inc.
SANTA ANA, CA 92702

Fred Hatfield Fitness Systems
VAN NUYS, CA 91406

Health-for-Life
LOS ANGELES, CA 90046

Orrin J. Heller
NORWALK, CA 90650

High-Tech Fitness, Inc.
LOS ANGELES, CA 90069

hiTech Sports & Fitness Products
SUNNYVALE, CA 94089

Howard's Equipment Co.
FOUNTAIN VALLEY, CA 92708

H. W. E., Inc.
LOS ANGELES, CA 90028

Ingenuts Enterprises
LOS ANGELES, CA 90049

Interface Products for Men
MARINA DEL REY, CA 90291

Inversion Therapy Equipment
FREMONT, CA 94539

Iron Co.
SAN DIEGO, CA 92110

Iron Man's Gym
OCEANSIDE, CA 92054

Jabel Products
BEVERLY HILLS, CA 90210

Jewelry by Roger
WHITTIER, CA 90609

Keiser Sports Health Equipment
FRESNO, CA 93706

Betty Kerr Enterprises
MARINA DEL REY, CA 90291

L. H.'s Art
NORWALK, CA 90650

The Library
VAN NUYS, CA 91406

Lifecycle, Inc.
IRVINE, CA 92714

Life Cycle Vitamin Co.
VAN NUYS, CA 91401

Life Style Products
MOUNTAIN VIEW, CA 94043

Light Force Spirulina Co.
BOULDER CREEK, CA 95006

Linquist
DAVIS, CA 95616

LIVE
FULLERTON, CA 92634

Bill Lopez Gym Equipment
CARSON, CA 90745

Lyons Health & Fitness
GLENDALE, CA 91203

Marathon Distributing Co.
PALOS VERDES ESTATES, CA 90274

Mav-Rik
LOS ANGELES, CA 90065

Rachel McLish
SANTA MONICA, CA 90406

Mill Creek Natural Products
ROLLING HILLS, CA 90274

Mills Enterprises
MIDWAY CITY, CA 92655

Minitec Marketing, Inc.
CARSON, CA 90746

V. Moon
OCEANSIDE, CA 92054

Muscle Dynamics, Ltd.
CARSON, CA 90746

Muscle Mart
SAN DIEGO, CA 92111

MusclePower International USA
AZUSA, CA 91702

Muscle Shorts
SANTA MONICA, CA 90405

Natural Peak
SACRAMENTO, CA 95813

Natural Source Products, Inc.
CANOGA PARK, CA 91304

The North Light
BURBANK, CA 91505

Nutrabiotics
CAPITOLA, CA 95010

Nutri Biotics
SANTA CRUZ, CA 95062

Nutri-Foods
CANOGA PARK, CA 91303

Nutri-Source Nutritional Products
ORANGE, CA 92667

Nutritional Factors
CONCORD, CA 94524

O.E.M. Publishing
SANTA MONICA, CA 90405

Olympia Health & Exercise Products
LOS ANGELES, CA 90036

Ooh La La!, Inc.
MONTEREY PARK, CA 91754

Ortho Support Wraps
NORCO, CA 91760

Danny Padilla
SANTA MONICA, CA 90406

Paramount Fitness Equipment Corp.
LOS ANGELES, CA 90058

Bob Paris Fashions
LOS ANGELES, CA 90046

Bill Pearl's Physical Fitness Architects
PASADENA CA 91106

Performance Plus Sports Products
ORANGE, CA 92667

Tom Platz, Inc.
SANTA MONICA, CA 90406

Plus Products
IRVINE, CA 92714

Polaris
SAN DIEGO, CA 92110

Product Support
SAN DIEGO, CA 92122

Pro-tron
NEWPORT BEACH, CA 92660

Queststar
SANTA MONICA, CA 90401

Rain Beau
SAN FRANCISCO, CA 94107

Steve Reeves
VALLEY CENTER, CA 92082

Robby Robinson
VENICE, CA 90291

Roseglen Ironworks
EL MONTE, CA 91732

Don Ross
VALLEJO, CA 94590

R & R Industries
TARZANA, CA 91356

Saf-T-Gym
HEALDSBURG, CA 95448

Samra Nutrition
SANTA MONICA, CA 90406

San Carlos Exercise Equipment Co.
SAN CARLOS, CA 94070

Arnold Schwarzenegger
SANTA MONICA, CA 90406

S.G.S. Enterprises
RAMONA, CA 92065

Shannon Publishing and Mail Order
DUBLIN, CA 94568

The Sharper Image
SAN FRANCISCO, CA 94111

SHE-BEAST by Pillow
VENICE, CA 90294

Silver Solarium
SAN FRANCISCO, GA 94103

Skin Control Systems, Inc.
BEVERLY HILLS, CA 90211

SKY Products
GARDEN GROVE, CA 92643

Solana, Inc.
IRWINDALE, CA 91706

Spartacus Fitness Systems
LOS ANGELES, CA 90004

Sports Conditioning Services
VAN NUYS, CA 91406

Sports Discount Center
SAN FRANCISCO, CA 94128

Sports Medical Nutrition
CONCORD, CA 94518

Sports Research Corp.
SAN PEDRO, CA 90731

Sterling Labs
VALLEY CENTER, CA 92082

L. D. Stokes Studios
LONG BEACH, CA 90804

Strength Source Unlimited
LOS ANGELES, CA 90041

Strong Barbell Co.
SACRAMENTO, CA 95838

Strong-Lon of California
NORTHRIDGE, CA 91325

Stroud's Lifeline
CARLSBAD, CA 92008

Sunshine Express
MARINA DEL REY, CA 90296

Superbodies Fitness Centers
COSTA MESA, CA 92627

Surgrip
MODESTO, CA 95354

Mandy Tanny
WOODLAND HILLS, CA 91365

Tickets of California
LOS ANGELES, CA 90007

Dennis Tinerino
NORTHRIDGE, CA 91328

Total Gym, Inc.
SAN DIEGO, CA 92111

Travolta by Carushka
NORTH HOLLYWOOD, CA 91605

Triple L Enterprises
ROSEMEAD, CA 91770

Kathy Tuite
CONCORD, CA 94524

Ujena
LOS ANGELES, CA 90067

Ultimate Aminos
SAN DIEGO, CA 92138-1886

Unicorn Press
RESEDA, CA 91335

United World Bodybuilders, Inc.
LOS ANGELES, CA 90069

Venus Food Supplements
THOUSAND OAKS, CA 91360

Video Associates
LOS ANGELES, CA 90006

Video 4 Productions
WOODLAND HILLS, CA 91367

Vita-Fresh Vitamin Co.
GARDEN GROVE, CA 92642

The Voight Fitness Center
LOS ANGELES, CA 90069

Russ Warner's Exercise Equipment Co.
SAN JOSE, CA 95126

Weider Health and Fitness, Inc.
WOODLAND HILLS, CA 91367

Weightlifter's Warehouse
LAKEWOOD, CA 90713

The Weight Room
LOS ANGELES, CA 90009

Werling
VENICE, CA 92091

West Coast Fitness Center
SAN FRANCISCO, CA 94116

Western Natural Products
SOUTH PASADENA, CA 91030

Wheeler's Fitness and Strength Enterprises
BAKERSFIELD, CA 93302

Claudia Cornell Wilbourn
SANTA MONICA, CA 90406

Wilson Sports Vitamins
GARDEN GROVE, CA 92641

World Gym
SANTA MONICA, CA 90405

World of Health
ALHAMBRA, CA 91801

Frank Zane
SANTA MONICA, CA 90406

Zane Haven
PALM SPRINGS, CA 92263

Zestron, Inc.
CAMPBELL, CA 95008

COLORADO

Earthrise Spirulina
BOULDER, CO 80306

Float to Relax, Inc.
LAKEWOOD, CO 80214

Ilona of Hungary
DENVER, CO 80206

Kellogg, Inc.
DACUNA, CO 80514

PS Products
MONUMENT, CO 80132

Rocky Mountain Gym Equipment Co., Inc.
COMMERCE CITY, CO 80022

Skyhook
ENGLEWOOD, CO 80155

Ultimate Fitness Enterprises
BUENA VISTA, CO 81211

United States Weightlifting Federation, Inc.
COLORADO SPRINGS, CO 80909

Casey Viator
NIWOT, CO 80544

CONNECTICUT

Jay Casagrande
NORWALK, CT 06851

Charlton Publications, Inc.
DERBY, CT 06418

Corbin-Gentry, Inc.
SOMERSVILLE, CT 06072

Muscle Factory
ROWAYTON, CT 06853

Ken Passariello
ORANGE, CT 06477

R and R Brass
ROWAYTON, CT 06853

Scrub Duds
CHESHIRE, CT 05410

Steroids
ORANGE, CT 06477

Wallingford Barbell Co.
WALLINGFORD, CT 06492

DELAWARE

L. Rolfe's Leather
NEWARK, DE 19711

FLORIDA

Bahama Tanning Products
FT. LAUDERDALE, FL 33301

Barbell Sportswear
JACKSONVILLE, FL 32205

BioTechnology, Inc.
MIAMI, FL 33166

The Body Shoppe
JACKSONVILLE, FL 32205

Frank Calta's Super Fitness
TAMPA, FL 33617

Darden Research Corp.
LAKE HELEN, FL 32744

Donkey Raise Machine
APOPKA, FL 32703

Fitness & Nutrition Center, Inc.
NORTH MIAMI BEACH, FL 33160

Future Equipment Co., Inc.
CLEARWATER, FL 33515

Steve Lennard
MIAMI, FL 33129

Mike Mentzer
DELAND, FL 32720

Jim Michaels Art Co.
PALM HARBOR, FL 33563

C. Miller
FT. LAUDERDALE, FL 33302-1234

Joe Mullen
DELAND, FL 32720

Natures Best
FT. WALTON BEACH, FL 32548

Nautilus Sports/Medical Industries, Inc.
DELAND, FL 32720

Nu Life
ST. PETERSBURG, FL 33710

Nutri-Data, Inc.
MIAMI, FL 33116

Nutri-Research
FT. LAUDERDALE, FL 33307

Nutritional Athletic Products
DAVIE, FL 33328

Leonard Poole
APOPKA, FL 32703

Powers Gym
FT. WALTON BEACH, FL 32548

Rubber Products
TAMPA, FL 33614

Softouch Co., Inc.
HOLLYWOOD, FL 33021

Suncoast Exercise Equipment
PALM HARBOR, FL 33563

Superior Health Studios for Men & Women
TAMPA, FL 33612

Titan Bodybuilding, Inc.
JACKSONVILLE, FL 32205

Vegebody
ST. PETERSBURG, FL 33733

Venus Bodywear Ltd.
JACKSONVILLE BEACH, FL 32250

GEORGIA

Arbol
ATLANTA, GA 30362

Bob Cornelius
VILLA RICA, GA 30180

C.W.S.
SYLVESTER, GA 31791

Doc's Sports
COLLEGE PARK, GA 30349-0338

Malepak
ATLANTA, GA 30349

Orion
ATLANTA, GA 30329

Betty Williams
CARTERSVILLE, GA 30120

HAWAII

ELF Research
PAUILLO, HI 96776

Hawaiian Resources
HONOLULU, HI 96816

The Power Pit
AIEA, HI 96701

IDAHO

Strength, Inc.
TWIN FALLS, ID 83301

The Weight Room Co.
POCATELLO, ID 83201

ILLINOIS

A.R.P.-Rhombus
OAK FOREST, IL 60452

Elmo's Exercise Equipment
EVERGREEN PARK, IL 60642

Exercircle
GENEVA, IL 60134

Ferrero Designs
DEPUE, IL 61322

Fox Marketing
BLOOMINGTON, IL 61701

Ernie and Diane Frantz Health Studio
AURORA, IL 60504

John LeGear
CHICAGO, IL 60606

Cindy Martin
NORTHBROOK, IL 60062

E. H. McDowell
CHICAGO, IL 60606

Mr. Universe Enterprises
OAK FOREST, IL 60452

Obertini Publishing Co.
EAST KANKAKEE, IL 60901

Olympic Trophy and Awards Co.
CHICAGO, IL 60630

R. J.'s Kitchen
WORTH, IL 60482

Joe Roark's Musclesearch
ST. JOSEPH, IL 61873

Search Labs
NILES, IL 60648

T.A.F. Enterprises, Inc.
PALOS HEIGHTS, IL 60463

VIOBIN Corp.
MONTICELLO, IL 61856

INDIANA

Body Dynamics, Inc.
INDIANAPOLIS, IN 46201

CPC
MICHIGAN CITY, IN 46360

Fraco, Inc.
MIDDLETOWN, IN 47356

G & S Distributors
WASHINGTON, IN 47501

High-Performance Products
LAWRENCEBURG, IN 47025

Power Place Products, Inc.
WEST LAFAYETTE, IN 47906

Sportsscreen
WHITELAND, IN 46184

Sunmaker, Inc.
FT. WAYNE, IN 46898

Suntron Corp.
FT. WAYNE, IN 46802

IOWA

AMF American
JEFFERSON, IA 50129

Green Valley Gym Equipment
CRESTON, IA 50801

Superior Gym Equipment
IOWA CITY, IA 52240

Universal Gym Equipment, Inc.
CEDAR RAPIDS, IA 52406

KANSAS

Adonis Herbs
LAWRENCE, KS 66044

Blackmon Enterprises
WICHITA, KS 67213

Peggy Guthridge
WICHITA, KS 67207

T & C Health Foods
TOPEKA, KS 66605

LOUISIANA

Body Masters Sports Industry, Inc.
RAYNE, LA 70578

Ken Broussard
NEW IBERIA, LA 70560

Gartrell Travel Service
NEW ORLEANS, LA 70130

Ripley Custom Shirtmakers
NEW ORLEANS, LA 70119

MARYLAND

Adonis Prductions
JOPPA, MD 21085

Atlantic Fitness Products
GLEN BURNIE, MD 21061

Baystar
OWINGS MILLS, MD 21117

Body World Enterprises
LAUREL, MD 20708-0644

D. Ann Browne
RANDALLSTOWN, MD 21133

Fenton Products
SILVER SPRING, MD 20910

High-Tech Tools, Inc.
COLUMBIA, MD 21045

Amelia Lavin
BALTIMORE, MD 21201

Joe Miller
COLLEGE PARK, MD 20783

National Sports Warehouse
BALTIMORE, MD 21221

C. L. Pohlmar
LEXINGTON PARK, MD 20653

Savage Enterprises
CASCADE, MD 21719

Sheritha Enterprises
BALTIMORE, MD 21214

The SunTan People
ROCKVILLE, MD 20850

MASSACHUSETTS

ARMS
FITCHBURG, MA 01420

Bee Pollen from England
NEWTON LOWER FALLS, MA 02161

Brad's Gym
ACUSHNET, MA 02743

Ken Charles, Inc.
BROCKTON, MA 02403

Clarendex Corp.
CATAUMET, MA 02534

Concepts Unlimited
WORCESTER, MA 01601

Fitness and Physiology
AMHERST, MA 01004

Health from the Sun Products, Inc.
DOVER, MA 02030

Jubinville Weight Exercising Equipment
HOLYOKE, MA 01040

K & D Co.
SALEM, MA 01971

Jeff King
SPRINGFIELD, MA 01108

Douglas James Leger
LEOMINSTER, MA 01453

MAGAZINES
HOLYOKE, MA 01040

PS Co.
WELLESLEY, MA 02181

Sports Science Consultants
NATICK, MA 01760

Stone Enterprises, Inc.
HANOVER, MA 02339

Train Right Fitness Center
HINGHAM, MA 02043

MICHIGAN

American Exercise & Gym Equipment Co.
SOUTHFIELD, MI 48034

Doug Brolus
DETROIT, MI 48224

Bud Charniga
LIVONIA, MI 48150

Creative Health Products
PLYMOUTH, MI 48170

Dragonfly Enterprises
CLIMAX, MI 49034

Great Lakes Sports Academy
MARQUETTE, MI 49855

Hastings Barbell Co.
HASTINGS, MI 49058

William F. Hinbern
FARMINGTON, MI 48024

Mark Horn
SOUTHFIELD, MI 48075

Katch's-FAT
ANN ARBOR, MI 48106

Ron Kosloff
DETROIT, MI 48205

Mighty Muscle Mugs
DETROIT, MI 48208

Morden Weightlifting Products
LANSING, MI 48915

Powerhouse Gym
HIGHLAND PARK, MI 48203

Quantum Productions
ROMEO, MI 48065

Reid's Fitness Equipment
MARYSVILLE, MI 48040

S & J Studios
LATHRUP VILLAGE, MI 48076

Wate-Man Sales, Inc.
LIVONIA, MI 48152

Wysong Medical, Inc.
MIDLAND, MI 48640

MINNESOTA

Collector's Casting
MORA, MN 55051

Decathlon Exercise Equipment Co.
ST. PAUL, MN 55102

Exercise Dynamics
BEMIDJI, MN 56601

Fitness King
MINNEAPOLIS, MN 55411

Mike MacDonald Systems
DULUTH, MN 55802

New Health Marketing
MINNEAPOLIS, MN 55423

ParaBody, Inc.
MINNEAPOLIS, MN 55413

Power Plus
ARTESIA, MN 88210

Pow'r Body Building
MINNEAPOLIS, MN 55413

RCM
ANOKA, MN 55303

Viking Gym, Inc.
BROOKLYN CENTER, MN 55429

Woman to Woman
EDEN PRAIRIE, MN 55344

MISSOURI

DLC Fabricating Co., Inc.
ST. LOUIS, MO 63110

Fitness Library
ST. ANN, MO 63074

Gateway Graphics
ST. LOUIS, MO 63118

Jay's Gym
LIBERTY, MO 64068

Mid-West T-Shirt Art
ARNOLD, MO 63010

Personal Training
HAZELWOOD, MO 63042

G. Potter
PACIFIC, MO 63069

Royal American Food Co.
BLUE SPRINGS, MO 64015

MONTANA

Free Weight Systems, Inc.
BUTTE, MT 59701

NEBRASKA

Body Culture Equipment Co.
ALLIANCE, NE 69301

Iron Man Magazine
ALLIANCE, NE 69301

J & B Albrights
ELKHORN, NE 68033

NEVADA

Masterworks
RENO, NV 89509

Physique Boutique
LAS VEGAS, NV 89112-1855

NEW HAMPSHIRE

Börlind of Germany
GRANTHAM, NH 03753

Futurebiotics, Inc.
W. CHESTERFIELD, NH 03466

Ortho Molecular Nutrition International
MANCHESTER, NH 03108

NEW JERSEY

Baldinger Insurance Group, Inc.
FT. LEE, NJ 07024

BioFitness
GUTTENBERG, NJ 07093

Country Life Farm
NEWTON, NJ 07860

Fitness Factory
EDISON, NJ 08818

FP Products
SADDLE BROOK, NJ 07662

Gainers
GARWOOD, NJ 07027

Health Culture
ROCKAWAY, NJ 07866

R. Hubbard
SCOTCH PLAINS, NJ 07076-0311

I. Gym
RIDGEFIELD, NJ 07657

Angelo Iuspa
NEWARK, NJ 07107

K & K Arm Strong Fitness Equipment
VINELAND, NJ 08360

Susan Koch
LITTLE SILVER, NJ 07739

Bob Krech-Art
WILLINGBORO, NJ 08046

Lederle Labs
WAYNE, NJ 07470

L & S Research
TOMS RIVER, NJ 08753-0550

Miss Olympia
MT. HOLLY, NJ 08060

Natural Stuff, Inc.
ROCKAWAY, NJ 07866

Pat's Mug
ROSENHAYN, NJ 08352

Tom Petro's Health Emporium
TRENTON, NJ 08611

P. C. House
ROCKAWAY, NJ 07866

Paul Roberts
PLAINFIELD, NJ 07060

Songgram
MERCERVILLE, NJ 08619

Sontegra
FT. LEE, NJ 07024

Spong Studios
KIRKWOOD, NJ 08043

Alan Tuck Associates
UNION, NJ 07083

Universal Supplements Corp.
LINDEN, NJ 07036

Viamonte Design, Inc.
CHERRY HILL, NJ 08034

Viking Barbell Co. & Health Club
BELLEVILLE, NJ 07109

Work Out
BOONTON, NJ 07005

W.S.P.
HOHOKUS, NJ 07423

NEW MEXICO

Clarence Bass RIPPED Enterprises
ALBUQUERQUE, NM 87108

Golden Eagle Jewelry Co.
ALBUQUERQUE, NM 87108

Pro Gym Fitness Center
ALBUQUERQUE, NM 87123

Rejuvenators
SANTA FE, NM 87501

Suncorp
SANTA CRUZ, NM 87567

Valley Machine Shop
FARMINGTON, NM 87401

NEW YORK

AB Video
NEW YORK, NY 10019

Aerobic Wear, Inc.
HUNTINGTON STATION, NY 11746

American Studio Arts
ONEONTA, NY 13820

Karen Angelone
RIDGEWOOD, NY 11385

Associated Products
COLD SPRING HARBOR, NY 11724

Athletes Additions
WOODMERE, NY 11598

Athletic Fitness Co.
AUBURN, NY 13022

Charles Atlas
NEW YORK, NY 10010

Beacon Enterprises, Inc.
NEW YORK, NY 10001

Jeffrey Bernard
NEW YORK, NY 10024

Body Bar Systems
BRONX, NY 10460

Bristol Sports Corp.
BOHEMIA, NY 11716

David Campbell, New Rochelle Fitness Center
NEW ROCHELLE, NY 10801

Chelsea Gym
NEW YORK, NY 10011

K. K. Clark
NEW YORK, NY 10019

Cybex
RONKONKOMA, NY 11779

Diamant Trading Co.
BROOKLYN, NY 11219

East Coast Body Building
FARMINGDALE, NY 11735

Exerco, Inc.
PLEASANTVILLE, NY 10570

Fitness Fashions
LOCUST VALLEY, NY 11560

Gershon Jewelers
CEDARHURST, NY 11516

Hammer Fist
BELLMORE, NY 11710

Healthy 'N Fit
BRONX, NY 10461

Improvement Products Corp.
NEW YORK, NY 10017

Steve Karas Enterprises
RICHMOND HILL, NY 11419

Gordon Lee Products
NEW YORK, NY 10021

Dan Lurie Barbell Co., Inc.
SPRINGFIELD GARDENS, NY 11413

MacLevy Products Corp.
ELMHURST, NY 11373

Magenst Publications
NEW YORK, NY 10028

Matt Physique Photography
QUEENS, NY 11415

Mojo Manor Studios
SYRACUSE, NY 13224

Muscle-Gram, Inc.
NEW YORK, NY 10128

National Health Products
UTICA, NY 13502

Kay King-Nealy
NEW YORK, NY 10010

New Horizons
NEW YORK, NY 10016

G. Pacillo Co., Inc.
BUFFALO, NY 14216

Pawling Rubber
PAWLING, NY 12564

P. J. Jewelry
SUNNYSIDE, NY 11104

Nancy Pollak
NEW YORK, NY 10024

Pro-Power Supplements
QUEENS VILLAGE, NY 11428

RayCo
NEW YORK, NY 10185

Sport Medical Technology Corp.
CENTER MORICHES, NY 11934

Standard Gym Equipment, Inc.
ROCHESTER, NY 14624

Jan Stuart Natural Skin Care Ltd.
NEW YORK, NY 10022

Tanning Hut, Inc.
ALBANY, NY 12205

TDS Barbell & Gym Equipment
BROOKLYN, NY 11222

Russ Testo
TROY, NY 12180

T. K. Equipment
MT. VERNON, NY 01550

Mike Torchia
HAWTHORNE, NY 10572

United Food & Fitness, Inc.
BRIARCLIFF, NY 11803

V.B.M.
NEW YORK, NY 10019

Vitacrown, Inc.
HICKSVILLE, NY 11801

Vita-Life Products
STATEN ISLAND, NY 10314

World Gym Supplements
REGO PARK, NY 11374

NORTH CAROLINA

Athtex
GASTONIA, NC 28052

Carolina Fitness Equipment
CHARLOTTE, NC 28234

Diet-Labs, Inc.
CLIMAX, NC 27233

The Good News Shirt Shop
REIDSVILLE, NC 27320

Jim Moore's World Gym
CHARLOTTE, NC 28210

NORTH DAKOTA

Doug's Gym & Health Studio
BISMARCK, ND 58502

OHIO

Adria Labs, Inc.
COLUMBUS, OH 43215

Berry's Barbell and Equipment Co.
COLUMBUS, OH 43209

Black's Health World
CLEVELAND, OH 44111

Buckeye Barbell
POWELL, OH 43065

Conan Research Corp.
MACEDONIA, OH 44056

A. W. Diciolla, Jr., Co.
CLEVELAND, OH 44102

D & L Publishing
MIDDLETOWN, OH 45042

Fitness Marketing Co.
COLUMBUS, OH 43215

Laser Publications
MOGADORE, OH 44260

Randy Morris
AKRON, OH 44320

Steve Mott
COLUMBUS, OH 43214

Natural Health Foods and Barbell Center
YOUNGSTOWN, OH 44512

North American Competitions International
COLUMBUS, OH 43223

Nutri-Tech
AKRON, OH 44319

Olympic Health Equipment, Inc.
CINCINNATI, OH 45239

Pacifico Enterprises
DAYTON, OH 45414

Power By Cash
DAYTON, OH 45420

Qualiform, Inc.
WADSWORTH, OH 44281

Samco
NORTH RIDGEVILLE, OH 44039-0088

Shake Recipes
CINCINNATI, OH 45275

Sweat, Inc.
CINCINNATI, OH 45201

Sword Enterprises
COLUMBUS, OH 43215

Vienna Health Products
VIENNA, OH 44473

VIM
CUYAHOGA FALLS, OH 44223

OKLAHOMA

Bicep Booster
TULSA, OK 74155

Body Building Unlimited
MOORE, OK 73153

Dick Burke's Mail Order Co.
OKLAHOMA CITY, OK 73101

Crain Power-Plus
SHAWNEE, OK 74801

C. W. Stapp Sportswear
MOORE, OK 73160

Mike Hiebert
BETHANY, OK 73008

R. Hughes
ADA, OK 74820

Muscle World
CLAYTON, OK 74536

Royal House
OKLAHOMA CITY, OK 73101

Strength Tech, Inc.
STILLWATER, OK 74076

OREGON

Little Grunt Productions
PORTLAND, OR 97205

Natural
MCMINNVILLE, OR 97128

Nutritional Charts
PORTLAND, OR 97230

Soloflex
HILLSBORO, OR 97123

V. V., Inc.
PORTLAND, OR 97232

PENNSYLVANIA

Billard Barbell Co.
READING, PA 19602

Charles & Associates
PITTSBURGH, PA 15235

Custom Gym Equipment
SINKING SPRING, PA 19608

Dolfin Corp.
SHILLINGTON, PA 19607

D & S Manufacturing & Marketing, Inc.
LITITZ, PA 17543

EARN Fitness
IMPERIAL, PA 15126

Edgewood Enterprises
GROVE CITY, PA 16127

General Nutrition Corp.
PITTSBURGH, PA 15222

Good Sports
PITTSBURGH, PA 15224

Dave Groscup
BIRDSBORO, PA 19508

The Grow-Eery
PHILADELPHIA, PA 19151

Kisha Fitness System
DUQUESNE, PA 15110

Kuc's Total Fitness Systems
MOUNTAINTOP, PA 18707

Lancon's Vitamins
BETHLEHEM, PA 18016

J. F. Loccisano
LANCASTER, PA 17603

Muscle Grams
READING, PA 19601

Muscle Head
PITTSBURGH, PA 15205

Northeast Power & Fitness
EASTON, PA 18042

Olympus Gym
WARRINGTON, PA 18976

Pitt Barbell & Healthfood Corp.
PITTSBURGH, PA 15235

Power Grip
CATASAUQUA, PA 18032

SAN
IRWIN, PA 15642

Smith's
PHILADELPHIA, PA 19132

Streamline Gym & Fitness Equipment
EAST STROUDSBURG, PA 18301

Vita Chart
SOUTHAMPTON, PA 18966

World Barbell & Healthfoods
UNIONTOWN, PA 15401

York Barbell Co., Inc.
YORK, PA 17405

RHODE ISLAND

Appian Way Sculpture Studio
JOHNSTON, RI 02919

SOUTH CAROLINA

Bodybuilders Cookbook
QUINBY, SC 29501

The Caines Co.
GREER, SC 29652

Greenville Health Club
GREENVILLE, SC 29609

Irmo Sports
COLUMBIA, SC 29210

Total Living Communications, Inc.
ISLE OF PALMS, SC 29451

TENNESSEE

American Athletic Supply, Inc.
KNOXVILLE, TN 37901

Fireworks by Julie St. Anne
NASHVILLE, TN 37212

Kreis Sports, Inc.
NASHVILLE, TN 37212

Richards Medical Co.
MEMPHIS, TN 38116

Rock & Row
CORRYTON, TN 37721

Simmons Co.
CHATTANOOGA, TN 37404

TEXAS

R. J. Bauer
DALLAS, TX 75220

Mike Benton
AUSTIN, TX 78758

Mike Bridges Systems
ARLINGTON, TX 76011

Builders Sportswear
ADDISON, TX 75001

Champion Barbell Manufacturing Div.
ARLINGTON, TX 76010

Champion Sports Nutrition
ARLINGTON, TX 76010

Derma-Research
HOUSTON, TX 77042

Dynamics Health Equipment Manufacturing Co., Inc.
SOUTH HOUSTON, TX 77587

Sam Easterwood
SAN ANTONIO, TX 78210

Elite Sales, Inc.
AUSTIN, TX 78764

Elmer's Weights, Inc.
LUBBOCK, TX 79490

Fitness Consultants & Supply
WICHITA FALLS, TX 76302

Fitness Management Service
SNYDER, TX 79549

Hammel Training
EULESS, TX 76039

Hydra-Gym Athletics, Inc.
BELTON, TX 76513

Inzer Power Shirts
LONGVIEW, TX 75606

Kelso
BULLARD, TX 75757

Mac Barbell Equipment
GRAND PRAIRIE, TX 75050

Magnum Exercise Equipment, Inc.
AUSTIN, TX 78758

McCain Productions
AUSTIN, TX 78704

Mike Minor Enterprises
NACOGDOCHES, TX 75961

Milton T. Moore, Jr.
DALLAS, TX 75214-0280

The Muscle Shop
ARLINGTON, TX 76010

Oakglade Industries
HOUSTON, TX 77071

Oasis Relaxation Tank Co., Inc.
HOUSTON, TX 77098

Regal Enterprises
DALLAS, TX 75206-2908

Tim Roberts
KATY, TX 77449

Simply Healthy Products
SEABROOK, TX 77586

Sure Grips
DALLAS, TX 75235

Texas Imperial American, Inc.
TYLER, TX 75710

Titan Suits
CORPUS CHRISTI, TX 78412

T. R. Enterprises
KATY, TX 77449

Vita Pro Products Co.
DALLAS, TX 75228

UTAH

Hoggan Health Equipment
SALT LAKE CITY, UT 84107

Larry Scott
NORTH SALT LAKE, UT 84054

Trace Minerals
CEDAR CITY, UT 84720

Wild Herbs & Specialties
SALT LAKE CITY, UT 84110

VERMONT

Campbell Enterprises
BURLINGTON, VT 05402

Jogbra, Inc.
BURLINGTON, VT 05401

Sportscience Laboratories
ESSEX JUNCTION, VT 05452

VIRGINIA

Body Mechanics, Ltd.
RICHMOND, VA 23226

Colonna's Gym
CHESAPEAKE, VA 23323

Colonna Health Products, Inc.
NORFOLK, VA 23523

Carlos DeJesus, The School of Natural Bodybuilding
RICHMOND, VA 23231

Richard Muldez
VIRGINIA BEACH, VA 23454

WASHINGTON

AMEREC Corp.
BELLEVUE, WA 98009

Discovery Publishing
TACOMA, WA 98401

Edward, Gregory, Leigh
SEATTLE, WA 98124

Jim Hix
SPOKANE, WA 99213-3453

L. E. Jacobson
SEDRO WOOLLEY, WA 98284

ORG Products
SEATTLE, WA 98168

Port-A-Gym Co.
LONGVIEW, WA 98632

Power Design
SEATTLE, WA 98111-1204

S.C.A. Corp.
REDMOND, WA 98052

Sky's the Limit
SUMNER, WA 98390

Wammer International Delivery
SEATTLE, WA 98166

WISCONSIN

Bill Bronk
CUSTER, WI 54423

Clean Water Systems
EAU CLAIRE, WI 54701

Huffy Corp.
MILWAUKEE, WI 53207

Lifeline Production and Marketing, Inc.
MADISON, WI 53715

Muscle-Up
JANESVILLE, WI 53547

Quality Designs
SUPERIOR, WI 54880

Research Specialties
GREEN BAY, WI 54308

WYOMING

BIO-SPORT
DOUGLAS, WY 82633

L & J Enterprises
CASPER, WY 82602

Tom Platz and Ed Guiliani

International Listings

AUSTRALIA

The Fitness Generation
271 CAMBERWELL RD., CAMBERWELL,
VICTORIA 3124, AUSTRALIA-03-813-3244
(see Weider Health and Fitness, Inc.)

W. Gallasch
PO BOX 17, BROOKLYN PARK, SOUTH
AUSTRALIA 5032
*films, magazines, protein supplements,
videos*

Genesis Trading Co.
PO BOX 208, GLEBE 2037, AUSTRALIA/
02-808-1342
*books, courses, martial arts supplies,
nutritional supplements, photos, posters,
tapes*

**Paul & Carole Graham's Gym &
Fitness Centre**
288 GRAND PARADE, RAMSGATE BEACH,
SYDNEY, AUSTRALIA/529-7658

Paul Graham
PO BOX 234, WOOLLAHRA 2025 NEW
SOUTH WALES, AUSTRALIA
T-shirts of the 1980 Mr. Olympia contest

Paul Graham's Mr. Universe Gym
PO BOX 27, BRIGHTON LE SANDS, NEW
SOUTH WALES 2215, AUSTRALIA
*videos of the 1982 and 1983 Mr.
Olympia contest*

Leisure Time Fitness Equipment
81 JOHNSTON, ST., FITZROY, VICTORIA,
AUSTRALIA/03-419-8866
*books, equipment, health foods, lifting
belts, posters, waist trimmers*

Leisure World Ltd.
CNR. GT. NORTH RD. & POLLEN ST., GREY
LYNN, AUCKLAND, AUSTRALIA/767-335

**Melbourne Gymnasium
Equipment**
14 LT. OXFORD ST., COLLINGWOOD,
VICTORIA, AUSTRALIA/03-419-6193
equipment

**North Shore Body Building
Supplies**
UNIT 1, 28 ALBERT ST., HORNSBY, NEW
SOUTH WALES, AUSTRALIA/477-5390

**Sportsman's Leisure & Hobby
Warehouse Pty. Ltd.**
PO BOX 5690, GOLD COAST MAIL CENTRE
BUNDALL, QUEENSLAND 4217
AUSTRALIA

**Suisse Naturopathics Pty.
Ltd.**
PO BOX 2, NIDDRIE, VICTORIA
NEW SOUTH WALES 3042
AUSTRALIA/03-330-1159
minerals, protein, vitamins

John Terilli
PO BOX 27, BRIGHTON LE SANDS, NEW
SOUTH WALES 2216, AUSTRALIA/529-7658

**Universal Sport and Body
Building Equipment**
UNIT 11-53, MYROORA RD., TERRY HILLS
2084, AUSTRALIA
equipment

BARBADOS

**Roy Callender's Family Fitness
Center**
SPEED BIRD HOUSE, FAIRCHILD ST.,
BRIDGETOWN, BARBADOS

BELGIUM

ACB Gym/Weider International
9 HOGE LANE, B 8200 BRUGGE,
BELGIUM/
050-31-64-94/telex: 82168 acbgym b
(see Weider Health and Fitness, Inc.)

CANADA

Active Creations
1 DAVIES CRES., TORONTO, ONTARIO,
CANADA M4J 2X4
T-shirts

Apex Athletics
1923 QUADRA ST., VICTORIA, BRITISH
COLUMBIA, CANADA V8T 4C1/604-381-1210
equipment

**Sherry Atton
c/o Scotty's Gym**
303 FIRST AVENUE NORTH, SASKATOON,
SASKATCHEWAN,
CANADA S7K 1X5
306-244-8330
seminars

Canusa Products
PO BOX 2009, BRAMALEA, ONTARIO,
CANADA L6T 3S3
tank tops

Dalgam Enterprises
2305 YONGE ST., SUITE 219, TORONTO,
ONTARIO, CANADA M4P 2C7
equipment, supplements, vitamins

Fitness Emporium
7555 GOREWAY DR., UNIT 80,
MISSISSAUGA, ONTARIO, CANADA L4T 3M9
sweatshirts, tank tops, T-shirts

Health Zone Fitness Equipment
100 WOODROW ST., SUITE 207, ST.
CATHARINES, ONTARIO, CANADA L2P 2A3
416-685-6690
equipment

Hercules Belts
0230 YPRES BLVD., WINDSOR, ONTARIO,
CANADA N8W 1S8
lifting belts

**International Fellowship of
Christian Iron Men**
PO BOX 75, NANAIMO, BRITISH COLUMBIA,
CANADA V9R 5K9
posters, tank tops, T-shirts

David Lasker
23 ALLOWAY AVE., WINNIPEG, MANITOBA,
CANADA R3G OZ7

classical posing music

Mohamed Makkawy
2110 DUNDAS ST. EAST, MISSISSAUGA,
ONTARIO
CANADA L4X 1L9

*nutritional manuals, posing workouts,
training courses*

G. Monnery
#502, 913 13 AVE., SW, CALGARY, ALBERTA,
CANADA T2R OL3

recipes for high-protein drinks

MuscleMag International
UNIT 2, 52 BRAMSTEELE RD., BRAMPTON,
ONTARIO,
CANADA L6W 3M5
416-457-3030/416-791-8590

*arm blasters, barbells, belt massagers,
belts, benches, books, bullworkers,
chinning bars, collars, courses, dumbbell
rods, dynotrainers, elbow support caps,
ergometers, equipment, exer-dials,
gloves, grips, headstraps, inversion bars
and boots, iron boots, iron claws, jump
ropes, kettlebells, knee supports,
magazines, posing trunks, power
crushers, protein powders, rowing
machines, scissors "V" builders, steel-
cable barbells, strands, support wraps,
training straps, triceps bars, triceps
bombers, T-shirts, weight-gain products,
weight stands*

ODIN
432-3868 SHELBOURNE, VICTORIA, BRITISH
COLUMBIA, CANADA, V8P 5J1/604-721-4166

*fine jewelry (sterling silver and gold-
plated medallions available in three
styles; each medallion comes with a free
20-inch gold-filled chain)*

Reid's Fitness Equipment
648 HURON ST., PO BOX 7147, LONDON,
ONTARIO, CANADA N5Y 4J9

equipment

Reps Champion, MuscleMag International
UNIT 2, 52 BRAMSTEELE RD., BRAMPTON,
ONTARIO, CANADA L6W 3M5/416-457-1019

equipment

The Sport and Fitness Academy
100 CENTENNIAL PARKWAY SOUTH, STONEY
CREEK, ONTARIO, CANADA L8G 2C8

Video Four Productions
UNIT 2, 52 BRAMSTEELE RD., BRAMPTON,
ONTARIO, CANADA L6W 3M5

videos of the 1983 Mr. Olympia contest

Weider Sports Equipment Co., Ltd.
WEIDER BLDG., 2875 BATES RD., MONTREAL,
QUEBEC
CANADA H3S 1B7/514-731-3783/
telex: 05-827669

equipment

Stephen Winter
39 MARIA ST., ACTON, ONTARIO, CANADA
L7J 2C6

paintings

Zen-Tec
202-1702 ELLICE AVE., WINNIPEG,
MANITOBA, CANADA R3H OB1

equipment

DENMARK

Form & Figur
GENTOFTAGADE 43, 2820 GENTOFTA,
DENMARK/01-65-25-30

gym wear

Solana, Scan Fit
HAVREHOLMVEJ 19B, 3120
DRONNINGMÖLLE, DENMARK/02-20-00-70

tanning equipment

ENGLAND

Bellow Equipment Co.
ELLERBY LANE, LEEDS, ENGLAND LS9 8LE

equipment

The Bodyshop
33 LEEDS RD., DEWSBURY, WEST
YORKSHIRE, ENGLAND WF12 7BB/
0924-467507

*ankle weights, digestive aids, equipment,
gyms, lifting belts, minerals, posing trunks,
protein powders, supplements, training
suits, vitamins, waist belts*

Chester
2 HEDLEY VILLAS, NOTTINGHAM N97 7BN,
ENGLAND

Sandow chest expander

Craven House
22 CHURCH ST., GODALMING, SURREY,
ENGLAND

(see Weider Health and Fitness, Inc.)

Davina Health Products
1 CAMBRIDGE CT., CAMBRIDGE ST.,
SHEFFIELD, ENGLAND S1 4HN

*minerals, protein, supplements, vitamins,
weight-gain products*

Dee Kay Leisure Ltd.
5-8 DUKES CT., DUKE ST., BRIGHTON,
SUSSEX, ENGLAND
0273-24968

sweatshirts, T-shirts

Brian Eastman
70 CONINGSBY GARDENS, LONDON,
ENGLAND E4 9BD

Titan deluxe multi-purpose bench

Europa International Sports Aids Co., Ltd.
47/49 TALBOT RD., BLACKPOOL,
LANCASTER, ENGLAND FY1 1LL

*minerals, protein powders,
supplements—endorsed by Gordon
Pasquil*

FINBARR
16 TURKETEL RD., FOLKESTONE, KENT,
ENGLAND

books and courses

Health & Leisure
88 WOOD ST., WALTHAMSTOW, LONDON
E17, ENGLAND/01-521-8092

equipment

Health Product Supplies
43 BALBY RD., DONCASTER, ENGLAND/
0302-25163

*glandulars, protein powders,
supplements, vitamins*

Hill Barbell
GREETS GREEN RD., WEST BROMWICH,
WEST MIDLANDS, ENGLAND B70 9EL/
021-557-2101

equipment

Hometrain
55 HEAVYGATE RD., SHEFFIELD, ENGLAND
S10 1PE

jewelry

International Swedish School of Physical Culture
BCM—SWEDISH HOUSE, LONDON WC1V
6XX, ENGLAND

*home-study courses that provide
diplomas for careers in: beauty diuretics,
dietetics, health and beauty culture,
physical training, Swedish massage and
physiotherapy*

Chris Lund
18 CRAIGSHAW SQUARE, HYLTON CASTLE
ESTATE, SUNDERLAND, TYNE AND WEAR,
ENGLAND SR5 3NG

*books, courses, magazines, Vince
Gironda's books and courses, official
distributor of Mike Mentzer products,
British representative for MuscleMag
products*

MUSCLE
DEPT. B., PO BOX 16, HARLTEPOOL,
CLEVELAND,
ENGLAND TS26 8RZ

Multi-Language Publications, Ltd
PAYNE HOUSE, 23-24 SMITHFIELD ST.,
LONDON, ECI,
ENGLAND

books, magazines

Muscle Machine Products
FERN LEA, CHASE RD., ROSS-ON-WYE,
HEREFORDSHIRE,
ENGLAND

women's competition suits

P. J. Equipment
205 LEA BRIDGE RD., LONDON, ENGLAND
E10/01-539-4689
equipment

Polaris
CASTLEFIELDS HOUSE, MAIN CENTER, DERBY DE 12 PE, ENGLAND/0332-45369
equipment, gym-planning service

R.P.M. Enterprises
PO BOX 26, KENDAL, CUMBRIA, ENGLAND
LA9 6LJ
T-shirts

S.P.S. Productions
49 REDHILL DR., FISHPONDS, BRISTOL, ENGLAND BS16 2AG
videos of Mohamed Makkawy

Steel City Sports Equipment Co., Ltd.
1 CAMBRIDGE CT., SHEFFIELD, YORKSHIRE, ENGLAND S1 4HN/0742-738090/ 0433-30898
equipment, Davina products

Sunset Marketing Ltd.
PO BOX 25, LEYLAND, LANCASTER, ENGLAND PR5 2QX/07744-33315
tanning cream

Total Fitness
537 RAINHAM RD. SOUTH, DAGENHAM, ESSEX, ENGLAND/01-593-2584
equipment, minerals, supplements, vitamins

Tropicana Food Products
UNIT 9, BEVERLY HOUSE, 133-157 TYBURN RD., BIRMINGHAM, ENGLAND B24 8AN/ 021-326-8311
caps, digestive aids, glandulars, minerals, power packs, protein powders, shorts, supplements, tank tops, T-shirts, vitamins, weight-gain formulas

Video 4 Ltd.
213 SUSSEX GARDENS, LONDON, ENGLAND W2/01-262-4063
videos of the 1983 Mr. Olympia contest

Wander Ltd.
STATION RD., KING'S LANGLEY, HERTFORDSHIRE, ENGLAND WD4 8LJ
protein foods and drinks

Weider Health and Fitness, Inc.
GODALMING, SURREY, ENGLAND/ 04868-25544
(see Weider Health and Fitness, Inc.)

WOT Productions Ltd.
20 ORANGE ST., LONDON, ENGLAND WC2H 7EW/930-8631/930-5896
videos of the 1983 Mr. Universe and Miss Bikini contests

Harold Wrigley
DEPT. BB, 11 GAIL CLOSE, FAILSWORTH, MANCHESTER, ENGLAND M35 OJ4
custom-made heat belts (Super Trim Gard and Bermuda Trim Gard)

FINLAND

Solana
SUN FLOWER OY, SAKARINKATU 3, 00500 HELSINGFORS 50, FINLAND/90-701-36-80
tanning equipment

Wrange Co.
VALIMOTIE 1A, 00380 HELSINKI 38, FINLAND/55-85-95
(see Weider Health and Fitness, Inc.)

FRANCE

Dominique Dumont
B.P. 362 R9, 67009 STRASBOURG CEDEX, FRANCE
French bodybuilding publication for women called Force & Beauté

GREECE

Athlitis
56 PANEPISTIMIOU ST., ATHENS, GREECE

ICELAND

Arni Hrobjartsson, Heimaval
PO BOX 39, KOPAVOGUR, ICELAND/1-42116
(see Weider Health and Fitness, Inc.)

ITALY

Fassi Sport
STRADA FRANCESCA, 42, ANGOLO STATALE DEL TONALE, 24040 ZINGONIA (BERGAMO), ITALY/035-885034
(see Weider Health and Fitness, Inc.)

JAPAN

Joe Weider Foods K.K.
MIYAJIMA BLDG. #303, 1-30-10 NIHONBASHI KAKIGARA-CHO, CHAU-KU, TOKYO, JAPAN/303-664-0551
(see Weider Health and Fitness, Inc.)

MALTA

Tony Gambin
FLAT 3, "OAKMORE", SUR FONS STR., ST. JULIANS, MALTA
muscle movies, slides, videos, photos of the champions

NEW ZEALAND

Polaris
PO BOX 9124, N. HAMILTON, NEW ZEALAND/ 071-394-671
equipment, gym-planning service

NORWAY

Chr. Mobech A/S
MOLLERGT 20, OSLO 1 NORWAY/2-201218
(see Weider Health and Fitness, Inc.)

Gym & Sun Equipment A/S
HOJBRATENVEJEN 25B, OSLO 10, NORWAY/ 02-308998

Solana
BOLUX AS, MÖLLEGAT 24, OLSO 1, NORWAY/02-20-72-60
tanning equipment

SCOTLAND

Webster
43 WEST RD., IRVINE, AYRSHIRE KA12 8RE, SCOTLAND
books and magazines

SINGAPORE

Paul Chua, Good Health Distributors
35 TANNERY RD., 09-10, RUBY INDUSTRIAL COMPLEX, TANNERY BLOCK, SINGAPORE 1334
(see Weider Health and Fitness, Inc.)

SOUTH AFRICA

Tableland-Fithealth-Products
2 UFFHER ST., SELBY, JOHANNESBURG, SOUTH AFRICA
(see Weider Health and Fitness, Inc.)

SWEDEN

Atlantis Import
BOX 23040, 750 23 UPPSALA, SWEDEN
equipment

Bodybuilding & Kraftsport
KUNDNUMMER 32-63-80-17, 104-30 STOCKHOLM, SWEDEN
books, gloves, gym bags, jewelry, magazines, posing briefs, sportswear, sweatshirts, T-shirts

Combi Produkter
BOX 15057, 200-31 MALMO, SWEDEN/ 046-11-11-13
gloves, training belts

Dexal Sportprodukter AB
BOX 45 224, S-104 30 STOCKHOLM, SWEDEN
gym wear, T-shirts, sweatshirts

Esselte Sport
BOX 134, 577-00 HULTSFRED, SWEDEN/ 0495-126-30
equipment

Firma Sjöfijaru
INGRID CAHLING, KÅLHAGSGATAN 2, 802-25 GAVLE, SWEDEN-026-18-51-52
Andreas Cahling products, books, gloves, minerals, spirulina

Heavy Gym
TRÄDGARDSGAT., 821-00 BOLLNÄS, SWEDEN
equipment

I. Leiner
NOORSGATAN 5, 761-00 NORRTÄLJE, SWEDEN
specialized hand grips

Silver Solarium
SILVER GRUPPEN AB, FOLKETSHUSVÄGEN, 26061 HYLLINGE, SWEDEN/042-225797
tanning equipment

Sjöbergs Lågpriser
BOX 6168, 800-06 GAVLE, SWEDEN/026-120 09-05
T-shirts

Svarspost
KUNDNUMMER 7167004, 200-11 MALMO, SWEDEN
minerals, supplements, vitamins

Trend Import
BOX 6007, 600-06 NORRKÖPING, SWEDEN
equipment

Uddeholm Kraftsport
BOX 703, 68301 HAGFORS, SWEDEN/ 0563-11000
equipment

Ulf Bengtsson Gym Products
ATLASGATAN 4, 113-20 STOCKHOLM, SWEDEN/08-31-24-12
gym wear

Viking Rehab AB
BOX 15144, 161-15 BROMMA, SWEDEN/ 08-26-25-20 VX
equipment

W-Sport
O. FORSTADSGAYAN 23, 211-31 MALMO, SWEDEN/040-23-20-01
(see Weider Health and Fitness, Inc.)

Fig. 102

SWITZERLAND

UTC Sport Div.
ST. ANNAGASSE 16, 8001 ZURICH, SWITZERLAND
(see Weider Health and Fitness, Inc.)

TAHITI

Weider Dynamic
B.P. 6185 FAAA, PAPEETE, TAHITI/2-69-68
(see Weider Health and Fitness, Inc.)

VENEZUELA

Jendomer S.R.L.
APARTADO 75-251, CARACAS 107, VENEZUELA/(2) 35-94-10
(see Weider Health and Fitness, Inc.)

WEST GERMANY

Firma Ludwig Brummer
LINDWURMSTR. 125, 8000 Munchen 2, WEST GERMANY/089-76-81-21
(see Weider Health and Fitness, Inc.)

Sport & Fitness
POSTFACH 2644, 4150 KREFELD, WEST GERMANY

YUGOSLAVIA

Body Building
POŠTANSKI FAH 97, 21400 BACKA PALANKA, YUGOSLAVIA

Petar Cĕlik
ŠUMSKA 32, 21400 BAČKA PALANKA, YUGOSLAVIA

Herkules
P. P. 97, 21400 BAČKA PALANKA, YUGOSLAVIA

Men of Iron

This list of names just begins to account for the growing population of male bodybuilders. We have tried to include as many individuals as space would allow.

Congratulations to the bodybuilders who are listed here.

Apache
John Abl
Steve Adell
Ray Adner
Jim Agigian
Danilo Aguilar
Douglas Aiello
Martin Alamango
Fatholomein Ali
Dennis Allen
Jon Aranita
Len Archambault
Billy Arlen
Pierre Asselin
Bronston Austin, Jr.

Jusup Wilcosz

Van Banks
Samir Bannout
Bob Barraclough
Clarence Bass
James Bass
Ray Beaulieu
Darcey Beccles
Albert Beckles
Tim Belknap
Rick Benedetto
Ulf Bengtsson
Greg Berbenuik
Mike Bergsma
Larry Bernstein
Renato Bertagna
Les Berthelette
Bob Birdsong
Steve Bohnstedt
Ray Boone
Doug Brignole
Mark Briscoe
Allen Brown
Eddie Brown
John Brown
Vince Brown
Winston Brown
Joe Bucci
Gerard Buinoud
Steve Burns
Charles Buser

Franco Columbu

Andreas Cahling
Roy Callender
Frank Calta
Pete Caputo
Steve Cavanaugh
Roy Chavez
Ming Chew
Jerry Chow
Mike Christian
Dennis J. Ciancio
Robert Ciancio
John Citron
Ron Clark
Barry Clothier
Ralph Coccio
Boyer Coe
Craig Cole
Donald Coleman
Lamar Collins
Franco Columbu
Greg Comeaux
Steve Conjar
Vinny Conzo
Ed Corney
Rick Cox
Abe Cuesta

Ed Corney

Mario DaSilva
William Dabish
Paul Daniels
Robert Dantlinger
Neal Davis
Steve Davis
Joseph Dawson
John DeFendis
Greg DeFerro
Carlos DeJesus
James DeMelo
Berry de Mey
Chris Dickerson
Joseph Disinti
Thomas Donato
Ian Dowe
Lance Dreher
Carl Dungy

Tom Platz

Tony Emmott
Ahmet Enunlu
Christer Eriksson
Ellis Evans
Jeff Everson

Lou Ferrigno
Larry Ferris
Tim Fish
Bertil Fox
Johnny Fuller

Bob Gallucci
Albert Garcia
Richard Gaspari
James Gaubert
Jesse Gautreaux
Charles Glass
Joe Gold
Joey Gomex
John Gourgot
Alan Graham
Bill Grant
Glenn Gravenbeek
Bill Gray
Michael Grieco
Manfred Grossler
Pete Grymkowski
Ed Guiliani
Jose Guzman

Bertil Fox

Mohamed Makkawy

Greg DeFerro

Mike Katz
John Kemper
Russell Kight
Jeff King
Alan Kirsch
Reijo Kivioja
Michael Klinefelter
Bill Knight
Don Knipp
Erwin Knoller
Rod Koontz
Yasushi Koyama
Eduardo Kuwak

Graeme Lancefield
Ulf Larson
Eugene Laviscount
Nick Lavitola
Ian Lawrence
Jean LeBlanc
Grant Ledbetter
Rory Leidelmeyer
Alain Leroy
Angelito Lesta
Gary Lewer
Karl Link
Tony Little
Scott Livingstone
Anibal Lopez
Eddie Love
Ron Love
Cal Lueneburg
Jesse Lujan
Lars Lunde

Ken Waller

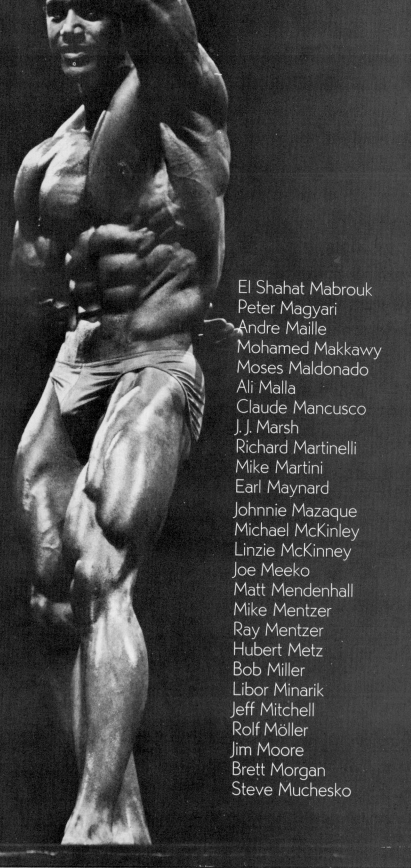

El Shahat Mabrouk
Peter Magyari
Andre Maille
Mohamed Makkawy
Moses Maldonado
Ali Malla
Claude Mancusco
J. J. Marsh
Richard Martinelli
Mike Martini
Earl Maynard
Johnnie Mazaque
Michael McKinley
Linzie McKinney
Joe Meeko
Matt Mendenhall
Mike Mentzer
Ray Mentzer
Hubert Metz
Bob Miller
Libor Minarik
Jeff Mitchell
Rolf Möller
Jim Moore
Brett Morgan
Steve Muchesko

Moses Maldonado

Ken Naughton
Alfred Neugebauer
Jacques Neuville
Pat Neve
Peter Nielsen
Erwin Note
Serge Nubret
Calvin Nyali

Sergio Oliva
Walter O'Malley
Juan Ojeda
Phil Outlaw

Bob Paris

Danny Padilla
Anthony Pandolfo
Luis Pardo
Bob Paris
Sam Pasco
Phil Pasquale
Ken Passariello
David Paul
Peter Paul
Tony Pearson
Peter Peck
Alois Pek
Charles Perez
Don Peters
Mike Petrella
Terry Phillips
Graham Pierce
Eric Pieters
Mike Piliotis
Tom Platz
Benny Podda
Rick Porcelli
Rick Poston
Jeffrey Primm
Ivan Putski

Tony Pearson

Jose Rabanal
Dwane Rankin
Jorma Raty
Bill Register
Keijo Reiman
Steven Reiter
Max Reppel
Phil Rhode
Bill Richardson
Claude Rigon
Robby Robinson
Carlos Rodriguez
Danny Rogers
Dave Rogers
Steve Romanelli
Steve Rosati
Gunnar Rosbo
Richard Roy
Dale Ruplinger

Bob Reis

Mike Sable
Heinz Sallmeyer
Rick Sampson
Pete Samra
Dan Samuda
Gerardo San Antonio
Billy Sanchez
Ernie Santiago
Frank Santoriello
Jerry Scalesse
Arnold Schwarzenegger
Tom Sims
Butch Smith
Jeff Smullen
Carlos Sotolongo
Doug Splittgerber
Joe Spooner
Neal Spruce
Dennis Stanton
Dirk Starke
Appie Steenbeck
Lawrence Story
Lionel Strongfort
Kozo Sudo
Shigeru Sugita
Tony Sullivan
Kalman Szkalak

Ernie Santiago

Taz Tally
Greg Tefft
John Terilli
Victor Terra
Russ Testo
Bill Tierney
Steve Timmreck
Dennis Tinerino
Mike Torchia
Dean Tornabene
Mark Torrance
Ron Teufel

Tevfik Ulusoglu
Tim Underwood

Timothy Vargo
Casey Viator
Marty Vranicar

Steve Davis

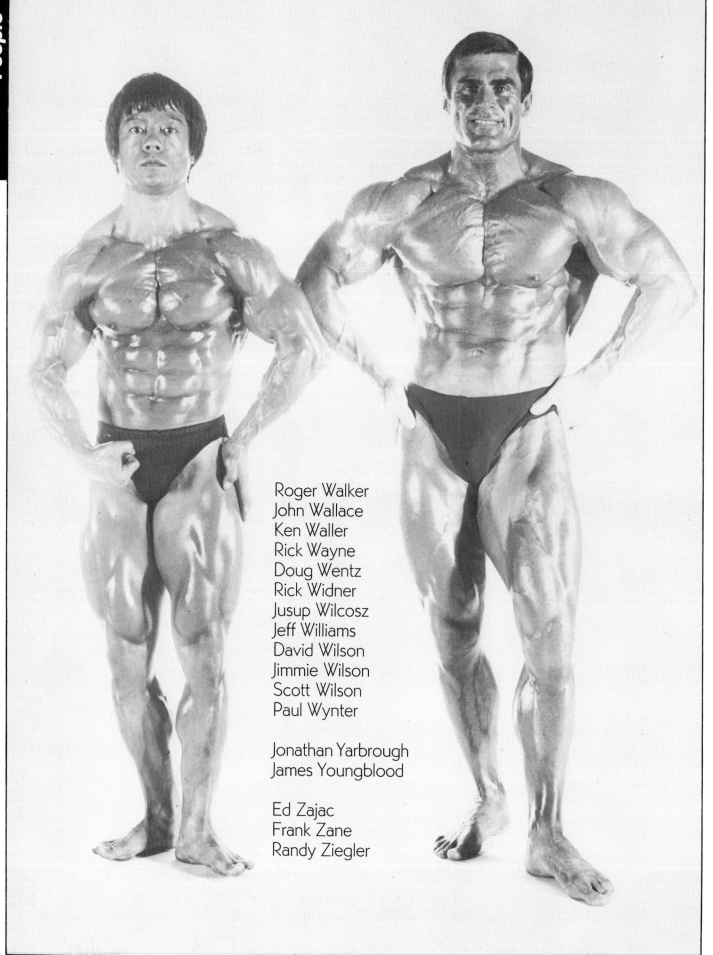

Roger Walker
John Wallace
Ken Waller
Rick Wayne
Doug Wentz
Rick Widner
Jusup Wilcosz
Jeff Williams
David Wilson
Jimmie Wilson
Scott Wilson
Paul Wynter

Jonathan Yarbrough
James Youngblood

Ed Zajac
Frank Zane
Randy Ziegler

Francois Chung and Terry Phillips

Women of Iron

The ranks of female bodybuilders are increasing every day. Here is a list to salute as many of them as possible.

Josiane Ackermans
Denise Agostini
Kris Alexander
Sally Allemang
Lisa Alvanos
Dinah Anderson
Rita Anderson
Lena Andersson
Suzie Andrews
Athena Annis
Astrid Aschwander
Sherry Atton

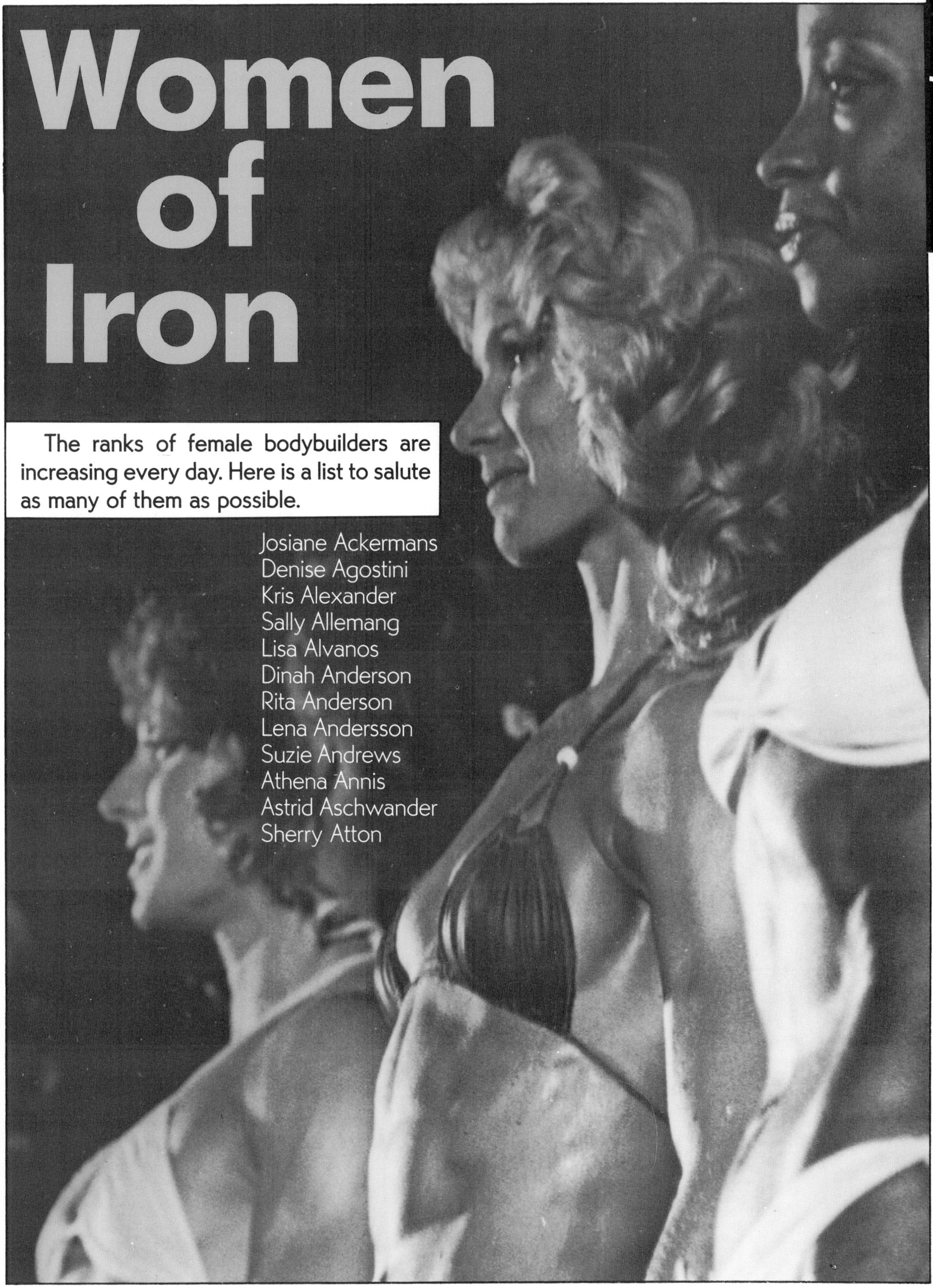

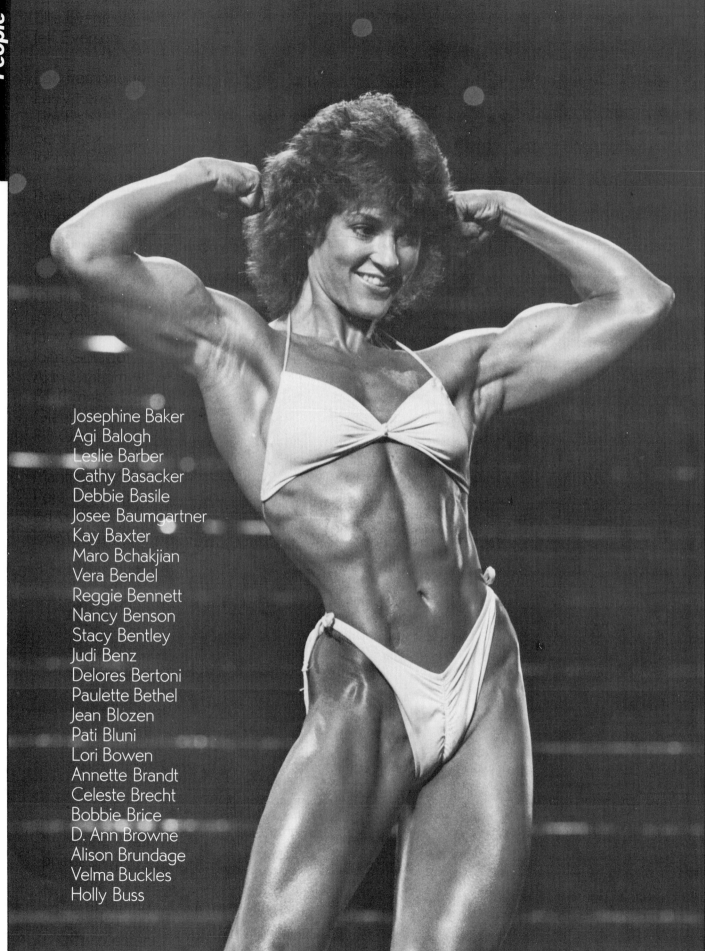

Josephine Baker
Agi Balogh
Leslie Barber
Cathy Basacker
Debbie Basile
Josee Baumgartner
Kay Baxter
Maro Bchakjian
Vera Bendel
Reggie Bennett
Nancy Benson
Stacy Bentley
Judi Benz
Delores Bertoni
Paulette Bethel
Jean Blozen
Pati Bluni
Lori Bowen
Annette Brandt
Celeste Brecht
Bobbie Brice
D. Ann Browne
Alison Brundage
Velma Buckles
Holly Buss

Lori Bowen

Candis Caldwell
Helene Calmels
Joanne Cameron
Mary Lou Carberry
Eileen Carda
Diane Cariedo
Maureen Casper
Lindy Champion
Patsy Chapman
Renee Chavez

Lydia Cheng
Carolyn Cheshire
Lynda Chicado-Sendow
Teri Clavell
Helene Clive
Kim Clouse
Valerie Coe
Lorraine Colavito
Valerie Collins
Laura Combes

Lynn Conkwright
Kathy Cosentino
Patty Cox
Allana Crielley
Candy Csencsits

Laura Combes and Claudia Wilbourn

Lucette Daulcle
Rebecca Davis
Chris Dawkins
Jenny Dawson
Laurin De Stefano
Devona
Robyn DeVoist
Patsy Delaender
Diana Dennis
Deborah Diana
Darci D'mitrenko
Joy Dobson
Leslie Dorazio
Marianne Duffy
Carla Dunlap

Lisa Elliot
Kike Elomaa
Brenda Eppey
Gaye Evanikoff
Cory Everson

Rachel McLish

Pat Filinick
Melissa Fisher
Kim Fonza
Thea Fox
Dori Frame
Bev Francis
Bessie Frank
Glennis Fraser
Doris Frederick
Lisser Frost-Larsen
Claire Furr

Cindy Gablehouse
Linda Gagliano
Gwynn Gambit
Anita Gandol
Judy Gillette
Chris Glass
Dawn Gnaegi
Trish Godtis
Maria Gonzales
Vicki Gore
Angela Graham
Judy Grayson
Susan Greene
Shelley Gruwell

Shelley Gruwell

Pirjo Haapalo
Vigdis Hagen
Marion Hammang
Audrey Harris
Cheryl Harriss
Melissa Hartland
Gale Haston
Kim Hawkins
Charlotte Hiller-Anderson
Marilyn Holmes
Mary Alice Horne
Terri Hughes
Yolanda Hughes

Pillow

Kathy Illingworth
Jill Ingels
Maria Issa

Diana James
Mary Ellen Jerumbo
Jane Jones
Sandra Jones

Keerie Keenan
Georgia Keller
Breigh Kelley
Shirley Kemper
Janice Killion
Debbie Kishel
Laurie Knecht
DeDe Koukus
Kim Kowalkowski
Lesley Kozlow
Mona Krause

Maryse Labranche
Diane Langone
Cindy Laub
Christine Laurant
Josie Lemmi
Terry LoCicero
Robin Locatash
Ginger Lord
Cammie Lusko
Lisa Lyon

Bev Francis

Corinne Machado-Ching
Diane Maddalo
Karin Marin
Lynn Marks
Susan Martin
Stella Martinez
Jillian Matey
Nancy Maychuk
Valerie Mayers
Rebecca McCrerey
Kathy McGrath
Sue Ann McKean
Sheritha McKenzie
Rachel McLish
Julie McNew
Dinise McPhail
Erika Mes
Terri Miladinovich
Heidi Miller
Georgia Miller-Fudge
Kathy Mischler
Mae Mollica
Salbiah Morris
Ellen Morrow
Elsie Mraz
Diana Mull

Anne Nelson
Kyle Newman
Teri Noor

Lori Okami
Rosa Olafsdottir
Debbie Orgorzat

Gladys Portugues

Camilla Palazzi
Polly Palestri
Auby Paulick
Aida Perez
Audrey Perryman
Lorna Peterson
Karen Pica
Jocelyn Pigeonneau
Pillow
Anita Pinnock
Lynn Pirie
Tina Plakinger
Helen Pollak
Gladys Portugues
Debbie Poston
Cheryl Prizio

Esi Rainwater
Maritza Ramos
Chris Reed
Kathy Richmond
Judy Riedel
Marsha Robbins
Mary Roberts
Susan Roberts
Diane Rook
Jackie Roos
Barbara Rosenburg
Renee Rossier
Ilse Rubin
Kathy Ruth
Sherry Ruth

Lisa Lyon

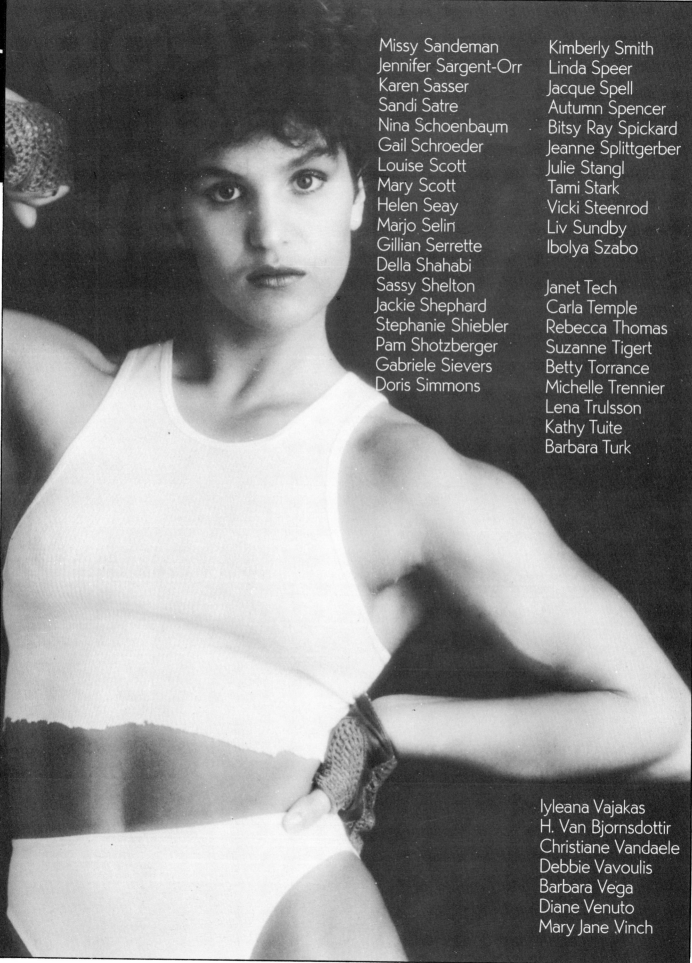

Missy Sandeman
Jennifer Sargent-Orr
Karen Sasser
Sandi Satre
Nina Schoenbaum
Gail Schroeder
Louise Scott
Mary Scott
Helen Seay
Marjo Selin
Gillian Serrette
Della Shahabi
Sassy Shelton
Jackie Shephard
Stephanie Shiebler
Pam Shotzberger
Gabriele Sievers
Doris Simmons

Kimberly Smith
Linda Speer
Jacque Spell
Autumn Spencer
Bitsy Ray Spickard
Jeanne Splittgerber
Julie Stangl
Tami Stark
Vicki Steenrod
Liv Sundby
Ibolya Szabo

Janet Tech
Carla Temple
Rebecca Thomas
Suzanne Tigert
Betty Torrance
Michelle Trennier
Lena Trulsson
Kathy Tuite
Barbara Turk

Iyleana Vajakas
H. Van Bjornsdottir
Christiane Vandaele
Debbie Vavoulis
Barbara Vega
Diane Venuto
Mary Jane Vinch

Marjo Selin

Lory Walkup
Celia Walsh
Zoe Warick
Anne Marie Webber
Gema Wheeler
Carrol White
Claudia Wilbourn
Cindy Williams
Myrna Loy Williams
Tina Woddley-Van Duyn
Lynda Wolf
Joan Wood
Linda Wood-Hoyte
Cindy Wright
Mary Wright
Jeanineq Wuytack

Charlotte Yarbrough

Janet Zagaro
Donna Zaitz
Mari Zegeling
Inger Zetterqvist

Vera Bendel

Iron Adagio: Couples

Here is a salute to a number of noteworthy duos in the bodybuilding world.

Erika Mes and Tony Pearson

Pierre Asselin and Lydia Cheng
Ronnie Ayres and Lisa Alvanos

Michael Barbieri and Terry Sally
Bob Barraclough and Pat Grimmel
Rick Basacker and Cathy Basacker
Jean-Marc Batiste and Veronique Bourgeois
Daniel Baumgartner and Josee Baumgartner
Albert Beckles and Kris Alexander
Ed Bertling and Kathy Cafaro
Dan Bailey and Linda Gagliano
Bob Birdsong and Carla Dunlap
Ray Boone and Ellen Morrow
Terry Brooks and Pam Brooks
John Brown and Shelley Gruwell

Ron Clark and Sharon Wells
Mike Coco and Colette Michelland
Boyer Coe and Valerie Coe
Lamar Collins and Adrienne Foster
Steve Curtis and Bitsy Spickard

Jim Davidson and Robin Franklyn
Steve Davis and Ellen Davis
Berry de Mey and Erika Mes
Greg DeFerro and Chris Dawkins
Phil Dempsey and Tina Plakinger
Harry Derglin and Marlene Fuhrer
Chris Dickerson and Stacy Bentley
Chris Dickerson and Lynn Conkwright
Eric Dowey and Brenda Dowey
Dave Dupre and Patty Sanchez
Jim Dziak and Denise Martin

Jeff Everson and Cory Everson
Roy Evola and Cynthia Sabia

Ken Fabregas and Claire Furr

Skip Gilkerson and Kim Kowalkowski

Dan Helgart and Lisa Coe
Ron Hester and Marilyn Holmes
Ed Holmes and Esi Rainwater
Monroe Huel and Ann Williams
Steve Hull and Louise Johnson
Steve Hyde and Norma Steverson

Derrick Jackson and Sheritha McKenzie
Royce Johnson and Heidi Miller

John Kemper and Carla Dunlap
Ron Kidd and Paula Kidd
Kirk Killion and Janice Killion

Kevin Lawrence and Diana Dennis
Angelito Lesta and Carolyn Cheshire

Bob Magersupp and Lisl Dutterer
Moses Maldonado and Lydia Cheng
Hubert Metz and Ingeborg Doree
Baron Molner and Donna Gulley
Serge Moreau and Mimi Rivest

Steve Newton and Lindsay Summers

Tony Pearson and Carla Dunlap
Tony Pearson and Shelley Gruwell
Tony Pearson and Gladys Portugues
Don Peters and Brenda Lieberman
Harold Poole and Janette Fricks

Keijo Reiman and Marjo Selin
Steve Rhone and Holly Schramm
Gerry Roberts and Susan Roberts
Ben Rodriguez and Gladys Portugues
Carlos Rodriguez and Melinda Perper

Mike Sable and Charlotte Yarbrough
Tim Sandatt and Pat Sawley
Lance Scurvin and Innes Merced
Andrew Searle and Carolyn Cheshire
Tom Sims and Sally Sims
Randy Souza and Agi Balogh
Doug Splittgerber and Jeanne Splittgerber
Bob Stanley and Connie Rouse
Elmer Streater and Tina LaBlanc
Walter Streets and Katherine Thomas

Taz Tally and Enita Mullen
Eddie TeQuiere and Monica Kozat
Russ Testo and Deborah Bouchard
Bill Tierney and Amanda Boulderson

Frank Wainwright and Karen Wainwright
Roger Walker and Kim Rogers

Ted Matush

Gabriel Wild and Hildegard Schafer
Rick Wilkens and Annette Clayton
Scott Wilson and Corinne Machado-Ching

Jonathan Yarbrough and Charlotte
Yarbrough
James Youngblood and Nancy Schrull

Ed Zajac and Agi Balogh
Lance Zavela and Tammy Oliver
John Zenda and Thea Fox

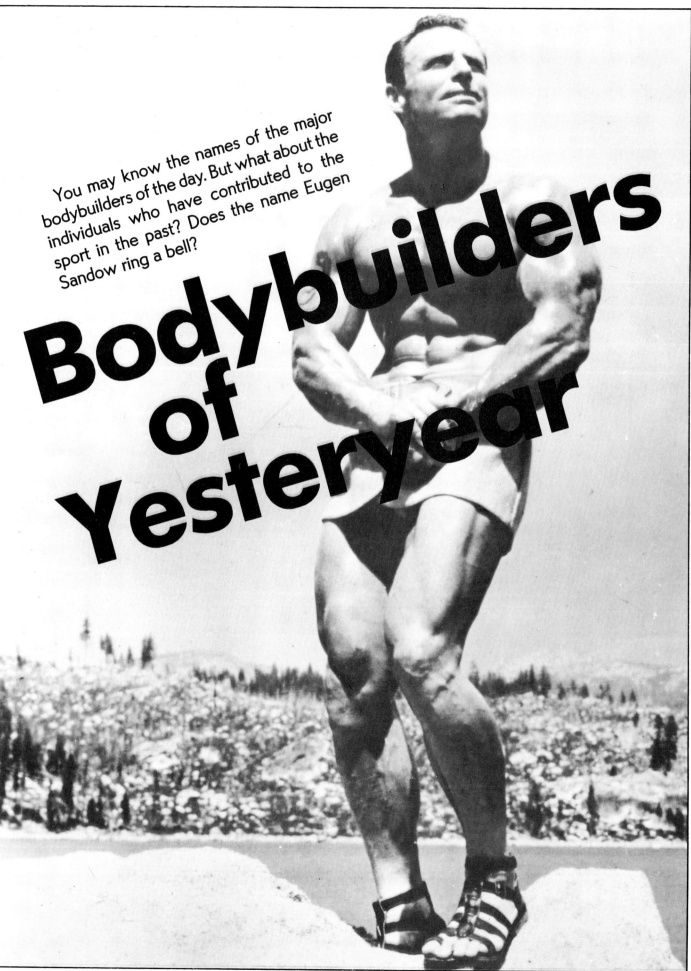

You may know the names of the major bodybuilders of the day. But what about the individuals who have contributed to the sport in the past? Does the name Eugen Sandow ring a bell?

Bodybuilders of Yesteryear

Chuck Sipes

Joe Abbenda
Otto Arco
Charles Atlas

Jules Bacon
Doris Barrilleaux
Laurie Baumert
Gene Bohaty
Joe Bonomo
Malcolm Brenner
Relna Brewer-McCrane

John Citrone
Brandt Clark
W. T. Coggins
Leroy Colbert

Jerry Daniels
Andre Dapp
John Decola
Jack Delinger
Dave Draper
Dick DuBois
Jim Dugger
Roy Duval

George Eiferman
Launceston Elliot
Roland Essmaker

John Farbotnik
Mike Ferraro

Bob Gajda
Vince Gironda
Bert Goodrich
John Grimek

Jack Delinger

George Hackenschmidt
Jim Haislop
Oscar Heidenstam
Paul Hill
Roy Hilligen
Barton Howath
Don Howorth

Roy Hilligen with wife and child

Vince Gironda

Frank Quinn

Bruce Randall
Steve Reeves
Edna "Connie" Rivers
Leo Robert
Arthur Robin
Andre Rolet
Clarence Ross
Jerry Ross
Ray Routledge

PHOTO WARNER

Clancy Ross

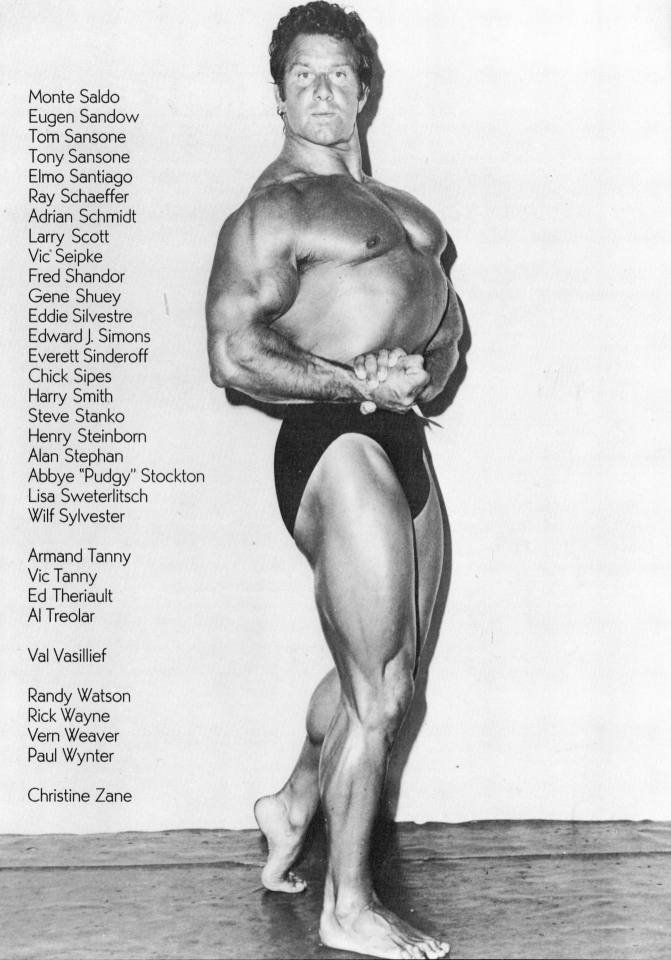

Monte Saldo
Eugen Sandow
Tom Sansone
Tony Sansone
Elmo Santiago
Ray Schaeffer
Adrian Schmidt
Larry Scott
Vic Seipke
Fred Shandor
Gene Shuey
Eddie Silvestre
Edward J. Simons
Everett Sinderoff
Chick Sipes
Harry Smith
Steve Stanko
Henry Steinborn
Alan Stephan
Abbye "Pudgy" Stockton
Lisa Sweterlitsch
Wilf Sylvester

Armand Tanny
Vic Tanny
Ed Theriault
Al Treolar

Val Vasillief

Randy Watson
Rick Wayne
Vern Weaver
Paul Wynter

Christine Zane

Reg Park

Nicknames of the Stars

Samir Bannout

Nearly every major bodybuilder has been dubbed with a nickname by the press or the public. It's always interesting—and a lot of fun—to think about how well the name suits the individual. The following list identifies the most well-known nicknames in the bodybuilding world.

Arms—Julie McNew/Leslie Barber
Austrian Oak—Arnold Schwarzenegger
Barbarians, The—David and Peter Paul
Bayonne Thunder—John Hnatyschak
Beast from the East—Benny Podda
Black Prince—Robby Robinson
Blond Bomber—Dave Draper
Cajun King—Boyer Coe
Cobra—Mike Huber
Demon—Ken Passariello
East Coast Tim Belknap—Richard Gaspari
Father of Physical Culture—Bernarr MacFadden
First Lady of Bodybuilding—Lisa Lyon
Fox/Foxy—Bertil Fox
Gentle Giant—Reid Schindle

Arnold Schwarzenegger

Giant from the Midwest—Matt Mendenhall

Giant Killer—Danny Padilla

Greek God—Steve Reeves

Incredible Hulk—Lou Ferrigno

Ingenious George—George Eiferman

Iron Guru—Vince Gironda

King—Jeff King

Lady Soul—Carla Dunlap

Larry the Legend—Larry Scott

Lean Machine—Tony Pearson

Legs/The Golden Eagle—Tom Platz

Lion of Lebanon—Samir Bannout

Little Miss Muscle—Mae Mollica

Magic Egyptian—Mohamed Makkawy

Martha Graham of Bodybuilding—Kay Baxter

Master Blaster/Trainer of Champions—Joe Weider

Master Poser—Ed Corney

Mentzer the Younger—Ray Mentzer

Merchant of Venom/Rick Vain—Rick Wayne

Monarch of Muscledom—John Grimek

Mr. Elegance—Chris Dickerson

Mr. Heavy Duty—Mike Mentzer

Mr. Robot—Russ Testo

Mr. T—Tim Belknap

Ms. Flex Appeal—Rachel McLish

Muscle Princess—Sheritha McKenzie

Myth, The—Sergio Oliva

Natural Champion—Dennis Tinerino

Phantom—Steve Michalik

Rocky/Man of Iron—Greg DeFerro

Sexy Eyes—Diana Dennis

She-Beast—Pillow

Shoulders—Serge Nubret

Steve Reeves II—Bob Paris

Superstar—Lynn Conkwright

Swedish Steel—Inger Zetterqvist

Thee Animal—Rod Koontz

Zipper, The—Mike Sable

Promoters and Sponsors

It requires a special individual to be a successful contest promoter or sponsor. This aspect of bodybuilding is an art unto itself. Money, publicity, facilities, trophies, bodybuilders, entertainment, and spectators must all be integrated for each event. Here are some of the companies and people who do it.

ACB Gym
Delores Ali

Bath Beach Health Spas
John Barbero
Ulf Bengtsson
Charles Blake
Julien Blommaert
Wally Boyko Productions, Inc.
Bradshaw Physique Productions
Gene Brasher Promotions, Ltd.
Albert Busek
George Butler

Canon Business Machines
Richard Cavaler
Paul Chua
Coors Beer Company
Corbin-Gentry, Inc.
Curtis Crebar

Jim Dandrow
Davina Health Products
Wayne and Karen DeMilia

Paul Edney

Flex Gym Equipment
Bob and Jeanette Fuchs

Frank Gall
James Gaubert
Mike Glass
Paul Grant
Rafael Guerrero

Ron Holden Promotions
Bobo Holmqvist

Mits and Dot Kawashima
John Kemper
Tom Kinney

Bud Leonard
Jim Lorimer
Love's Health Club
Dan Lurie

Roger Mervau
Milo Health Drink
Stan Morey
Muscle Mart

National Fitness Trade Journal
Natural Physique Center
Vince Napoli
Doc Neely
F. Nicolini
Onni Nordstrom

George Paine
Physique Productions, Inc.

David Riley
Dick Roberts

Russ Warner, Bill Pearl, and Rick Wayne

Ben and Joe Weider

Joseph Schmidt
Casey Schneider
Arnold Schwarzenegger
Singapore Tourist Promotion Board
Vicki Smith
George Snyder
Solana, Inc.
Oscar State
Charles Stone
Stone Gym Equipment

Tampa Bodybuilding Association
Titan Promotions
Joe Tete Promotions
TK Equipment Company

Russ Warner
Mary Washco Productions
Ben and Joe Weider
Weider Health and Fitness, Inc.

With the large number of contests being held every week around the world, it is a wonder that qualified judges can be found to participate. Theirs is not an easy or popular job.

Among the many hundreds of judges, here are just a few of the more well-known ones.

Judges

Dolores Ali
Bradley Annis
Janet Atherton

Doris Barrilleaux
Clarence Bass
Art Bedway
Robert Binafl
Denise Black
Jacques Blommaert
Julien Blommaert
Charles Bradshaw

John Calasione
Jan Caswell
Richard Cavaler
Dominic Certo
Anita Columbu
Candy Csencsits

Jim Dandrow
Marilyn Davies
Ron Davies
Carole Dequay
Carla Dunlap
Rosemarie Durfee
Jeannette Dyer

Doug Evans

Franco Fassi
Monica Froelich
Susan Fry

Carole Graham

Mary Hastings
Janet Heim
Michael Hekel
Sheila Herman

Erich Janner
Marie Jay
Walter Jekot

Mike Katz
John Kemper
Doreen Kennedy

Carlos Rodriguez

Lori Bowen and Shelley Gruwell

Kay King-Nealy
Anna Knight
Sue Koch

Jim Lensveld
Paul Love
Pat Luthy

Jim Manion
John Martin
John Carl Mese

Ken Neely
Ludek Nosek

Mary Orlando

B. Peterson
Peter Potter

Sandy Ranalli
Dick Roberts
Winston Roberts

Gus Salerno
Clark Sanchez
Nina Schoenbaum
Roger Schwab
Charles Simkovich
Jim Smith
Vicki Smith
Arne Svedsen

Mandy Tanny
Sven-Ole Thorsen

Walter van den Branden

Gema Wheeler
Bill Wick
Claudia Wilbourn

Oscar State

Judges

Photographers

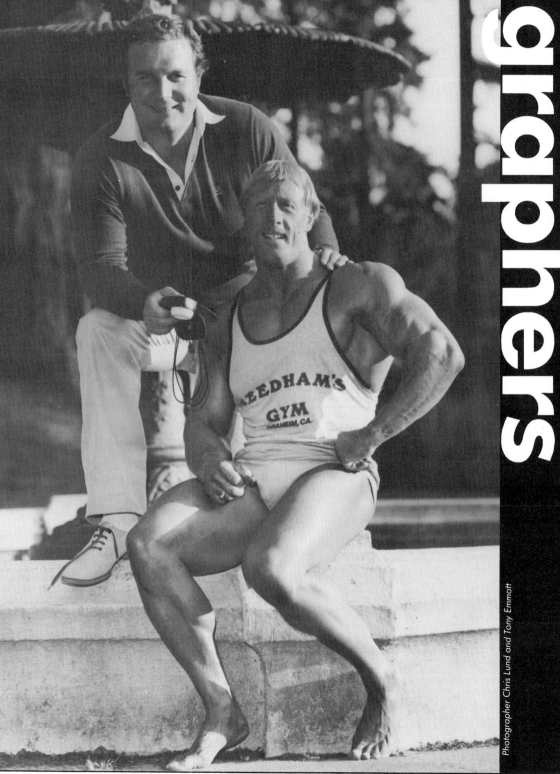

Photographer Chris Lund and Tony Emmott

Here is a list of some of the great photographers in the business. Has your picture been taken by any of them? If so, consider yourself very fortunate!

Larry Agron
Al Antuck

Mike Bailey
John Balik
Doris Barrilleaux
Garry Bartlett
Peter Brenner
Albert Busek
George Butler

John Campos
Jimmy Caruso
Karen Clark
Geoff Collins
James Cordean

D'arbanville
Benno Dahmen
Don Y. Dan
Pete Daniels
Craig Deitz
Denie
Bil Dobbins
Steve Douglas

Gino Edwards

Dick Falcon
Bob Flippin
Jerry Frederick

Wayne Gallasch
Bob Gardner
George Greenwood
Joe Griffith
Bob Gruskin

Edward Hankey
Bill Heimanson
Max Helweg
Monty Heron
Mike Hopkins

Bill Jentz
Art and Ben Jones

David Keith
Robert Kennedy
Bruce Klemens

Tony Lanza
Bob Long
Chris Lund
Mark Lurie

Robert Mapplethorpe
Jim Marchand

John Nafpliotis
Robert Nailon
Gary Nathan
Pat Neve
Mike Neveux
Neal Nordlinger

Richard Ortiz

Allan Paul
Peter Potter

David Randall
Bill Reynolds
Rob Robson
Rich Ruoti

Dave Sauer
Rick Semple
Roger Shelley
Robert Spector

Kathy Tuite
Samuel Tyus

Joe Valdez

Doug White
Bill Wick
Jim Wilmer
Steve Winnerstrom

Art Zeller

John Balik

Tim Belknap

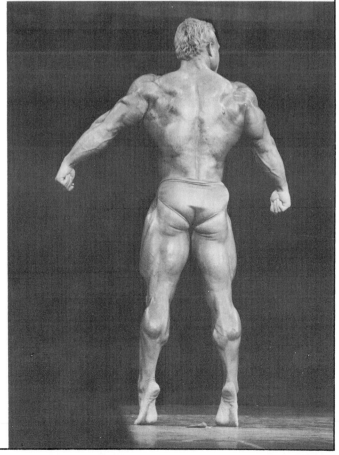

IFBB

Greg DeFerro

International Federation of Bodybuilders

Bertil Fox

IFBB

The International Federation of Body-builders (IFBB) is the official governing organization for men and women body-builders (amateur and professional).

In 1947, Ben and Joe Weider founded the IFBB, which was quickly endorsed by the top champions of the sport worldwide. In 1970, the IFBB joined the General Assembly of International Sports Federations (GAISF), an organization which coordinated Olympic and non-Olympic amateur sports. This merger increased the IFBB's membership to include 130 nations, making it the seventh-largest international amateur sports federation in the world.

The IFBB serves: to promote total physical fitness, scientific training principles, and exercise as a way of life; to develop the whole person and encourage individual potential; to foster bodybuilding as a highly beneficial, competitive, and positive sport; and to obtain Olympic recognition for the sport.

The credo is a reflection of the organization: "Bodybuilding is important for nationbuilding."

IFBB OFFICERS

President
Ben Weider
2875 Bates Rd., Montreal, Quebec, Canada H3S
1B7/514-731-3783/telex: 055-61488

Executive Vice-President
Oscar State
4 Godfrey Ave., Twickenham, TW2 7PF, England
1-898-5288

Executive Council Vice-Presidents
Julien Blommaert—Europe
Paul Chua—Asia
Victor A. Copra—Caribbean Islands
Paul Graham—Oceania
Abd El Hamid El Guindy—Middle East
Jim Manion—North America
Laercio Martine—South America
Tom O'Omuombo—Africa

General Secretary
Winston Roberts

Assistant Secretary
Harris Kagan

Patrons
President Ferdinand E. Marcos
Joe Weider

Treasurer
Lucille Lamarre

Legal Counsel
George Lengvari

Medical and Research Committee
Professor Ernst Jokl, M.D. (Chairman)
Dr. Charles Garfield (Secretary)

Judge's Committee
Jacques Blommaert (Chairman)
Oscar State (Secretary)

Women's Committee
Doris Barrilleaux (Chairperson)
Susan Fry (Secretary)

Professional Judging Director
Roger Schwab

Liaison for Professionals
Wayne DeMilia

IFBB Historian
David Webster

Official Journal
Flex Magazine

IFBB Women's Committee

Chairwoman
Doris Barrilleaux
PO Box 937, Riverview, FL 33569

General Secretary
Susan Fry
PO Box 363, Niwot, CO 80544-0363

Members
Carole Bennett
PO Box 27, Brighton Le Sands
New South Wales 2216, Australia
Carolyn Cheshire
6 Woburn Ct., Stanmore Rd.
Richmond, Surrey, England

National Physique Committee

In 1978, the National Physique Committee (NPC) was recognized as the official governing organization for men's amateur bodybuilding. Prior to that, the NPC was a committee of the Amateur Athletic Union (AAU). However, the AAU relinquished control, and the NPC became a separate entity. Under its guidance, amateur men's bodybuilding became unified and began to grow. When this occurred, the AAU decided to re-enter the sport, which caused some divisions regarding contests and memberships. Via legal channels, the NPC still retained its function as the official governing organization for men's amateur bodybuilding.

The AAU still gives contests and is working to expand membership. Yet it is the NPC that works to unify the sport, to offer high-level competitions, to supply a superior amateur bodybuilding organization and program for all members, to support Olympic recognition, and to promote and develop the sport to its utmost potential.

Membership is presently $10/year.

Harry and Ray Clarke

NPC OFFICERS

President
James Manion
140 East Mall Plaza, Carnegie, PA 15106

Vice-Presidents
Clarence Bass
528 Chama, NE, Albuquerque, NM 87108

Wayne DeMilia
PO Box 1490, Radio City Station, New York, NY
10019

Pete Grymkowski, c/o Gold's Gym
360 Hampton Dr., Venice, CA
90291/213-392-3005

Paul Love
3050 Story Rd., San Jose, CA 95127

Secretary
John Carl Mese
170 NE 99th St., Miami Shores, FL 33138

Treasurer
Harry Wulff
633 Racine Ave., Pittsburgh, PA 15216

Extra Trustee
Clark Sanchez
322 Muriel NE, Albuquerque, NM 87123

Athlete Trustees
Charles Glass
742 E. 88th Pl., Los Angeles, CA 90002
Lee Haney
PO Box 185, Santa Monica, CA 90406

Members-at-Large
Heine Fountaine
Tim Kimber
Rod Miller
Peter Potter
John Simkovich

Athlete Representatives
Donald Ausmus
608 Esperanza, McAllen, TX 78501

Daniel Berumen
11150 Loch Avon Dr., Whittier, CA 90606

Charles Colson
1416 W. Tennessee St., Tallahassee, FL 32304

Charles Glass
742 E. 88th Pl., Los Angeles, CA
90002/213-971-4235

Lee Haney
PO Box 185, Santa Monica, CA 90406

Don Knipp
624 Warner Ave., #17-G, Huntington Beach, CA
92647

Benny Podda
217 Lake St., South Fork, PA 15956

NPC DISTRICT CHAIRMEN

Alabama—Southeastern District
Mike Kiser
7624 Nubbin Ridge Rd., Knoxville, TN 37919

Alaska
Lawrence S. Gordon
604 Highlander Circle, Anchorage, AK 99502

Arizona
Pat Neve
4127 W. Cavalier, Phoenix, AZ 85019

Arkansas
Rion Weiner
8 Cottage Ct., North Little Rock, AR 72118

California—Los Angeles District (zip codes:
900–919, 923–931, 934, 935)
Richard Roberts
202 W. 20th St., Santa Ana, CA 92706

California—San Diego District (zip codes: 920–922)
Lou Duarte, Lou's Gym
124 E. 30th St., #A, National City, CA 92050

California—Central District (zip codes: 932, 933, 936, 937)
Casey Schneider
3233 N. Cedar, Fresno, CA 93726

California—North (zip codes: 939–961)
Paul Love
3050 Story Rd., San Jose, CA 95127

Colorado
Jim Smith
7335 Mt. Meeker Rd., Longmont, CO 80501

Connecticut
Jim Howley
985 Farmington Ave., Bristol, CT 06010

Delaware
Rick Williams
514 N. Ford Ave., #2, Wilmington, DE 19805

District of Columbia
Thomas Moffett
805 Montpelier St., Baltimore, MD 21218

Florida—North District (zip codes: 320–322, 326–329, 335–339)
Richard Collis, c/o Mr. Gym
2490 12th St., Sarasota, FL 33577

Florida—West District (zip codes: 323–325)
John Powers
169 Miracle Strip Plaza, Ft. Walton Beach, FL 32548

Florida—South District (zip codes: 330–334)
John Carl Mese
170 NE 99th St., Miami Shores, FL 33128

Hawaii
Bill Nelson
PO Box 23161, Honolulu, HI 96822

Idaho
Mike Shine, Boise YMCA, 1050 W. State St., Boise, ID 83702

Illinois
James Marchsand
9103 Franklin Ct., #102, Orland Park, IL 60462

Indiana
Troy Beck
18210 Promise Rd., Noblesville, IN 46060

Iowa
Gary Glanzer
c/o Des Moines Athletic Club, 1120 Walnut, Des Moines, IA 50309

Kansas—Missouri Valley District
John R. Erter
208 Lake Village Blvd., Blue Springs, MO 64015

Kentucky
Franklin Page
9 Rebel Rd., Louisville, KY 40206

Louisiana
James A. Gaubert
1421 Avenue G, Marrero, LA 70072

Maine
Rich Labbe
50 S. Main St., Auburn, ME 04210

Maryland
Thomas Moffett
805 Montpelier St., Baltimore, MD 21218

Massachusetts
Bruce Stone
14 Hanover St., PO Box 2024, Hanover, MA 02339

Michigan
Richard Cavaler
5914 12th St., Detroit, MI 48208

Mississippi—Southern District
James A. Gaubert
1421 Avenue G, Marrero, LA 70072

Missouri
John R. Erter
208 Lake Village Blvd., Blue Springs, MO 64015

Montana
Phillip J. Balland
908 W. 31st St., Cheyenne, WY 82001

Nebraska
Andy Fry
c/o Sweep Left Athletic Club, 815 O St., Lincoln, NE 68508

Nevada
Harold Wooten
14055 Perlite Dr., Reno, NV 89511

New Hampshire
Bruce Stone
14 Hanover St., PO Box 2024, Hanover, MA 02339

New Jersey
James Dandrow
PO Box 21, Bloomfield, NJ 07003

New Mexico
Clark Sanchez
322 Muriel NE, Albuquerque, NM 87123

New York—Metropolitan District (zip codes: beginning with 10, 11)
Richard Roach
171 W. 81st St., New York NY 10024

New York—East District (zip codes: beginning with 12, 13)
Michael Mashuta
5 Kenaware Ave., Delmar, NY 12054

New York—West District (zip codes: beginning with 14)
James Rockell
c/o Samson's Gym, 572 Lyell Ave., Rochester, NY 14606

North Carolina
Alan R. Hoffman
PO Box 687, Hope Mills, NC 28348

North Dakota
Bob Norland
203 E. Arbor Ave., #306-F, Bismarck, ND 58501

Ohio—North District (zip codes: beginning with 44)
Raymond Gingo
3698 Argonne St., Mogadore, OH 44260

Ohio—South District (zip codes: beginning with 43, 45)
John Parrillo
936 North Bend Rd., Cincinnati, OH 45224

Oklahoma
Allan Levine
905 W. Mitchell, Midwest City, OK 73110

Oregon
Charles Amato
12185 SE 108, Portland, OR 97266

Pennsylvania—East District (zip codes: beginning with 17, 18, 190—196)
Jeff Wolfe
c/o Lancaster County Racquetball Club
1319 Millersville Park, Lancaster, PA 17603

Pennsylvania—West District (zip codes: beginning with 15, 16)
Harry Wulff
633 Racine Ave., Pittsburgh, PA 15216

Rhode Island
Leonard Meglio
1800 Post Rd., Airport Plaza, Warwick, RI 02886

South Carolina
Phil Outlaw
5322 Trudy St., Charleston, SC 29405

South Dakota
Bob Norland
203 E. Arbor Ave., #306-F, Bismarck, ND 58501

Tennessee
Mike Kiser
7624 Nubbin Ridge Rd., Knoxville, TN 37919

Texas—North District (zip codes: beginning with 75, 76)
Michael Graham
603 W. 13th St., Austin, TX 78701

Texas—East District (zip codes: beginning with 77)
Michael Graham
603 W. 13th St., Austin, TX 78701

Texas—South District (zip codes: beginning with 78)
Michael Graham, 603 W. 13th St., Austin, TX 78701

Texas—West District (zip codes: beginning with 79)
Michael Graham
603 W. 13th St., Austin, TX 78701

Utah
Ronald DeBry
1950 S. 1700 East #B, Salt Lake City, UT 84108

Vermont
Ron Evans
PO Box 337, Rutland, VT 05701

Virginia—Potomac District (zip codes: 220—223)
Thomas Moffett
805 Montpelier St., Baltimore, MD 21218

Virginia—Virginia District (zip codes: 224—246)
Alan Hoffman
PO Box 687, Hope Mills, NC 28348

Washington
Geoffrey Ross
c/o Iron Works Gym, 12708 Northrup, Bellevue, WA 98005

West Virginia
Art Bedway
100 W. Circle Dr., Weirton, WV 26062

Wisconsin
Robert Plakinger
c/o Wedgewood Fitness Center, 6807 W. Morgan Ave., Milwaukee, WI 53220

Wyoming
Phillip J. Balland
908 W. 31st St., Cheyenne, WY 82001

If you are in the military service and your address is an APO or FPO box number, you are in the Armed Forces District.

If you reside in any territory, protectorate, etc., of the United States (except Puerto Rico and the Virgin Islands, which have special federations allied with the IFBB), you are in the Overseas District.

The Military and Overseas Districts have no committee and no chairmen; they are directly handled by the NPC National Office. If there is no representative for a particular state, contact the NPC National Office for further information.

NPC National Office
Jerome D. Weis, Administrator
PO Box 37, Dayton View Station, Dayton, OH 45406

NPC National Athlete Registration Service
American Sports Management, Inc.
27208 Southfield Rd., Lathrup Village, MI 48076

Amateur Athletic Union

The Amateur Athletic Union of the United States, Inc. (AAU) controls a variety of amateur sports. For many years, the sport of physique was run by a subcommittee of the AAU Weightlifting Committee, but separated to form its own organization—the National Physique Committee (NPC)—in 1978 by a congressional act.

When the NPC eventually broke away from the AAU, it became affiliated with the IFBB. However, when the AAU wanted to re-enter the sport of bodybuilding, the IFBB refused to grant the organization official recognition. Legal battles ensued which only seemed to foster conflict and confusion between the organizations.

These lawsuits are not completely settled, but the AAU continues to hold the registered trademark of the Mr. America title.

Presently, the AAU is working: to organize the promotion of bodybuilding at the local, state, and national levels; to consolidate amateur involvement in all areas of physique competition; and to develop a cohesive work force for the total unification of the sport of bodybuilding.

AAU OFFICERS

President
Josiah Henson
    3468 Mildred Dr., Falls Church, VA 22042

Vice President
Richard E. Harkins
    620 W. 26th St., Kansas City, MO 64108

Secretary
Gussie Crawford
    900 Weidmann Rd., Manchester, MO 63011

Treasurer
Joseph D. Murphy
    260 Pleasant Hill Blvd., Palatine, IL 60067

Membership is presently $10/year.

AMERICA EXECUTIVE COMMITTEE

Chairman

Cliff Sawyer
64 June St., Worcester, MA 01602

Members

Ken Alexander
c/o Coordinated Hosp. Svs., 5410 Homberg Dr.
Knoxville, TN 37916

Robert Crist
19 Barnes St., Hampton, VA 23664

Irish Gale
PO Box 416, Maywood, CA 90270

Ira Hurley
PO Box 1013, Glendale Heights, IL 60137

Kay Hurley
One Wheaton Ctr., #1205
Wheaton, IL 60187

Suzanne Kosak
8304 Elkwood Lane, Tampa, FL 33615

James Lowe
538 E. Huntington Rd., Rossville, GA 30741

Dave Mayor
7653 Wyndale Ave., Philadelphia, PA 19151

Pete Miller
1831 Gilson St., Falls Church, VA 22043

Tom Minichiello
250 W. 49th St., New York, NY 10019

Stan Morey
12101 N. 56th St., Tampa, FL 33617

Jack O'Bleness
3901 W. 111th St., Inglewood, CA 90303

Peary Rader
c/o *Iron Man* Magazine, PO Box 10
Alliance, NE 69301

Michael Walczak
4901 Van Nuys Blvd., #110
Sherman Oaks, CA 91403

Alternate Members

Jon Reiger
1320 Lydia St., Louisville, KY 40217

Frank Peffer
c/o Peffer Athletic Club, 1501 Albright Ave.
Scranton, PA 18508

Jerry Bianucci
5926 Cauba Ct., Alexandria, VA 22301

AAU ASSOCIATION PHYSIQUE CHAIRMEN

Adirondack

Joe Berlino
c/o Steel Pier Athletic Club, 1301 Hutton St.
Troy, NY 12181

Arizona

Mark Melkouski
1850 E. University, Tempe, AZ 85281

Carlos Rodriquez
703 E. Broadway, Tucson, AZ 85719

Central

Ira Hurley
PO Box 1013, Glendale Heights, IL 60137

Connecticut

Lyle Hayes
97 Cedar Hill Rd., Huntington, CT 06484

Florida

Stan Morey
12101 N. 56th St., Tampa, FL 33617

Georgia

James Lowe
538 E. Huntington Rd., Rossville, GA 30741

Indiana

Perry Winn
c/o The Winner's Edge, 5922 E. 10th St.
Indianapolis, IN 46219

Iowa

Nick Ganakas
c/o Nick's Fitness Center, 419 Jefferson
Burlington, IA 52601

Kentucky

Dr. Jon Reiger
1320 Lydia St., Louisville, KY 40217

Maine

Susan Fides
17 Palmer St., Portland, ME 04102

Metropolitan

Tom Minichiello
c/o Mid-City Gym, 224 W. 49th St.
New York, NY 10019

Middle Atlantic
Bob O'Leary
c/o Health Food Dist., 101 El Drive
Taylor, PA 18517

Midwestern
Doug Lindzey
3810 "Q" St., Omaha, NE 68107

Minnesota
Jim Youngner
c/o The Gym, 670 Mendelssohn Ave. North
Golden Valley, MN 55427

New England
Cliff Sawyer
64 June St., Worcester, MA 01602

Niagara
Dave Davis
4000 Harlem Rd., Snyder, NY 14226

North Carolina
Jack King
122 S. Hawthorne
Winston-Salem, NC 27103

Ohio
Richard Torio
4025 Berwick Dr.
Toledo, OH 43612

Oklahoma
Dave Keener
c/o Gold's Gym of Tulsa, 2117-B S. Garnett
Tulsa, OK 74129

Oregon
Roger Sandvold
4119 Riverview Dr., West Linn, OR 97068

Ozark
Rick King
c/o Eagle Gyms, 2561 Woodson Rd.
St. Louis, MO 63114

Pacific
Mike Dayton
PO Box 6410, Concord, CA 94524

Potomac Valley
Pete Miller
1831 Gilson St., Falls Church, VA 22043

South Atlantic
Jim Wilmer
204 Chell Rd., Joppa, MD 21085

Southeastern
Ken Alexander
c/o Coordinated Hosp. Svs.
5410 Homberg Dr., Knoxville, TN 37916

Southern
Frank Mule
3970 Downman Rd., New Orleans, LA 70126

Virginia
Robert Crist
19 Barnes Ct., Hampton, VA 23364

West Virginia
Larry Robinson
65 Skyline Dr., St. Albans, WV 25177

If you live in an area that is not listed, please contact Mimi Sherman at the National AAU House, 3400 W. 86th St., Indianapolis, IN 46268 (317) 872-2900.

American Federation of Women Bodybuilders

The American Federation of Women Bodybuilders (AFWB) was established in 1980. It is the official governing organization for amateur women bodybuilders in the United States. The AFWB is the only organization recognized by the IFBB for female physique athletes.

Each state has an AFWB representative who works with all contest promoters to help organize competitions and to set up clinics, seminars, and workshops. The state representatives also function to meet legal, administrative, disciplinary, and medical needs of their members.

The primary goals of the AFWB are to promote the positive growth of women's bodybuilding and to further the values, aims, and ideals of the federation.

Membership is presently $15/year.

Rachel McLish

AFWB OFFICERS

President
Vicki Smith
PO Box 363, Niwot, CO 80544-0363

Vice-President
Doris Barrilleaux
PO Box 937, Riverview, FL 33569

General Secretary
Candy Csencsits
R.D. 1, PO Box 726, Lenhartsville, PA 19534

Treasurer
Gema Wheeler
8334 Whitefield, Dearborn Heights, MI 48127

National Sanction Secretary
Anna Knight
2807 Flakewood, Little Rock, AR 72207

AFWB EXECUTIVE COMMITTEE

Public Relations
Jan Caswell
1120 N. Flores, #10, Los Angeles, CA 90069

Promotions
Linda Evans
PO Box 726, Rutland, VT 05701

Judge's Committee
Candy Csencsits
R.D. 1, PO Box 726, Lenhartsville, PA 19534
Sandy Ranalli
2534 Reading Blvd., W. Lawn, PA 19609
Gema Wheeler
Judges Clinics Official, 8334 Whitefield, Dearborn
    Heights, MI 48127

National Judge's Card Coordinator
Mary Hastings
14800 Robson, Detroit, MI 48227

Judge's Clinic Coordinator
Andrea Ferenc
31345 Tamarack, Apt. 2213, Wixom, MI 48096

Technical Committee
Deborah Moore
PO Box 23104, Kansas City, MO 64141

Disciplinary Committee
Patty Sanchez
322 Muriel NE, Albuquerque, NM 87123

Medical Committee
Dr. Lynn Pirie
413 N. 16th St., Phoenix, AZ 85016

Election Committee
Pat Luthy
PO Box 8803, Boise, ID 83707

Council Members
Patty Sanchez
322 Muriel St. NE, Albuquerque, NM 87123
Jeanne Splittgerber
513 E. Mitchell, Appleton, WI 54911

Consultants
Doris Barrilleaux
Kim Cassiday
Sheila Herman
Susan Koch
Claudia Wilbourn

AFWB REGIONAL DIRECTORS

Northeast
Julie McNew
PO Box 67276, Los Angeles, CA 90067

Northwest
Kelly Nelson
1200 Eastmont, #33, East Wenatchee, WA 98801

North Central
Cindy Gablehouse
7912 Broadview Dr., Lincoln, NE 68505

Southeast
Maryann Wettstein
1503 S. 9th St., Leesburg, FL 32748

South Central
Dinah Anderson
1529 N. 11th St., Abilene, TX 79601

Southwest
Jeanne Jelcick
c/o Alley Health Club, PO Box 932, Freedom, CA 95015

AFWB REGIONAL SANCTION SECRETARIES

Northeast
Janet Heim
R.D. 4, White Rd., Watertown, NY 13601
(Maine, New Hampshire, Vermont, Massachusetts, Rhode Island, Connecticut, Delaware, Maryland, Ohio, Washington, DC, Indiana)

North Central
Jeanne Splittgerber
513 E. Mitchell, Appleton, WI 54911
(Michigan, Wisconsin, Illinois, Iowa, Nebraska, Minnesota, North Dakota, South Dakota)

Northwest
Pat Luthy
PO Box 8803, Boise, ID 83707
(Washington, Oregon, Idaho, Wyoming, Montana, Alaska)

Southeast
Rosemarie Durfee
4167 Arrow Lane, Sarasota, FL 33582
(West Virginia, Virginia, North Carolina, South Carolina, Kentucky, Tennessee, Georgia, Alabama, Mississippi)

South Central
Anna Knight
2807 Flakewood, Little Rock, AR 72207
(Arkansas, Louisiana, Texas, Oklahoma, New Mexico, Missouri, Kansas, Colorado)

Southwest
Stephanie Johnson
PO Box 86490, San Diego, CA 92138-6490
(California, Nevada, Utah, Arizona, Hawaii)

AFWB STATE REPRESENTATIVES

Alabama
Cheryll Phifer
31 Sunscape Dr., Birmingham, AL 35215

Alaska
Pat Beers
c/o Gold's Gym, 5011 Artic Blvd., Anchorage, AK 99503

Arizona
Vicki Neve
4127 W. Cavalier, Phoenix, AZ 85019

Arkansas
Anna Knight
2807 Flakewood, Little Rock, AR 72207

California (Northern)
Brenda Renz
10 W. Locust, Lodi, CA 95240

California (Southern)
Mae Mollica
PO Box 81886, San Diego, CA 92138

Connecticut
Maribeth Maia-Debrizzi
100 Overland Ave., Bridgeport, CT 06606

Delaware
Cindy Williams Reichert
514 N. Ford Ave., #2, Wilmington, DE 19805

Florida (Central)
Maryann Wettstein
1503 S. 9th St., Leesburg, FL 32748

Florida (South)
Suzanne Arthur
23 W. Granada Ave., Ormond Beach, FL 32074

Hawaii
Cathy Chang c/o Physique World, Inc.
1668 B South King Ave., Honolulu, HI 96826

Idaho
Bitsy Ray Spickard
2304 Bodily, Idaho Falls, ID 83402

Illinois (East)
Deborah Kuhn
2444 W. Ainslie, Chicago, IL 60625

Illinois (West)
Monica Hurt
7619 Sussex Creek, Darien, IL 60559

Indiana
Jo Berta
2519 E. 10th, Suite 6, Anderson, IN 46012

Kansas
Jana Oliver
610 Shefford, Wichita, KS 67212

Louisiana
Vicki Panebiango
PO Box 2343, Lafayette, LA 70502

Maryland
Denise Bazemore
2206 Water Vale Dr., Fallston, MD 21047

Michigan
Gema Wheeler
8334 Whitefield, Dearborn Heights, MI 48127

Mississippi
Andrea Moody
PO Box 3604, Gulfport, MS 39503

Missouri
Jackie Harrington, Apt. A311
5502 NE Scandia Lane, Kansas City, MO 64118

Montana
Bonnie Doucett
2201 Dearborn, Missoula, MT 59801

Nebraska
Linda Krussel
RR #2, PO Box 299 E, Nebraska City, NE 68410

Nevada
Doreen Kenedy
1062 Palmerston St., Las Vegas, NV 89110

New Hampshire
Lucy Scheerr
PO Box 1292, New London, NH 03257

New Jersey
Josephine Baker, c/o East Coast Gym
242 Dover Rd., South Toms River, NJ 08757

New Mexico
Patty Sanchez
322 Muriel St., NE, Albuquerque, NM 87123

New York City
Kay King-Nealy
12 E. 22nd St., #PHD, New York, NY 10010

New York State
Janet Heim
R.D. #4, White Rd., Watertown, NY 13601

North Carolina
Susan Hoffman
PO Box 687, Hope Mills, NC 28348

North Dakota
Sylvia Fossen
2493 W. 4th Ave., Dickinson, ND 58601

Ohio
Denise Black
11934 Lorain Ave., Cleveland, OH 44111

Oregon
Cindy Wright
10915 SW Hall Blvd., #10, Tigard, OR 97223

Pennsylvania
Sandy Ranalli
2534 Reading Blvd., W. Lawn, PA 19609

South Carolina
Winnie Machado
172 Cobbs Way, Anderson, SC 29621

Tennessee
Sassy Shelton
3220 Gleason Dr., #68, Chattanooga, TN 37412

Texas (North)
Laurie Fuller
c/o Texas Health Club
140 N. 5th, Silsbee, TX
      77656

Texas (South)
Janet Atherton
6211 Brookgate Dr., Spring, TX 77373

Utah
Vikki Alred
3848 S. 2215 East, Salt Lake City, UT 84109

Vermont
Linda Evans
PO Box 337, Rutland, VT 05701

Virginia
Cindy Zurmuhlen
c/o Horizon House, 1300 Army Navy Dr., #104,
      Arlington, VA 22202

Washington
Colleen Fisher, NE 1100 Old Highway, Belfair, WA
      98528

Wyoming
Karen Minchow,
PO Box 1314, Evansville, WY
      82636

Wisconsin
Jeanne Splittgerber
513 E. Mitchell, Appleton, WI 54911

If no state representative is listed, contact the General Secretary (Candy Csencsits) for more information.

Carla Dunlap

Frank Zane

Men's Competitions

*The abbreviations used are: BW, bantamweight; LW, lightweight; MW, middleweight; LHW, light-heavyweight; and HW, heavyweight.
†This indicates the overall title winner.

Mr. Olympia

1965	Larry Scott
1966	Larry Scott
1967	Sergio Oliva
1968	Sergio Oliva
1969	Sergio Oliva
1970	Arnold Schwarzenegger
1971	Arnold Schwarzenegger
1972	Arnold Schwarzenegger
1973	Arnold Schwarzenegger
1974	Arnold Schwarzenegger
1975	Arnold Schwarzenegger
1976	Franco Columbu
1977	Frank Zane
1978	Frank Zane
1979	Frank Zane
1980	Arnold Schwarzenegger
1981	Franco Columbu
1982	Chris Dickerson
1983	Samir Bannout

IFBB Mr. America

1949	Alan Stephan
1950	Chuck Sipes
1960	Gene Shuey
1962	Larry Scott
1963	Reg Lewis
1964	Harold Poole
1965	Dave Draper
1966	Chet Yorton
1967	Don Howorth
1968	Frank Zane
1969	John Decola
1970	Mike Katz
1971	Ken Waller
1972	Ed Corney
1973	Lou Ferrigno
1974	Bob Birdsong
1975	Robby Robinson
1976	Mike Mentzer
1977	Danny Padilla

IFBB Mr. World

1962	Jose Castaneda Lence
1963	Jorge Brisco
1965	Kinglsey Poitier
1966	Sergio Oliva
1967	Rick Wayne
1968	Chuck Sipes
1969	Frank Zane
1970	Dave Draper
1971	Franco Columbu
1972	Mike Katz
1973	Ken Waller
1974	Bill Grant
1975	Robby Robinson
1976	Darcey Beccles

IFBB Mr. Europe

1981

LW	Jose Rabanal
MW	Anton Holic
LHW	Libor Minarik
HW	Gunnar Rosbo

1982

LW	Herman Hoffend
MW	Erwin Note
LHW	Libor Minarik
HW	Berry de Mey

IFBB Mr. International

1974	Lou Ferrigno
1976	Robby Robinson
1977	Mohamed Makkawy
1978	Joe Nazzario
1979	Greg DeFerro
1980	Andreas Cahling
1981	Scott Wilson

IFBB Pro Mr. Universe

1975	Bob Birdsong
1978	Roy Callender
1979	Roy Callender
1980	Jusup Wilcosz
1981	Dennis Tinerino

IFBB Mr. Universe

(With the introduction of bodyweight classes, this contest was then termed "The World Amateur Bodybuilding Championships.")

1959	Eddie Silvestre
1961	Chuck Sipes
1962	George Eiferman
1963	Harold Poole
1964	Larry Scott
1965	Earl Maynard
1966	Dave Draper
1967	Sergio Oliva
1968	Frank Zane
1969	Arnold Schwarzenegger
1970	Arnold Schwarzenegger

World Amateur Bodybuilding Championships (IFBB Mr. Universe)

1971

Short Class
1. Deiana
2. Renato Bertagna
3. Plumans

Medium Class
1. Albert Beckles
2. Ahmet Enunlu
3. Ed Corney

Tall Class
1. Bloemmer
2. Reidmeir
3. Mike Katz

1972

Short Class
1. Suetmisue
2. Pierre Van Den Steen
3. Mohamed Makkawy

Medium Class
1. Ed Corney
2. Rudman
3. Annette

Tall Class
1. Mike Katz
2. Baldo Lois
3. Ali Algayar

1973

Short Class
1. Deiana
2. Plumans
3. Berange

Medium Class
1. Albert Beckles
2. Ahmet Enunlu
3. Annette

Tall Class
1. Lou Ferrigno
2. Ken Waller
3. Mike Katz

1974

Short Class
1. Pierre Van Den Steen
2. Mohamed Makkawy
3. Renato Bertagna

Medium Class
1. Ahmet Enunlu
2. Bob Birdsong
3. Cesarion

Tall Class
1. Lou Ferrigno
2. Ken Waller
3. Bill Grant

Roy Callender and Franco Columbu

Scott Wilson

Bob Birdsong

Dave Johns and Kal Szkalak

Franco Columbu (left)

Greg DeFerro

1975

Short Class
1. Wilf Sylvester
2. Renato Bertagna
3. Kemp

Medium Class
1. Robby Robinson
2. Albert Beckles
3. Gerard Buinoud

Tall Class
1. Ken Waller
2. Roger Walker
3. Bill Grant

1976

Short Class
1. Mohamed Makkawy
2. Danny Padilla
3. Adolph Zeigner

Medium Class
1. Robby Robinson
2. Mike Mentzer
3. Ahmet Enunlu

Tall Class
1. Roger Walker
2. Darcey Beccles
3. Karl Kainrath

1977

Short Class
1. Danny Padilla
2. Mohamed Makkawy
3. Renato Bertagna

Medium Class
1. Roy Callender
2. Darcey Beccles
3. Stach

Tall Class
1. Kal Szkalak
2. Mike Mentzer
3. Bill Grant

1978

Short Class
1. Carlos Rodriguez
2. Renato Bertagna
3. Robert Dantlinger

Medium Class
1. Tom Platz
2. Stach
3. Darcey Beccles

Tall Class
1. Mike Mentzer
2. Jusup Wilcosz
3. Reid Schindle

1979

LW
1. Renato Bertagna
2. Heinz Sallmeyer
3. Teck Hin

MW
1. Roy Duval
2. Anton Baldwin
3. Anton Holic

LHW
1. Samir Bannout
2. Ron Teufel
3. Johnny Fuller

HW
1. Jusup Wilcosz
2. Mike Mentzer
3. Chen Wint

1980

LW
1. Heinz Sallmeyer
2. Ken Passariello
3. Ray Beaulieu

MW
1. Jorma Raty
2. Anton Baldwin
3. Jonker

LHW
1. Johnny Fuller
2. Bronston Austin, Jr.
3. Keijo Reiman

HW
1. Hubert Metz
2. Reid Schindle
3. Christian Janatsch

1981

LW
1. Ken Passariello
2. Jose Rabanal
3. Fikret Hodzic

MW
1. Gerard Buinoud
2. James Youngblood
3. Anton Holic

LHW
1. Jacques Neuville
2. Tim Belknap
3. Keijo Reiman

HW
1. Lance Dreher
2. Gunnar Rosbo
3. Josef Vesely

1982

LW
1. James Gaubert
2. Jean LeBlanc
3. Herman Hoffend

MW
1. Dale Ruplinger
2. Erwin Knoller
3. Erwin Note

LHW
1. Ahmet Enunlu
2. Keijo Reiman
3. Moses Maldonaldo

Harold Poole

Jim Morris

Ed Corney

Ali Malla

Steve Davis, Ken Passariello, and Cliff Koons

Robby Robinson

HW
1. Lee Haney
2. Gunnar Rosbo
3. Alois Pek

1983

BW
1. Herman Hoffend
2. Antonio Sella
3. Alain Leroy

LW
1. Appie Steenbeck
2. Jesse Lujan
3. Mike Piliotis

MW
1. Charles Glass
2. Erwin Note
3. Erwin Knoller

LHW
1. Chuck Williams
2. Keijo Reiman
3. Ian Dowe

HW
1. Bob Paris
2. Berry de Mey
3. Rolf Möller

IFBB World Professional Bodybuilding Championships

1982

1. Albert Beckles
2. Boyer Coe
3. Johnny Fuller

1983

1. Mohamed Makkawy
2. Greg DeFerro
3. Lee Haney

1984

1. Albert Beckles
2. Greg DeFerro
3. Bill Grant

Pro Mr. World

1971	Boyer Coe
1972	Boyer Coe
1973	Boyer Coe
1974	Boyer Coe
1975	Boyer Coe
1976	Tony Emmott
1977	Serge Nubret
1978	Anibal Lopez
1979	Tony Pearson
1980	Anibal Lopez

AAU Mr. America

1938	Bert Goodrich
1939	Roland Essmaker and Bert Goodrich
1940	John Grimek
1941	John Grimek
1942	Frank Leight
1943	Jules Bacon
1944	Steve Stanko
1945	Clarence Ross
1946	Alan Stephen
1947	Steve Reeves
1948	George Eiferman
1949	Jack Delinger
1950	John Farbotnik
1951	Roy Hilligen
1952	Jim Park
1953	Bill Pearl
1954	Dick Dubois
1955	Steve Klisanin
1956	Ray Schaeffer
1957	Ron Lacy
1958	Tom Sansone
1959	Harry Johnson
1960	Lloyd Lerille
1961	Ray Routledge
1962	Joe Abbenda
1963	Vern Weaver
1964	Val Vasilief
1965	Jerry Daniels
1966	Bob Gajda
1967	Dennis Tinerino
1968	Jim Haislop
1969	Boyer Coe
1970	Chris Dickerson
1971	Casey Viator
1972	Steve Michalik
1973	Jim Morris
1974	Ron Thompson
1975	Dale Adrian
1976	Kalman Szkalak
1977	Dave Johns
1978	Tony Pearson
1979	Ray Mentzer
1980	Gary Leonard
1981	Tim Belknap
1982	Rufus Howard
1983	Jeff King

AAU Junior Mr. America

1944	Steve Stanko
1945	Joseph Lauriano
1946	Everett Sinderoff
1947	Edward J. Simons
1948	Harry Smith
1949	Val Pasqua
1950	John Farbotnik
1951	George Paine
1952	Malcolm Brenner
1953	Steve Klisanin
1954	Gene Bohaty and Harry Johnson
1955	Vic Seipke
1956	Ray Schaeffer
1957	Jim Dugger
1958	Tom Sansone (East)
	Ray Routledge (West)

Dale Adrian

Bob Paris

1959	Elmo Santiago
1960	Joe Lazzaro (East)
	Frank A. Quinn (South)
	Gail Crick (Southwest)
	Hugo Labra (West)
1961	Joe Simon (East)
	Ronnie Russell (Southeast)
	John Gourgott (South)
	Lou Wolter (Midwest)
	Harold Poole (Central)
	Franklin Jones (West)
1962	Joseph Abbenda (East)
	Billy Lemacks (South)
	Tuny Monday (Midwest)
1963	Randy Watson
1964	John Decola
1965	Jerry Daniels
1966	Sergio Oliva
1967	Dennis Tinerino
1968	Jim Haislop
1969	Boyer Coe
1970	Chris Dickerson
1971	Casey Viator
1972	Pete Grymkowski
1973	Paul Hill
1974	Ron Thompson
1975	Willie Johnson
1976	Dave Johns
1977	Mario Nieves
1978	Tony Pearson
1979	Robert Jodkiewicz
1980	Ernie Santiago
1981	Marty Vranicar
1982	Michael Antonio

AAU Teenage Mr. America

1958	John Gourgott
1959	Joe Abbenda
1960	Jerry Doetrell (East)
	Gil Dimeglio (Central)
	John Corvello (West)
1961	Steve Boyer (East)
	John Piscareta (Midwest)
1962	Michael Liscio (East)
	Mickey Majors (Midwest)
1963	Jerry Daniels
1964	Bud Schosek
1965	Dennis Tinerino
1966	Boyer Coe
1967	Mike Dayton
1968	Ken Covington
1969	Bob Gallucci
1970	Casey Viator
1971	Scott Pace
1972	Sammie Willis
1973	Joe Ugolik
1974	Dan Tobol
1975	Ron Teufel
1976	Mike Torchia
1977	Jim Yasenchock
1978	Rudy Hermosillo
1979	Lee Haney
1980	Danny Berumen
1981	Michael Quinn

Bert Goodrich

Clancy Ross

John Grimek

Les Spendlove

John Terilli

AAU Over-40 Mr. America

1976 Vic Seiple
1977 Kent Kuehn
1978 Earl Maynard
1979 Phil Outlaw
1980 Paul Love
1981 O. J. Smith

AAU Mr. USA

1964 Mike Ferraro
1965 Bob Gajda
1966 Dennis Tinerino
1967 Jim Haislop
1968 Chris Dickerson
1969 Ken Waller
1970 Casey Viator
1971 Steve Michalik
1972 Jim Morris
1973 Paul Hill
1974 Pat Neve
1975 Clinton Beyerle
1976 Manuel Perry
1977 Rod Koontz
1978 Ron Teufel
1979 Robert Reis
1980 Dave Rogers
1981 Jesse Gautreaux

AAU Junior Mr. USA

1965 Dennis Tinerino
1966 Chris Dickerson
1967 James Morris
1968 Boyer Coe
1969 Ken Waller
1970 Carl Smith
1971 Pete Grymkowski
1972 Ron Thompson
1973 Paul Hill
1974 Dave Johns
1975 Floyd Odom
1976 Joe Means
1977 Dave Rogers
1978 Tony Pearson
1979 Jim Seitzer
1980 Ernie Santiago
1981 Robert Coburn

AAU Teenage Mr. USA

1975 Steve Shields
1976 Steve Borodinsky
1977 Rudy Hermosillo
1978 Casey Kucharyk
1979 Joe Fulco
1980 John Taylor
1981 Konstantine Spanoudis

AAU Over-40 Mr. USA

1979 Paul Yazolino
1980 Don Len
1981 Art Peacock

AAU Mr. World

1970 Ken Waller (amateur)
     Arnold Schwarzenegger
     (pro)
1971 Albert Beckles
1972 Paul Grant
1973 Ron Thompson
1974 Roy Duval
1975 Ian Lawrence
1976 Bertil Fox

NBBA Natural Mr. America

1978 Tyronne Youngs
     (amateur)
     Dennis Tinerino (pro)
1979 Ron Magnum (amateur)
     Tyronne Youngs (pro)
     Doug Brignole
     (teenage)
     Jerry Englebert
     (over-40)
1980 Chuck Buser (amateur)
     Rod Koontz (pro)
1981 Eddie Love

NABBA Mr. Britain

1930 W. T. Coggins
1931 C. Coster
1932 W. T. Coggins
1933 S. Ingleson
1934 W. Bower
1935 W. Purchon
1936 W. Archer
1937 O. Heidenstam
1938 T. Moreland
1939 H. Loveday
1940 G. Allan
1941 K. Paton
1942 no contest
1943 Don Dorans
1944 Gordon MacKay
1945 Bill Beaumont
1946 Charles Curzon
1947 Jim Elliot
1948 Charles Jarrett
1949 Reg Park
1950 Hubert Thomas
1951 Dennis Stallard
1952 Mervynne Cotter
1953 John Lees
1954 Wally Wright
1955 Bill Parkinson
1956 Henry Downs
1957 Len Sell
1958 John Hewlett
1959 Tony Rothwell
1960 Adrian Heryet
1961 Dave Stroud
1962 Ted Guttridge
1963 Paul Nash
1964 Terry Parkinson
1965 John Citrone
1966 John Citrone
1967 Wilf Sylvester

Roy Callender

Ivan Pjirlic

Brian de Mey

Bill Trotter

Tony Emmott

1968   Brian Eastman
1969   Frank Richard
1970   Albert Beckles
1971   Albert Beckles
1972   Paul Grant
1973   Roy Duval
1974   Eddie McDonough
1975   Ian Lawrence
1976   Bertil Fox
1977   Eddie McDonough
1978   Bill Richardson
1979   Terry Phillips
1980   Graham Brogden
1981   Eddie Millar
1982   Ian Dowe
1983   Jeff King

The Ironman

1953   Bert Elliot
1954   Tommy Kono
1955   Vic Nicoletti
1956   Doyle Brewer
1957   *no records available*
1958   Bill Stathes
1959   *no records available*
1960   Al Souza
1961   *no records available*
1962   Ralph McCoy
1963   Harold Love
1964   Leon Burks
1965   Gene Dickerson
1966   Joe Townsell
1967   Bob Kemper
1968   Mike Dayton
1969   Ed Corney
1970   Dave Ferradino
1971   Dominic Dibetta
1972   Charles Francillette
1973   Dennis Holmes
1975   Charles Glass
1976   Rod Koontz
1977   John Sandoval
1978   Glenn Maur
1979   John Lloyd
1980   Dolph Pierce
1981   George Bass
1982   Gerald Riley

NABBA Mr. Universe

1948   John Grimek
1950   Steve Reeves
1951   Reg Park

Amateur

1952   Mohammed Nasr
1953   Bill Pearl
1954   Enrico Thomas
1955   Mickey Hargitay
1956   Ray Schaeffer
1957   John Lees
1958   Earl Clark
1959   Len Sell
1960   Henry Downs
1961   Ray Routledge
1962   Joe Abbenda

Ernie Santiago

Paul Wynter

Jeff King

Dave Johns, Kal Szkalak, Sergio Oliva

1963	Tom Sansone
1964	John Hewlett
1965	Elmo Santiago
1966	Chester Yorton
1967	Arnold Schwarzenegger
1968	Dennis Tinerino
1969	Boyer Coe
1970	Frank Zane
1971	Ken Waller
1972	Elias Petsas
1973	Chris Dickerson
1974	Roy Duval
1975	Ian Lawrence
1976	Shigeru Sugita
1977	Bertil Fox
1978	Dave Johns
1979	Ahmet Enunlu
1980	Bill Richardson
1981	John Brown
1982	John Brown
1983	Jeff King

Professional

1952	Juan Ferrero
1953	Arnold Tyson
1954	Jim Park
1955	Léo Robert
1956	Jack Delinger
1957	Arthur Robin
1958	Reg Park
1959	Bruce Randall
1960	Paul Wynter
1961	Bill Pearl
1962	Len Sell
1963	Joe Abbenda
1964	Earl Maynard
1965	Reg Park
1966	Paul Wynter
1967	Bill Pearl
1968	Arnold Schwarzenegger
1969	Arnold Schwarzenegger
1970	Arnold Schwarzenegger
1971	Bill Pearl
1972	Frank Zane
1973	Boyer Coe
1974	Chris Dickerson
1975	Boyer Coe
1976	Serge Nubret
1977	Tony Emmott
1978	Bertil Fox
1979	Bertil Fox
1980	Tony Pearson
1981	Robby Robinson
1982	Eduardo Kuwak
1983	Eduardo Kuwak

WBBG Pro Mr. America

1967	Harold Poole
1968	Harold Poole
1969	Johnny Maldonado
1970	Rick Wayne
1971	Peter Caputo
1972	Bill Grant
1973	Chris Dickerson
1974	Warren Frederick
1975	Ralph Kroger
1976	Scott Wilson
1977	Don Ross

1978	Anibal Lopez
1979	Tommy Aybar
1980	Anibal Lopez

WABBA Mr. World

1977	Ahmet Enunlu (amateur)
	Sergio Oliva (pro)
1978	Ahmet Enunlu
1979	Tony Pearson
1980	Eduardo Kuwak (amateur)
	Sergio Oliva (pro)
1982	Eduardo Kuwak

WBBG Mr. World

1971	Boyer Coe
1972	Boyer Coe
1973	Boyer Coe
1974	Boyer Coe
1975	Boyer Coe
1976	Tony Emmott
1977	Serge Nubret
1978	Anibal Lopez
1979	Tony Pearson

Mr. California

1946	Steve Reeves
1951	Roy Hilligen
1953	Bill Pearl

1955	Jerry Ross
1960	Larry Scott
1961	Hugo Labra
1963	Don Howorth
1964	Joe Nista
1965	John Corvello
1966	Ralph Kroger
1969	Paul Love
1970	Chris Dickerson
1972	Ed Corney
1973	Mike Besikoff
1974	Scott Wilson
1975	Dale Adrian
1976	Kalman Szkalak
1977	Dave Johns
1978	Ron Teufel
1979	Larry Jackson
1980	Rory Leidelmeyer
1981	Ed Zajac
1982	Doug Brignole
1983	Mike Christian

Night of the Champions

1978	Robby Robinson
1979	Robby Robinson
1982	Albert Beckles
1983	Lee Haney

1980 Mr. Olympia

1. Arnold Schwarzenegger
2. Chris Dickerson
3. Frank Zane

1980 Canada Cup

1. Chris Dickerson
2. Boyer Coe
3. Dennis Tinerino

1980 Pennsylvania Grand Prix

1. Casey Viator
2. Chris Dickerson
3. Roy Callender

1980 Professional Grand Prix

Florida: Chris Dickerson
Louisiana: Casey Viator
California: Chris Dickerson
Pittsburgh: Casey Viator
New York: Chris Dickerson
Overall: Chris Dickerson

1980 Mr. California

Men

Short Class
1. Bronston Austin, Jr.
2. Mike Libby

Tall Class
1. Rory Leidelmeyer†
2. John Brown
3. Gary Leonard

Johnny Fuller, Lee Haney, Albert Beckles

Teenage

Short Class
1. Danny Berumen†
2. Richard Hills
3. Lorenzo Belzer

Tall Class
1. Robert Marsh
2. Michael McClellan
3. Tony DePina

1981 Mr. Olympia

1. Franco Columbu
2. Chris Dickerson
3. Tom Platz

1981 European Grand Prix

1. Boyer Coe
2. Albert Beckles
3. Jusup Wilcosz

1981 Professional Grand Prix

California: Chris Dickerson
Louisiana: Chris Dickerson
Washington, DC: Chris
 Dickerson
New England: Albert Beckles
New York: Chris Dickerson
Overall: Chris Dickerson

1981 Louisiana Grand Prix

1. Chris Dickerson
2. Albert Beckles
3. Roy Callender

1981 New York Grand Prix

1. Chris Dickerson
2. Albert Beckles
3. Boyer Coe

1981 Washington, DC Grand Prix

1. Chris Dickerson
2. Roy Callender
3. Boyer Coe

1981 New England Grand Prix

1. Albert Beckles
2. Chris Dickerson
3. Boyer Coe

1981 California Grand Prix

1. Chris Dickerson
2. Roy Callender
3. Boyer Coe

1981 Montreal Grand Prix

1. Boyer Coe
2. Albert Beckles
3. Johnny Fuller

1981 World Cup

1. Boyer Coe
2. Chris Dickerson
3. Bronston Austin, Jr.

1981 World Games I

LW
1. Renato Bertagna
2. Esmat Sadek
3. Joe Distinti

MW
1. James Youngblood
2. Billy Knight
3. Erwin Note

LHW
1. Jacques Neuville
2. Keijo Reiman
3. Ulf Bengtsson

HW
1. John Kemper
2. Wayne Robbins
3. Ahmed Ibrahim

1981 Mr. International

LW
1. Ralph Piers
2. Ray Beaulieu
3. Philip Dlamini

MW
1. Shigeru Sugita
2. Laurens Brazil
3. Henry Caulker

LHW
1. Ali Malla
2. Les Galvin
3. Bill Arlen

HW
1. Scott Wilson†
2. Larry Jackson
3. Rod Koontz

Ian Dowe

Chris Dickerson

Dale Ruplinger

1982 Mr. Olympia

1. Chris Dickerson
2. Frank Zane
3. Casey Viator

1982 Swedish Grand Prix

1. Mohamed Makkawy
2. Samir Bannout
3. Casey Viator

1982 Belgian Grand Prix

1. Mohamed Makkawy
2. Albert Beckles
3. Jusup Wilcosz

1982 NPC American Bodybuilding Championships

LW
1. James Gaubert
2. Dean Tornbene
3. Joseph Disinti

MW
1. Dale Ruplinger
2. Pat Neve
3. Bill Register

LHW
1. Moses Maldonado
2. Chuck Williams
3. Charles Glass

HW
1. Lee Haney†
2. Matt Mendenhall
3. Tim Belknap

1982 NPC USA Bodybuilding Championships

LW
1. Scott Livingstone
2. Terry Schiebel
3. Philip Lima

MW
1. Dale Ruplinger†
2. Steven Reiter
3. Sam Capelouto

LHW
1. Donald Gay
2. Richard Roy
3. Glenn Knerr

HW
1. Jon Jordon
2. Neal Spruce
3. Bob Paris

1983 Mr. Olympia

1. Samir Bannout
2. Mohamed Makkawy
3. Lee Haney

1983 Swedish Grand Prix

1. Mohamed Makkawy
2. Lee Haney
3. Jusup Wilcosz

1983 Swiss Grand Prix

1. Mohamed Makkawy
2. Bertil Fox
3. Lee Haney

1983 Colorado Grand Prix

1. Tony Pearson
2. Bob Birdsong
3. Ali Malla

1983 Portland Grand Prix

1. Scott Wilson
2. Tony Pearson
3. Johnny Fuller

1983 World Grand Prix

1. Mohamed Makkawy
2. Lee Haney
3. Jusup Wilcosz

1983 NPC USA Bodybuilding Championships

Men

LW
1. Billy Sanchez
2. Jose Guzman

MW
1. Ernie Santiago†
2. Michael Huber
3. Anthony Little

LHW
1. Benny Podda
2. Richard Roy
3. Steven Reiter

HW
1. Ron Clark
2. Lawrence Story
3. Robert Jordan

Teenage

LW Frank Santoriello
MW Victor Tierra†
LHW James DeMelo
HW Vinny Conzo

1983 NPC Junior National Championships

LW
1. Jose Guzman
2. Steve Romanelli
3. Tony Murphy

MW
1. Ralph Coccio
2. Amos McCoy
3. Ed Nieves

LHW
1. Dave Hawk
2. Rick Porcelli
3. Nick Lavitola

HW
1. Richard Gaspari†
2. Steve Adell
3. Dave Berman

1983 NPC Junior USA Championships

Men

LW
1. James Bass

MW
1. Paul Jean Guillaume
2. Alan Graham
3. Jose Guzman

LHW
1. Tim Underwood
2. Mike Hay
3. Terrell Roberson

HW
1. John Kemper†
2. Don Stenger
3. Troy Beck

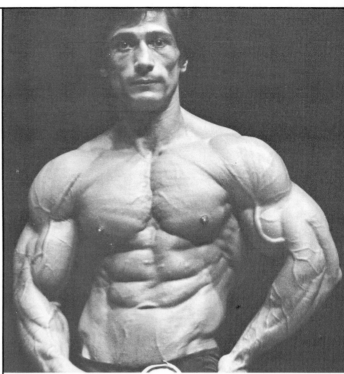

Danny Padilla

Bertil Fox, Tony Pearson, Mohamed Makkawy, Jusup Wilcosz

Bertil Fox

Men Over-40

LW
1. Eddy Ruiz
2. Tom Connor
3. Harold Collins

MW
1. Walt Tyndall
2. Ron Grosso
3. Mike Graham

LHW
1. Billy Joe Barrett
2. Chuck Siska
3. Rich Yarbro

HW
1. Ken Hamel
2. Paul Pigue, Jr.

1983 Amateur Mr. Universe

Short

1. Terry Phillips
2. Mike Sable
3. Larry Bernstein

Medium

1. Vince Brown
2. Eugene Laviscount
3. Robert Reis

Tall

1. Jeff King†
2. John Brown
3. Marty Vranicar

1983 Pro Mr. Universe

1. Eduardo Kuwak
2. Ian Lawrence
3. Rufus Howard

1983 NPC California State Championships

LW
1. Robert Iadevaia
2. Richard Scimeca
3. Grant Ledbetter

MW
1. Jon Aranita
2. Michael Grieco
3. Joe Fustor

LHW
1. Ray Boone
2. Dave Stevens
3. Rick Cox

HW
1. Mike Christian†
2. Jeff Smullen
3. John Abl

1983 NPC Teenage USA

LW
1. Frank Santoriello
2. Ulrick Bien Aime
3. Wayne Hugar

MW
1. Victor Terra†
2. Anthony Civiletti
3. Gerald Atkins

LHW
1. James DeMelo
2. Jerry West
3. Joby Saad

HW
1. Vinny Conzo
2. Dave Pebbles

1983 NPC National Championships

LW
1. Jesse Lujan
2. Dean Tornabene
3. Scott Livingstone

MW
1. Charles Glass
2. Linzie McKinney
3. Jon Aranita

LHW
1. Chuck Williams
2. Moses Maldonado
3. Benny Podda

HW
1. Bob Paris†
2. Rory Leidelmeyer
3. Mike Christian

1983 World Junior Men's Bodybuilding Championships

LW
1. Mohammed Faskham
2. Michael Innis
3. Rudiser Schmitz

MW
1. Giovanni Benyaniws
2. Greg Berbenuik
3. Paul Caldicott

HW
1. Arnold Buurman
2. John Fisher
3. Lennart Wilhelmsson

Arnold Schwarzenegger

Pillow

Women's Competitions

Miss Olympia

1980

1. Rachel McLish
2. Auby Paulick
3. Lynn Conkwright

1981

1. Kike Elomaa
2. Rachel McLish
3. Lynn Conkwright

1982

1. Rachel McLish
2. Carla Dunlap
3. Kike Elomaa

1983

1. Carla Dunlap
2. Candy Csencsits
3. Inger Zetterqvist

American Women's Bodybuilding Championships

1980

1. Laura Combes
2. Claudia Wilbourn
3. Carla Dunlap

1981

LW
1. Mary Roberts
2. Bobbie Brice
3. Kathy Cosentino

HW
1. Carla Dunlap†
2. Shelley Gruwell
3. Deborah Diana

Inger Zetterqvist

1982

LW
1. Debbie Basile
2. Dinah Anderson
3. Mae Sabbagh

MW
1. Leslie Barber
2. Maria Gonzales
3. Agi Balogh

HW
1. Carla Dunlap†
2. Deborah Diana
3. Lori Bowen

1983

LW
1. Susan Roberts
2. Stella Martinez
3. Mae Mollica

MW
1. Dinah Anderson
2. Dawn Gnaegi
3. Candis Caldwell

HW
1. Lori Bowen†
2. Lesley Kozlow
3. Sue Ann McKean

World Professional Women's Bodybuilding Championships

1982

1. Rachel McLish
2. Candy Csencsits
3. Sherry Atton

1983

1. Carla Dunlap
2. Kike Elomaa
3. Sherry Atton

USA Women's Bodybuilding Championships

1981

Deborah Diana

1982

LW
1. Stella Martinez†
2. Terri Miladinovich
3. Kathleen Mischler

MW
1. Annette Brandt
2. Leslie Barber
3. Valerie Mayers

Kay Baxter

HW
1. Lynn Pirie
2. Carla Dunlap
3. Julie McNew

1983

LW
1. Susan Roberts
2. Charlotte Yarbrough
3. Theresa Hensley

MW
1. Dinah Anderson
2. Lindy Champion
3. Mary Ellen Jerumbo

HW
1. Lori Bowen†
2. Velma Buckles
3. Lynn Pirie

World Women's Bodybuilding Championships

1979

1. Lisa Lyon
2. Claudia Wilbourn

1981

1. Lynn Conkwright
2. Kay Baxter
3. Corinne Machado-Ching

1982

1. Rachel McLish
2. Candy Csencsits
3. Lynn Pirie

1983

1. Carla Dunlap
2. Kike Elomaa
3. Sherry Atton

1984

1. Lori Bowen
2. Carla Dunlap
3. Mary Roberts

Ms. California

1980

1. Claudia Wilbourn
2. Shelley Gruwell
3. Jan Bowden

1982

LW
1. Stella Martinez†
2. Agi Balogh
3. Debbie Basile

Gladys Portugues

Inger Zetterqvist

Bev Francis and Carla Dunlap

Lori Bowen

Lucy Ming Kee

Caroline Cheshire

MW
1. Maria Gonzales
2. Jackie Shephard
3. Kristina May

The Ironwoman

1980   Stella Martinez
1981   Kathy Tuite
1982   Gayle Hall
1983   Agi Balogh

1980 Women's Nationals

1. Rachel McLish
2. Georgia Miller-Fudge
3. Claudia Wilbourn

1980 US Women's Bodybuilding Championships

1. Rachel McLish
2. Georgia Miller-Fudge
3. Kay Baxter

1981 World Games I

LW
1. Pam Brooks
2. Josee Baumgartner
3. Chris Reed

MW
1. Kike Elomaa
2. Gail Schroeder
3. Deborah Diana

1981 Montreal Grand Prix

1. Shelley Gruwell
2. Sherry Atton
3. Kay Baxter

1981 Night of the Champions

1. Carla Dunlap
2. Cindy Williams
3. Maro Bchakjian

1982 Ms. East Coast

LW
1. Gema Wheeler
2. Diane Maddalo
3. Maureen Casper

HW
1. Cory Kneuer
2. Maro Bchakjian
3T. Julie McNew
3T. Renee Rossier

1982 2nd California Gold Cup

1. Lynn Pirie
2. Kathleen Mischler
3. Charlotte Yarbrough

1982 1st Russ Warner Classic

LW
1. Terry Miladinovich
2. Charlotte Yarbrough
3. Sandi Sigona

Gladys Portugues

Rachel McLish

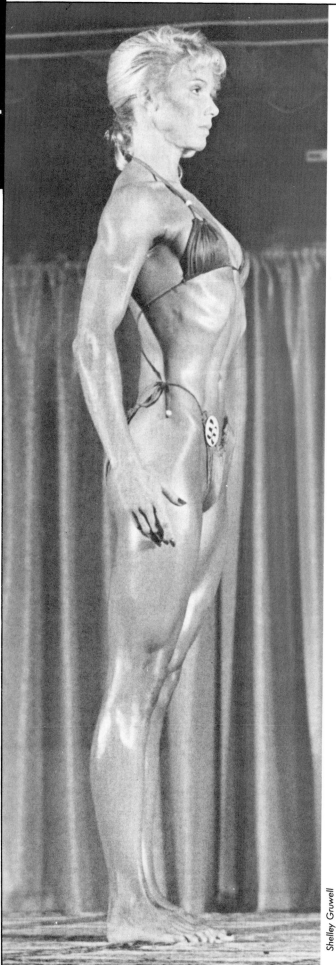

Shelley Gruwell

HW
1. Sandi Satre
2. Myrna Loy Williams
3. Reggie Bennett

1982 North American Women's Championships

LW
1. Shirley Kemper
2. Agi Balogh
3. Pam Brooks

MW
1. Cory.Everson
2. Maro Bchakjian
3. Jeanne Splittgerber

1982 Ms. Natural Western America

Short Class
1. Agi Balogh
2. Rita Anderson
3. Nancy Celestina

Tall Class
1. Myrna Loy Williams†
2. Nancy Dixon
3. Enid Fox

1982 AAU Ms. America

LW
1. Gloria Romo
2. Kathy Clarke

MW
1. Tina Plakinger†
2. Denise Martin
3. Gale Greenhouse

HW
1. Rebecca Thomas
2. Debbie DeWitt
3. Amy Goldwater

1982 2nd European Championships

LW
1. Jackie Roos
2. Lisser Frost-Larsen
3. Josee Baumgartner

HW
1. Marjo Selin
2. Angela Graham
3. Asa Gillberg

1982 Scandinavia vs. USA Women

1. Carla Dunlap
2. Kike Elomaa
3. Deborah Diana

1983 Women's California Bodybuilding Championships

LW
1. Susan Roberts†
2. Ellen Morrow
3. Cindy Kay Peterson

MW
1. Kim Fonza
2. Judy Grayson
3. Agi Balogh

HW
1. Sue Ann McKean
2. Sandi Satre
3. Cheryl Harriss

1983 World Women's Amateur Championships

LW
1. Erika Mes
2. Astrid Aschwander
3. Christine Laurant

MW
1. Inger Zetterqvist
2. Pirjo Haapalo
3. Lori Bowen

1983 WABBA World Championships

1. Gabriele Sievers
2. Jocelyne Pigeonneau
3. Hermine Klinger

1983 Texas Cup

LW
1. Betty Torrance
2. Autumn Spencer
3. Celeste Brecht

HW
1. Mary Alice Horne†
2. Lindy Champion
3. Lynda Wolf

1983 Eastern America

LW
1. Nina Schoenbaum†
2. Helen Pollak
3. Penelope Bassett

MW
1. Janet Zagaro
2. Aida Perez
3. Caroline Rosemoff

Couples' Competitions

American Mixed Pairs Bodybuilding Championships

1980
1. John Brown and Shelley Gruwell
2. John Kemper and Carla Dunlap

1981
1. Jeff Everson and Cory Kneuer
2. Rick and Cathy Basacker
3. Paul Daniels and Gail Schroeder

1982
1. Rick and Cathy Basacker
2. Randy Souza and Agi Balogh
3. Gerry and Susan Roberts

1983
1. Kevin Lawrence and Diana Dennis
2. Ray Boone and Ellen Morrow
3. Doug and Jeanne Splittgerber

Pro-Am World Mixed Pairs Championships

1982
Tony Pearson and Shelley Gruwell

1983
1. Tony Pearson and Shelley Gruwell
2. Bob Birdsong and Carla Dunlap
3. Scott Wilson and Corinne Machado-Ching

USA Mixed Pairs Bodybuilding Championships

1982
1. Troy Beck and Julie McNew
2. Sam Capelouto and Linda Meckles
3. Steve Broughton and Andrena Hawkins

1983
1. Jeff and Cory Everson
2. Gerry and Susan Roberts
3. Mike Sable and Charlotte Yarbrough

1981 World Couples Bodybuilding Championships

1. Chris Dickerson and Lynn Conkwright
2. Carlos Rodriguez and Melinda Perper
3. Boyer and Valerie Coe

1982 AAU American Mixed Pairs Championships

1. Phil Dempsey and Tina Plakinger
2. Sam Capelouto and Linda Meckles
3. Jim Dziak and Denise Martin

1982 North American Mixed Pairs Championships

1. Jeff and Cory Everson
2. Randy Souza and Agi Balogh
3. Terry and Pam Brooks

1982 European Couples Bodybuilding Championships

1. Berry de Mey and Erika Mes
2. Keijo Reiman and Marjo Selin
3. Gabriel Wild and Hildegard Schafer

Anibal Lopez and Doris Barrilleaux

Rufus Howard and Ian Lawrence

Combination Competitions

1981 American Natural Bodybuilding Championships

Men

Short Class
1. Dennis Wood
2. Dennis Beyer
3. Phil Pasquale

Medium Class
1. Bob Gallucci †
2. Eddie Love
3. Don Townes

Tall Class
1. Greg Tefft
2. Jack Farnetti
3. William Burge

Teenage

Short Class
1. Bohdan Narolsky †
2. Bob Gomez
3. Mike Ryan

Medium Class
1. Matt DeCaprio
2. Joe Romano
3. Steve Stanissich

Women

1. Darci D'mitrenko
2. Sissy Ceravolo
3. Shari Decker

Masters

Short Class
1. Phil Pasquale
2. Elliot Gilchrist
3. Jack King

Medium Class
1. Jim Karas †
2. Don Len
3. Art Peacock

Tall Class
1. Ormsby Marcelle
2. Kenny Hall
3. Dan Iacovone

1981 European Championships

Men

LW
1. Jose Rabanal
2. E. Hodzic
3. Reijo Kivioja

MW
1. Anton Holic
2. Erwin Knoller
3. Ereyetis Kurtural

LHW
1. Libor Minarik
2. Keijo Reiman
3. Angelito Lesta

HW
1. Gunnar Rosbo
2. Josef Vesely
3. Christian Janatsch

Women

LW
1. Astrid Aschwander
2. Sue Tonks
3. Jackie Roos

MW
1. Kike Elomaa
2. Lena Trulsson
3. Vera Bendel

1982 Superbowl of Bodybuilding II

Men

1. Greg Comeaux
2. Rick Cox
3. Apache

Women

LW
1. Leslie Barber
2. Annie Hess
3. Charlotte Yarbrough

MW
1. Lesley Kozlow
2. Diana Dennis
3. Missy Sandeman

Couples

1. Mike Sable and Charlotte Yarbrough
2. Kevin Lawrence and Diana Dennis
3. Monroe Huel and Ann Williams

1982 Bodybuilding Expo III

Women

LW
1. Charlotte Yarbrough
2. Chris Reed
3. Teri Clavell

MW
1. Lynn Pirie
2. Cory Everson
3. Joanne Cameron

Couples

1. Mike Sable and Charlotte Yarbrough
2. Jeff and Cory Everson
3. E. Holmes and Esi Rainwater

1982 WABBA World Championships

Men

Amateur Class 1
1. John Brown
2. Rufus Howard
3. Bob Esprit

Amateur Class 2
1. John Terilli
2. Ian Dowe
3. Vince Brown

Amateur Class 3
1. Terry Phillips
2. Francois Chung
3. Eric Pieters

Miss Bikini
1. Jocelyn Pigeonneau
2. Mary Scott
3. Lucy Ming Kee

1982 American Natural Bodybuilding Classic

Men

Short Class
1. Don Townes
2. Don King
3. Kim Lovett

Medium Class
1. Tony Cusack
2. Dave Jones
3. Ron Jumper

Tall Class
1. Greg Tefft †
2. John Ayers
3. Scott Baker

Women

1. Terri Rouviere
2. Janice Graser
3. Louise Johnson

Couples

1. Steve Hull and Louise Johnson
2. Bob Stanley and Connie Rouse
3. George Hrehocik and Amy Johnston

1982 Canadian Bodybuilding Championships

Men

LW
1. Jean LeBlanc
2. Ray Beaulieu
3. Giles Lepage

MW
1. Serge Moreau
2. Dan Kennedy
3. Winston Green

LHW
1. Les Berthelette
2. Winston Brown
3. Mark Morin

HW
1. Andre Maille
2. Wayne Robbins
3. Mark Hintz

Women

LW
1. Michelle Trennier
2. Carolyn Carpenter
3. Holly Buss

MW
1. Paula Dosne
2. Louise Wood
3. Lori Davis

1983 Canadian Bodybuilding Championships

Men

LW
1. Calvin Nyuli
2. Ray Beaulieu
3. Gilles Pommerlleau

MW
1. Mark Boulduc
2. Mike Watson
3. Winston Green

LHW
1. Les Berthelette
2. Mark Marshall
3. Bob Taylor

HW
1. Steve Keesa
2. Andre Maille
3. Louis Dickerson

Masters

LW
1. Norm Wickens
2. Henry Chang
3. Woody McCollough

HW
1. Clem McLaughlin
2. Morris Berthelette

Women

LW
1. Holly Buss
2. Dawn Isely
3. Donna Lea

HW
1. Carla Temple
2. Shelly Huber
3. Paula Dosne

1982 Natural Mr. and Ms. Universe

Men

Short Class
1. Howard Madison
2. Don Townes
3. Steve Reed

Medium Class
1. Chuck Buser†
2. Tony Cusack
3. Mike McCloud

Tall Class
1. Cecil Squires
2. Louis Pierrilo
3. Lou Perrotta

Teenage

1. Bob McKitrick
2. Bob Anderson
3. Matt Mannino

Masters

1. Don Len
2. Arthur Peacock
3. Ron Cuspard

Women

1. Renee Rossier
2. Heidi Miller
3. Sheritha McKenzie

1982 Night of the Champions

Men

1. Albert Beckles
2. Bertil Fox
3. Johnny Fuller

Women

1. Carla Dunlap
2. Cindy Williams
3. Maro Bchakjian

Johnny Fuller and Casey Viator

Johnny Fuller

Bob Paris

Charles Glass

Chuck Williams

Dave Johns

1983 Night of the Champions

Men

1. Lee Haney
2. Greg DeFerro
3. Johnny Fuller

Women

1. Gladys Portugues
2. Liv Sundby
3. Diane Maddalo

1983 Mr. and Ms. America

Men

Short Class
1. Larry Bernstein
2. William Hatcher
3. Alan Kirsch

Medium Class
1. Jesse Gautreaux
2. Bob Reis
3. J. J. Marsh

Medium-Tall Class
1. Jeff King †
2. Phil Rhode
3. Rick Poston

Tall Class
1. Marty Vranicar
2. Steve Cavanaugh
3. Jeff Monson

Women

Short Class
1. Diane Langone
2. Bessie Frank
3. Pam Shotzberger

Medium Class
1. Kerrie Keenan †
2. Julie Stangl
3. Ronda Williams

Medium-Tall Class
1. Rebecca Thomas
2. Judi Benz
3. Barbara Devio

Tall Class
1. Cheryl Harriss
2. Anne Hope
3. Cheryl Prizio

1983 Expo IV

Men

Short Class
1. Donny Wiggins
2. Bob Shry
3. Max Cordoba

Tall Class
1. Ron Thrash
2. Steve Bohnstedt
3. Isaac Curtis

Women

LW
1. Candis Caldwell
2. Annie Hess
3. Thea Fox

MW
1. Cory Everson
2. Elaine Craig
3. Mona Krause

Couples

1. Jeff and Cory Everson
2. John Zenda and Thea Fox

1983 East Coast Physique Championships

Men

LW
1. Juan Ojeda
2. David Wilson
3. Steve Burns

MW
1. John Hnatyschak †
2. Jose Guzman
3. Dan Samuda

LHW
1. Nick Lavitola
2. Claude Mancuso
3. Pierre Asselin

HW
1. Rick Widner
2. Mike Long
3. Mark Green

Women

LW
1. Barbara Vega
2. Mary Jane Vinch
3. Georgia Keller

HW
1. Maro Bchakjian †
2. Lydia Cheng
3. Terry LoCicero

Couples

1. Pierre Asselin and Lydia Cheng
2. Ben Rodriguez and Gladys Portugues
3. Ronnie Ayres and Lisa Alvanos

Bob Birdsong

Mohamed Makkawy, Lee Haney, and Samir Bannout

1983 California Muscle Classic

Men

LW
1. Melvin Staples
2. Joey Gomez
3. Elmer Streater

MW
1. Lance Zavela
2. Monroe Huel
3. John Poquignot

LHW
1. Earl Watts†
2. Max Cordoba
3. Dave Owens

HW
1. Mike Christian
2. Sulby Price
3. Floyd Scanlon

Seniors

1. Monroe Huel
2. Don Peters
3. David Owens

Women

LW
1. Jill Ingels
2. Charlotte Yarbrough
3. Donna Zaitz

MW
1. Diana Dennis†
2. Laurin DeStefano
3. Joanne Cameron

Couples

1. Jonathan and Charlotte Yarbrough
2. Lance Zavela and Tammy Oliver
3. Elmer Streater and Tina LaBlanc

1983 Gold's Bodybuilding Classic

Men

LW
1. Joseph Dawson
2. Russell Kight
3. John Ramirez

MW
1. Ernie Santiago†
2. Steve Davis
3. Geof Ross

LHW
1. Dan Dal Colletto
2. Brian Homka
3. David Campbell

Jacqueline and Serge Nubret

HW
1. Larry Ferris
2. Chris Greenleaf
3. Greg Schwarz

Women

LW
1. Lori Okami
2. Sally Allemang
3. Gayle Hall

MW
1. Alison Brundage
2. Audrey Perryman
3. Jill Ingels

HW
1. Pillow†
2. Sue Ann McKean
3. Dawn Gnaegi

1983 AAU Eastern US Bodybuilding Championships

Mr. Eastern US   Joe Meeko
Novice Mr. Eastern US   Walter
  Harner
Teenage Eastern US   Tom
  Silso
Jr. Teen Eastern US   Derrick
  Whitseth
Masters Eastern US   Bob
  Barraclough
Ms Eastern US   Nancy
  Maychuk
Couples   Tony Saceridote and
  Linda Larynkiewcz

1983 European Championships

Men

LW
1. Appie Steenbeck
2. Reijo Kivioja
3. Tevfik Ulusoglu

MW
1. Anton Holic
2. Karl Link
3. Robert Dantlinger

LHW
1. Angelito Lesta
2. Dirk Starke
3. Arnold Buurman

HW
1. Christer Eriksson
2. Manfred Grossler
3. Alois Pek

Women

LW
1. Astrid Aschwander
2. Camilla Palazzi
3. Christine Laurant

Sergio Oliva and Robby Robinson

Lance Dreher

Gunnar Rosbo

Ahmet Enunlu

Wilfried Dubbels

Rolf Muller

Vic Downs

MW
1. Inger Zetterqvist
2. Vera Bendel
3. Anita Pinnock

1983 European Cup

Men

1. Robert Dantlinger
2. Bill Tierney
3. Giovanni Curtarelli

Women

1. Christine Laurant
2. Josee Baumgartner
3. Ellen Van Maris

1983 AFWB Nationals

Women

LW
1. Mae Mollica
2. Sally Allemang
3. Breigh Kelley

MW
1. Debbie Vavoulis
2. Dawn Gnaegi
3. Cathy Basacker

HW
1. Diana Dennis
2. Cory Everson
3. Sue Ann McKean

Couples

1. Ed Zajac and Agi Balogh
2. Jeff and Cory Everson
3. Ray Boone and Ellen Morrow

1983 NABBA Universe

Men

Amateur Class 1
1. Jeff King†
2. John Brown
3. Marty Vranicar

Amateur Class 2
1. Vince Brown
2. Eugene Laviscount
3. Bob Reis

Amateur Class 3
1. Terry Phillips
2. Mike Sable
3. Larry Bernstein

Professional
1. Eduardo Kuwak
2. Ian Lawrence
3. Rufus Howard

Miss Bikini

1. Mary Scott
2. Beth Lopez
3. Lucy Ming Kee

1984 IFBB Caesar's Grand Prix

Men

1. Lee Haney
2. John Terilli
3. Albert Beckles

Women

1. Carla Dunlap
2. Tina Plakinger
3. Rachel McLish

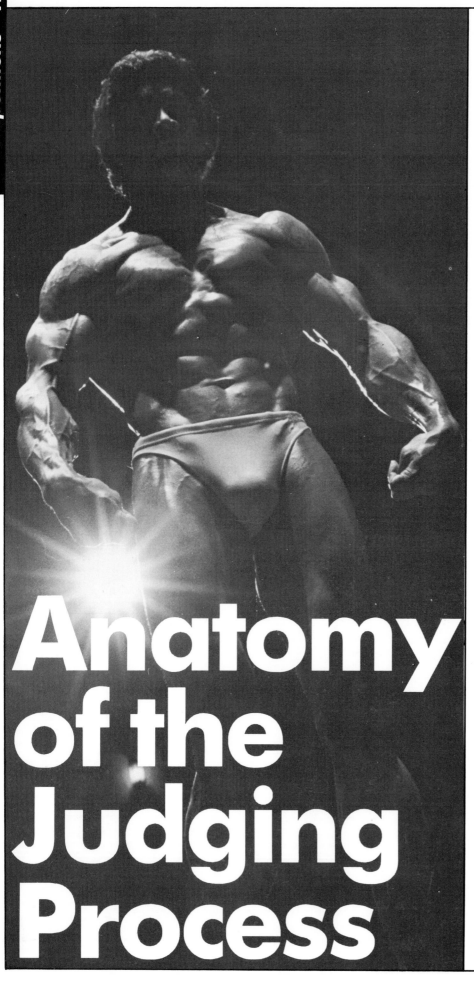

Anatomy of the Judging Process

Judging a physique contest is not a simple task since there are no exact standards for evaluating all body types. However, qualified, experienced judges usually find common denominators to agree upon as to what constitutes a prize-winning physique. Although there are some guidelines for the judges to use, the outcome of a bodybuilding contest remains largely a subjective decision. In the final analysis, it often comes down to the personal likes and dislikes of the judges regarding physique types, especially in extremely close decisions.

Obviously, this causes discrepancies between who the judges and the audience see as the obvious winners. This results in the countless controversial decisions made in bodybuilding contests over the years, which either leaves the audience suspecting the honesty and integrity of the judges or wondering if they have eyesight problems.

The purpose of this chapter is to examine some of the guidelines set down for judges by the International Federation of Bodybuilders (IFBB) and to explain what male and female bodybuilders are expected to show during each round of the judging process. With this information, the competing bodybuilder and the ardent fan can better understand how the judges arrive at their decisions.

Before we examine the actual judging procedures, it should be stated that the IFBB has made every effort to guarantee that judges and contests are fair. A list of accuracy marks is kept for each judge to ensure that he or she is honest and competent. If the marks are obviously out of line with the other judges, and/or show bias and incompetence, that judge is disqualified from judging at future IFBB contests.

When competing in an IFBB contest, each competitor must go through an official weigh-in to be placed in the proper weight class before taking part in the prejudging procedure, the evening presentation, plus (if he or she makes the finals) a posedown to determine the order of the top six finalists.

THE WEIGH-IN

All competitors must have their weight checked the evening before the prejudging day. The men must wear posing trunks while being weighed and the women must wear bikinis. Then the competitor is placed in his or her proper weight class.

In men's international competition, there are four categories:
1. Lightweight—up to and including 70 kilograms
2. Middleweight—up to and including 80 kilograms
3. Light Heavyweight—up to and including 90 kilograms
4. Heavyweight—over 90 kilograms

There are only two weight categories in women's international competition:
1. Lightweight—up to and including 52 kilograms
2. Middleweight—over 52 kilograms

In international competition, each country is allowed four competitors and up to three in one weight class. Of course, in pro contests there is no weight class and all competitors, regardless of weight, compete together.

A timetable for weighing in is published by the IFBB judge's committee and is strictly adhered to. Competitors who fail to weigh in within the time set or their category are automatically eliminated from the competition. Since the timetable is published well in advance of the weigh-in, there should not be any excuse for missing it.

An overweight competitor who may be one or two pounds over his or her intended weight class is given thirty minutes to try and lose the weight. If the bodybuilder is unable to shed the excess pounds or simply comes in over his or her nominated weight class, he or she may compete in the next higher category. However, it cannot result in more than three competitors in one weight class from the same federation.

During the weigh-in, the IFBB committee determines the order in which the competitors appear before the judges. Each competitor is issued the proper number corresponding to the order in which he or she will appear. This number is to be attached to the left side of the posing trunks and must be worn throughout the prejudging procedure and the final evening presentation.

THE PREJUDGING PROCEDURE

The prejudging procedure takes place the morning after the weigh-in for the world and continental championships. A timetable is published indicating the time of the prejudging for each weight category, so it is up to the competitor to find out when he or she is being prejudged and arrive early to prepare properly. The IFBB guidebook suggests that each competitor should be brought backstage at least thirty minutes prior to the prejudging to change and prepare for competition.

Each competitor should also be familiar with the IFBB rules concerning costumes. The men are not allowed to wear bikini-type trunks and the posing trunks must be "clean and decent." The women must wear "bikinis of a solid, nondistracting color which must conform to accepted standards of taste and decency." The fastenings of the bikini must also be plain with no ornamentation. Metallic materials such as gold or silver lamé are also forbidden. The bikinis must reveal the abdominal and lower-back muscles. Competitors are not allowed to wear "footwear, watches, rings, bangles, pendants, earrings, wigs, distracting ornamentation, or artificial aids to the figure." In addition, they must not chew gum or candy or smoke.

Artificial body coloring may be used, provided that it is applied at least twenty-four hours prior to the prejudging. The IFBB rules also state: "The excessive application of oil on the body is strictly forbidden, but body oils, skin creams, or moisturizers may be used in moderation."

The prejudging procedure and the evening contest are judged by seven knowledgeable, competent, and impartial judges, according to the following rules:

- They must not converse with the other judges.
- They must not attempt to influence the decisions of other judges.
- They must not take photographs while judging.
- They must not coach any of the competitors.
- They must not consume alcoholic beverages while judging.

There are two rounds of prejudging in IFBB amateur competition (compulsory posing and free posing) and for professional contests, three rounds (compulsory, relaxed, and free posing) plus the final posedown. Because there are far more competitors in amateur contests than in professional ones, the IFBB has combined the compulsory and relaxed rounds of posing into one round.

ROUND 1

Round 1 is the compulsory or the muscularity posing, in which the poser flexes his or her muscles prior to the contest to achieve a pumped-up appearance and then again for the judges. In the compulsory round, the judges look for muscularity, balanced development, density, definition, mass, shape, and tie-ins.

Each competitor is sent out individually onto the stage by the chief marshall in numerical order. Then the chief judge puts the male competitor through seven compulsory poses (five for women, which will be dealt with later). The following is a brief description of the poses and what the judges are instructed to look for according to the IFBB.

FRONT DOUBLE BICEPS

Facing the judge, the bodybuilder raises his or her arms and hits a double biceps shot. While the arms are the main muscle groups assessed, obviously the competitor should attempt to contract as many other frontal muscles as possible because the judges will be surveying the whole physique.

The IFBB guidebook instructs the judges to look first at the primary muscle group being displayed and

"then the judge should survey the whole physique starting at the head and looking at every part in a downward sequence, beginning with general impressions, looking for muscular bulk, balanced development, muscular density, and definition."

When doing any pose, it's always best to start at the bottom and work your way up. Set your feet, flex your legs and abs, and then flex your arms. Try and keep your face relaxed and try to smile as you pose. You have to make it appear easy and that you are enjoying yourself.

Even though the compulsory poses are supposed to be done in the same way by everyone to make comparisons more fair, there are certain tricks to individualize your double biceps pose. For example, Albert Beckles brings his arms straight out to his sides showing his incredible lats, giving the judges a different angle to view his fantastic arms before slowly raising his arms to the standard position to finish his pose.

FRONT LAT SPREAD

Although the purpose of this pose is to show the lat muscles from the front and shoulder width and V-shape, the competitor should always attempt to contract as many front muscles as possible. Again, start from the bottom—set your feet, tense the thighs, draw in the waist, and expand your chest and lats. The judges are instructed to survey the primary muscles and conclude with an overall survey.

SIDE CHEST

The competitor is allowed to do the side chest pose from either side to display his or her best arm. Dur-

ing this pose, the judges are required to pay "particular attention to the pectoral muscles, the arch of the rib cage; the biceps and forearms and the leg biceps and calves." The judge then will conclude his survey with an overall examination.

BACK DOUBLE BICEPS

The competitor is required to place one foot on the toes to allow the judges to see the development of the calf. The competitor should also contract the arms, shoulders, upper and lower back, and the leg biceps and calves.

This pose allows the judges to look at more muscles than in any other pose—biceps, triceps, forearms, neck, delts, traps, teres, infraspinatus, erectors, external obliques, lats, glutes, thigh biceps and calves. The competitor's shoulders and hip and waist widths are assessed along with considerations of balance, shape, muscle density, and definition.

BACK LAT SPREAD

Place one foot in back of your body to show the calf development. Place the hands on the hips and do a lat spread. The judges are primarily looking at the spread of the lats, but they are also scrutinizing the calves, leg biceps, width of the hips, waist and shoulders, arms, the thickness and density of the back, plus the separation of the lat, trap, and erector muscles. The judges are looking for lat balance (i.e., one lat shouldn't be more developed than the other). After assessing the primary muscle groups, the judges once again finish with an overall survey.

Note: Don't round your back instead of spreading your lats, which ruins the pose. Practice until you can spread the lats without unnecessary arching and rounding of the back.

SIDE TRICEPS

The competitor can pose from either side to show his or her best arm. The rules state that the competitor must bend at the knee, resting on the toes to show the calves from the side. Raise the chest and contract the abs and the thighs.

Remember, the judges are examining your whole physique. If you flex your triceps but forget to flex your calves, leg biceps, abs, and pecs, you're not going to look good, make a good impression, or score high. You simply must learn to control more than one muscle group at a time.

ABS AND THIGHS

The competitor must place both hands behind the head and extend one leg forward, simultaneously contracting the muscles of the abs and the thighs and calf of the forward leg. The judges are instructed to survey the abs and thigh-calf muscles first and then conclude with an overall examination.

After each competitor has gone through the seven compulsory poses, each judge is allowed to ask for certain competitors to come forward to be compared in particular poses. They are allowed as many comparisons as necessary to make a decision, but usually this amounts to only two or three comparisons each. The comparisons are considered extremely important in "deciding which competitor has the superior physique from the aspects of muscular bulk, balanced development, muscular density and definition."

An important point for competitors to remember while onstage is that they are being watched at all times, even when they are standing at the rear of the stage. If they relax their muscles, round their shoulders, or let their stomachs hang out, one of the judges could be influenced by a bad impression.

Frank Zane and Andreas Cahling are always at their best and very professional whether standing in line while others are compared, or on the posing platform themselves. They stand semi-tensed with their abs flexed and their arms slightly out to the sides to show their shoulder and lat width at all times. This makes a very positive impression on the judges. Always assume you're being watched!

In Gestalt psychology, it is often said that the whole is greater than the sum of all the parts. This is also true for physiques. While a competitor may have individually well-developed muscles, something can be missing, perhaps proper tie-ins, balance, shape, or an overall aesthetic appearance. It can also be a competitor's charisma and stage presence or even his or her reputation in past performances in contests. Unfortunately, judges are only human and are sometimes influenced by reputations. Judges can certainly be less critical of superstars like Arnold and Franco, overlooking faults they would mark down in a newer competitor.

The IFBB guidebook suggests that during Round 1 judges should not immediately try to start placing competitors. Rather, it is recommended that judges should make notes to sort the competitors into three groups: 1. the competitors deemed worthy of a high place; 2. the competitors whom they consider not good enough for a higher placing; and 3. the ones whom they consider will be placed lowest. The judges should also make notes of the competitors they wish to compare in order to be able to place them more accurately. Once delegated to one of the lower groups, it is extremely difficult to move to a higher place in your rating.

Generally, this is the time when judges start deducting or adding points for good or bad body parts. Of course, many discrepancies take place between the bodybuilders and judges, the fans and judges, and between the judges themselves. For instance, a judge must decide (everything else being equal) which is worth more: a 20-inch well-defined arm balanced with 16-inch calves or an 18-inch arm not quite as shapely but balanced with 18-inch calves.

At the 1982 Mr. Olympia contest in London, England, I discussed this aspect of judging with Winston Roberts, secretary of the IFBB and a regular judge at the Olympia and Grand Prix events. For him, it is easier to judge a top international or pro event than a local or regional event because the physiques are generally more balanced, symmetrical, and equal; it is usually the definition and muscularity and posing that separates the men. However, in a contest of lesser-caliber bodybuilders, one man may have great thighs, lats, and triceps, but no calves, pecs, biceps, or abs; another will have just the opposite of mismatched features. How do you judge who is better? It becomes entirely subjective at this point—what the judge personally likes or dislikes. The judge must weigh each factor and decide on the best physique.

After all the comparisons are made, the judges are instructed to mark their score sheets using the notes they have made during the comparisons. Each judge must place all competitors from first to last, without allowing for ties, using the number 1 for the best competitor, number 2 for second best, and so on. The marks are then collected by the judges' secretary and taken to the statisticians' table. The high and low marks of each competitor are discarded and the other five scores are totalled for each competitor's Round 1 Position. The judges' secretary has the authority to replace any judge whose scores are grossly out of line with the other judges or are obviously unfair or biased.

ROUND 2

In Round 2, the relaxed round, the judges are looking at the overall appearance of the competitors for the purpose of symmetrical evaluation. Each competitor is judged for total balance, size, shape, and muscular bulk, with the emphasis placed on proportion and balance. The body parts must be equally developed and how the muscles flow and tie in together is also considered.

The judges are instructed to look for good posture and athletic bearing, correct anatomical structure (body framework, broad shoulders, high chest, correct spinal curves, limbs and trunk in good proportion, straight legs), good skin tone with an absence of spots or acne or tattoos—which the IFBB considers as a skin blemish—hair tidily dressed, and well-shaped feet and toes.

The chief marshall lines up all the competitors in numerical order and the chief judge leads them in a line before the judges. According to IFBB rules: "The competitor must stand in a relaxed, erect position without any muscle flexing or contractions, head erect, eyes directed straight forward, arms hanging straight by the sides. The chief judge then directs the competitors to turn right four turns so that the judges will see them from the front, left side, rear view, right side, and front view again."

Again, the judges are first instructed to sort the competitors into three groups of the highest, middle, and lowest of calibers, and each judge can ask for comparisons between particular competitors. The IFBB advises judges: "When having difficulty in placing two or three competitors who seem to be on the same level, the judge should look for faults which will help him to differentiate between the competitors. Do not mark faults too harshly if the other more positive aspects of the physique are still of a high standard."

The guidebook states: "If any competitor deviates from the correct performance of the required poses in the first or second round, the chief judge will caution him or her. If the offense is repeated, the chief judge shall instruct the judges to penalize the offender by marking a plus against his or her number on their mark sheets." This results in the competitor being one placement lower.

After Round 2, the scores are collected and tallied, the high and low marks for each competitor discarded, with the total of five scores being the mark achieved for the second round. Most competitors don't place enough emphasis on the importance of the second round of relaxed posing, but it does account for at least 30 percent of the total score.

ROUND 3

Round 3, the freestyle posing round, is usually performed at the evening show. Each competitor performs his or her posing routine to a personal choice of music, which must be given to the official in charge of coordinating music for the contest. This is the theatrical portion of the competition where illusion can make mediocre bodybuilders appear even better than they really are if they are excellent posers.

The judges are instructed to look for a display of muscular physique in an artistic and well-choreographed routine, which should not be just a series of pretty movements. The competitor should show movement and control. Smooth transitions are therefore very important. He or she must display all sides of his or her physique and all major muscle groups. Marks can be deducted for poor posing and underdeveloped body parts.

At the end of Round 3, the six finalists are announced. The chief judge then directs them through the seven compulsory poses (five for women), which are performed simultaneously while the judges compare them.

Now the posedown starts, in which each competitor is free to do any posing of his choice, which again is performed simultaneously by all six finalists. This becomes a time of controlled chaos as competitors try to outpose each other and (hopefully) draw the judges' attention. During the posedown, the competitors are free to move around to be compared with different competitors as long as they do not push or shove anyone out of the way or indulge in any other unacceptable behavior.

At the end of the posedown, the six finalists are placed at the rear of the stage. The score sheets have been collected and totalled for each competitor. The names are then announced from sixth place to first place and appropriate trophies and/or cash prizes are awarded.

Each category has a victory ceremony immediately after the posedown final while the finalists are lined up at the back of the stage. A victory pedestal with three places is centered on the stage for the top three winners of each class.

WOMEN'S COMPETITION

The procedure for judging women's competitions is fundamentally the same as the men's. There is an official weigh-in and three rounds of prejudging for the women pros (two rounds for amateurs) with a posedown at the evening presentation for the six finalists. As in the men's competition, there are compulsory poses, but the women have only five of them:

• Front Double Biceps
• Side Chest
• Back Double Biceps
• Side Triceps
• Abs and Thighs

The poses are done in the same manner as the men's except for the front and back double biceps poses as the fists are not clenched and the arms are not completely bent in a fully contracted position. Also, one leg is extended to the rear slightly and raised up on the

toes. Each pose is also judged the same as the men's, that is, the primary and secondary muscle groups and then an overall assessment.

However, there are special guidelines judges are to consider in regard to female competitors. The IFBB guidebook states: "First and foremost, the judges must bear in mind that he or she is judging a woman's bodybuilding competition and is looking for an ideal feminine physique. Therefore, the most important aspect is shape, a feminine shape."

The other aspects are similar to those described for assessing men, but in regard to muscular development, it must not be carried to excess where it resembles the "massive muscularity of the male physique." The definition of women's muscles "must not be confused with emaciation, as the result of extreme weight loss whereby the excessive loss of body fat reveals the underlying muscles which will be flat, stringy, and underdeveloped."

In Round 2, judges are also instructed to look for other faults, not usually seen in men, like stretch marks, operation scars, cellulite, etc. They are also to observe whether the women competitors walk and move in a graceful manner. The rest of the contest is scored the same as the men's.

In conclusion, judging physique shows is a difficult task, and in most contests it is the finer points that separate the champs from the masses. While most bodybuilding fans vicariously enjoy the success of their idols and want them to win every time, they must also realize that this isn't always possible. Only

one person can win, and it is the competitor who shows the best physique over three rounds of posing and has the least amount of faults on a particular day.

Each individual has the right to choose his or her favorite, but that is only one person's opinion. It's easy to criticize when you're not in the hot seat. Seven experienced judges usually see to it that the right competitor wins. That's what judges are there for, and we owe them a debt of gratitude for it.

Shelley Gruwell

Routines and Exercises

Generally speaking, body-builders request more information about workout routines than any other topic, because every body-builder wants to maximize his or her progress. They want to follow an exercise routine that gives them the best possible results.

Many people wonder about the programs of the successful pro bodybuilders, although it could be argued that the routines of genetically superior bodybuilders will not necessarily be ideal for less gifted individuals.

There is a further point of consideration: Most bodybuilders change their routines from one month to the next. Accordingly, the exercises, sets, and reps which Danny Padilla, Greg DeFerro, and Tom Platz do this week, may be totally changed the next week. Some bodybuilders go so far as to *never* perform the same workout twice.

It is important for the aspiring bodybuilder, male or female, to understand that there is no single routine that will work for everyone. Bodybuilding is a trial-and-error adventure. A routine is only a collection of exercises—no more, no less. Its purpose is to maximally stimulate muscle growth while at the same time keeping below the duration and intensity level that would hinder full recuperation between workouts.

As a general rule, a bodybuilder should devote more time to training those body parts that are proportionately less developed than the rest of the physique. Women often do this; men, however, frequently devote more time to the areas that develop easily, and neglect the under-par muscle areas.

George Snyder, of the famous Olympus gyms in Warrington, Pennsylvania, published three volumes of a series entitled *Three More Reps*. Each book detailed the training

philosophy of numerous current champions of the sport of bodybuilding. The training programs and exercise philosophy included in Snyder's books was based on actual live seminars held by the respective champions at the Olympus gym. Accordingly, they accurately depict the truth.

Although there is constant change in a bodybuilder's routine, there can also be an underlying philosophy that remains unchanged. The following routines of the stars are reproduced with the kind permission of George Snyder, originator of the Miss Olympia contest, gym owner, entrepreneur, and promoter.

Following the routines of these championship men and women, you will find a helpful section listing a variety of exercises for the major body parts and a unique collection of bodybuilding tips for getting the most from your exercises and routines.

Samir Bannout's Routine

Day One

SHOULDERS

Front Raises (with barbell or dumbbells): 4 sets, 8–15 reps. (He increases the weight each set, with consequent decreases in repetitions.)

Lateral Raises (with dumbbells): 4 sets, 8–15 reps.

Bent-over Laterals (on cables): 4 sets, 8–14 reps.

Press behind Neck: 4 sets, 8–15 reps.

Upright Row (with barbell): 4 sets, 8–15 reps.

BICEPS

Alternate Dumbbell Curls: 4 sets, 8–12 reps.

Preacher Curls (varying grip widths): 4 sets, 8–12 reps.

Concentration Curls (with dumbbells): 4 sets, 8–12 reps.

(He increases training poundage each succeeding set.)

TRICEPS

Lat-machine Pressdowns: 4 sets, 8–12 reps.

One-arm Triceps Extensions (with dumbbells): 4 sets, 8–12 reps.

(Sometimes he does the Supine French Press or Supine Dumbbell Kickbacks.)

Parallel Bar Dips, or Reverse Dips (with weight attached to his body): 4 sets, 8–12 reps.

Day Two

THIGHS

Leg Extensions (machine): 8 sets, 10 reps; 4 sets, 5 reps.

Leg Biceps Curls: 5 sets, 10 reps.

Light Deadlifts (to stretch leg biceps): 4 sets, 10 reps.

Lunges or Hack Squats: 4 sets, 12 reps.

Regular Squats: 6 sets, 8–10 reps (heavy).

CALVES

(Sometimes he does his calf work in the evening.)

Calf Stretches (on a block, without weights, as warm-up).

Standing Heel Raises (very heavy!): 8 sets, 15 reps.

Seated Heel Raises (heavy): 8 sets, 15 reps. (More stretches of the muscle afterwards.)

ABDOMINALS (a 20-minute session)

Sit-ups: 4 sets, 25 reps (with weight).

Leg Raises (on chinning bar): 4 sets, 25 reps.

Intercostal Crunches (pulley machine): 4 sets, 30 reps.

Day Three

(He normally works groups individually, but at other times he does super sets.)

CHEST

Bench Press (Warms up with 135 pounds, 20–25 reps first set. Then increases poundages for each succeeding set.) Average: 6 sets, 8–10 reps.

Incline Press: 6 sets, 8–12 reps (increases weight each set).

Flyes (incline or flat, as mood hits him): 4 sets, 8–15 reps (uses both cables and dumbbells).

Dumbbell Pullover (across bench): 4 sets, 8–15 reps.

Parallel Bar Dips (weighted): 4 sets, 8–15 reps.

BACK

Lat Pulldowns (to back of neck or weighted chins): 6 sets, 8–12 reps.

Bent-over Row (varies grip widths on barbell): 5 sets, 8–12 reps.

T-bar Row: 5 sets, 8–12 reps.

Cable Row: 4 sets, 8–12 reps.

Note: Samir normally takes a 35-second rest between sets. He always trains as heavily as possible, without sacrificing reps or training style.

Roy Callender's Routine

Note: Roy trains each body part each third day, works three weeks without pause and takes one or two days off after the third training week. He varies body groupings from time to time. Trains weak areas each workout. Saves miniworkouts for areas that are slow gainers. Does not count reps or sets—works by instinct. Uses a three-day workout cycle.

Day One

CALVES

(1-hour routine)
Heel Raises (while seated at machine)
Toe Pushes (on leg-press machine with head at
  high end of platform)

THIGHS

(1-hour routine)
Sissy Squats (100 reps in 2 minutes)
Lunges (up to 200 reps)
Leg Extensions (toes pointed)
Leg Curls

BACK

(90-minute routine)
Chins (to clavicles and to back of neck on
  triangular bar)
Pulldowns (to front and back of neck)
Stiff-legged Deadlifts (on bench)
One-arm Dumbbell Row
Hyperextensions
T-bar Row

TRICEPS

(15-minute miniroutine)
Lat Pressdowns

Day Two

THIGHS

(30-minute routine)
Leg Extensions (on machine)

CHEST

Bench Press
Bench Press Super-setted with Flat Bench Flyes
Parallel Bar Dips
Pullovers (across bench)
Pulley Crossovers (varied angles)

SHOULDERS

(45-minute routine)
Heavy Barbell or Dumbbell Shrugs

BICEPS

(15-minute miniworkout)
Choice of Regular Barbell Curl, Incline Curl, or
    Concentration Curl. Uses only one.

TRICEPS

(45-minute routine)
Dumbbell Triceps Press (in lying position)
Lat Pressdowns
Reverse Dips (feet elevated, body down)

Day Three

CALVES

(30-minute routine)
Standing Heel Raises
Donkey Raises

RIB CAGE & SERRATUS

(15-minute routine)
Straight-arm Pullovers (across bench)

SHOULDERS

(1-hour routine)
Front Press (seated or behind the neck)
Seated Dumbbell Press
Alternate Dumbbell Press
Lateral Raises (with dumbbells in regular style
    and bent-over style). Also uses pulleys.

TRICEPS

(15-minute routine)
Lat-machine Pressdowns

BICEPS

(45-minute routine)
Regular Barbell or Dumbbell Curls, Seated or
    Alternate Dumbbell Curls, Preacher Bench
    Curls.

ABDOMINALS

(20-minute routine)
Sit-ups, Leg Raises, and Crunches. Aims for burn
    sensation in abdominal area. Trains abdomi-
    nals every day.

Lydia Cheng's Routine

Monday Morning

ABDOMINALS

Hanging Leg Raises: 3 sets, 15 reps.
Flat Leg Raises (weighted): 4 sets, 15 reps.
Crunches: 5 sets, 20 reps.

CALVES

Seated Calf Raises: 6 sets, 15 reps.
Leg-machine Toe Raises: 6 sets, 15 reps.
Donkey Calf Raises: 4 sets, 15 reps.

Monday Evening

CHEST

Incline Dumbbell Press: 4 sets, 10 reps.
Flat Dumbbell Flyes: 4 sets, 10 reps.
Cable Crossovers: 3 sets, 15 reps.

Tuesday Morning

BACK

Chin-ups (to front): 3 sets, as many reps as possible.
Wide-grip Pulldowns (behind neck): 4 sets, 10 reps.
Wide-grip Pulldowns (in front of neck): 4 sets, 10 reps.
Low Pulley Rows: 4 sets, 10 reps.
One-arm Dumbbell Row: 4 sets, 8 reps.
Straight-arm Pulldowns: 4 sets, 8 reps.

Wednesday Morning

BICEPS

Barbell Curls: 4 sets, 10 reps.
Incline Dumbbell Curls: 4 sets, 8 reps.
Concentration Curls: 4 sets, 8 reps.

TRICEPS

One-arm Triceps Extensions: 4 sets, 8 reps.
Triceps Pressdowns: 4 sets, 8 reps.
Dumbbell French Press: 4 sets, 10 reps.
Rope Pulls: 4 sets, 10 reps.

Wednesday Evening

LEGS AND LOWER BACK

Leg Extensions: 4 sets, 15 reps.
Squats: 4 sets, 15 reps.
Leg Press: 4 sets, 15 reps.
Leg Curls: 4 sets, 15 reps.

Method

Lydia trains on a six-day double split system (eight-day cycle, three days on, one day off).

Carolyn Cheshire's Routine

Day One

CHEST

Flat Bench Press: 4 sets, 10 reps.
Dumbbell Bench Press: 4 sets, 10 reps.
Supine Flyes: 4 sets, 10 reps.
Dumbbell Pullovers (across bench): 4 sets, 10 reps.

BACK

Wide-grip Chins: 3 sets, 10 reps.
Narrow-grip Chins: 3 sets, 10 reps.
Pulldowns (in front of neck): 4 sets, 10 reps.
Pulldowns (behind neck): 4 sets, 10 reps.
Close-grip Pulldowns: 3 sets, 10 reps.
Long Cable Row: 4 sets, 10 reps.
Bent-over Barbell Row: 4 sets, 10 reps.
Single-arm Row: 3 sets, 10 reps.

Method

Three days on, one day off. The routine is split three ways, occasionally single-rep limits are attempted in basic exercises.

Day Two

LEGS

Squats (vary foot position): 5–7 sets, 15 reps.
Leg Press: 5 sets, 15 reps.
Leg Extensions: 4 sets, 15 reps.
Stiff-leg Deadlifts (from bench): 4 sets, 10 reps.
Leg Curls (with forced reps): 4 sets, 10 reps.
Toe Raises (on leg press): 10 sets, 20 reps.

Day Three

SHOULDERS

Barbell Press: 5 sets, 10 reps.
Barbell Front Raises: 3 sets, 10 reps.
Lateral Raises: 3 sets, 10 reps.
Bent-over Flyes (face down on bench): 3 sets,
    10 reps.
Upright Row: 4 sets, 10 reps.
Heavy Dumbbell Shrugs: 3 sets, 10 reps.

BICEPS

Wide-grip Barbell Curls: 4 sets, 10 reps.
Reverse-grip Curls: 4 sets, 10 reps.
Concentration Curls: 3 sets, 10 reps.

TRICEPS

Close-grip Bench Press: 5 sets, 10 reps.
Lying Triceps Extensions (straight bar): 4 sets,
    10 reps.
Pressdowns: 4 sets, 10 reps.
Reverse Pressdowns: 3 sets, 10 reps.
Cable Kickbacks: 3 sets, 10 reps.

ABDOMINALS

Weighted Leg Raises: 3 sets, 30 reps.
Incline Sit-ups (with weight): 3 sets, 20 reps.

Boyer Coe's Routine

Method

Monday, Wednesday, Friday: Chest, Back Shoulders, Calves, and Waist.
Tuesday, Thursday: Thighs, Biceps, Triceps, Calves, and Waist.

CHEST

super set [Incline Press: 4 sets, 8–10 reps.
Dips: 4 sets, 8–10 reps.
Incline Dumbbell Press: 4 sets, 8–10 reps.

BACK

super set [Wide Chins to Chest: 4 sets, 8–10 reps.
Barbell Row: 4 sets, 8–10 reps.
super set [T-Bar Row: 4 sets, 8–10 reps.
Long Cable Row: 4 sets, 8–10 reps.
Lower Back Machine (or Hyperextensions,
    Good Morning): 8 sets, 8–10 reps.

SHOULDERS

super set [Press behind Neck: 4 sets, 8–10 reps.
Laterals: 4 sets, 8–10 reps.
super set [Rear Delt Machine (pec machine): 4 sets, 8–10
    reps.
Bent-over Rear Laterals: 4 sets, 8–10 reps.
Dumbbell Shrugs: 8 sets, 8–10 reps.

THIGHS

super set [Squats: 4 sets, 8–10 reps.
Sissy Squats (or Leg Press): 4 sets, 8–10 reps.
super set [Leg Extensions: 4 sets, 8–10 reps.
Leg Curls: 4 sets, 8–10 reps.

CALVES

super set [Standing Toe Raises: 10 sets, 15–20 reps.
Lying Toe Raises (on leg-press machine): 10 sets,
    15–20 reps.

WAIST

super set [Hanging Knee Raises: 5 sets, 25 reps.
Crunch Sit-ups (with weight): 5 sets, 25 reps.
Twists: 5 sets, 25 reps.

BICEPS

super set [Curling Machine: 4 sets, 8–10 reps.
Standing Curls (dumbbell or barbell): 4 sets,
    8–10 reps.
super set [Lying Flat Curls: 4 sets, 8–10 reps.
E-Z Bar Curls (standing): 4 sets, 8–10 reps.

TRICEPS

super set [Pressdown: 4 sets, 8–10 reps.
French Press (lying or seated): 4 sets, 8–10 reps.
super set [Standing French Press: 4 sets, 8–10 reps.
Kickbacks: 4 sets, 8–10 reps.

FOREARMS

Barbell Wrist Curls: 8 sets, 15–20 reps.

Greg DeFerro's Routine

Note: The exercises are performed 4 sets each movement, 25 reps each, except for the twists which are performed in sets of 50 reps.

Monday & Thursday

CHEST

Incline Press (warm-up with moderate weight):
    2 sets, 15 reps.
Crunches (pec-dec machine): 3 sets, 10 reps.
Incline Barbell Press: 3 sets, 8–10 reps.
Dumbbell Flyes (on flat bench): 3 sets, 10 reps.
Bench Press (with barbell); 3 sets, 10 reps.
Parallel Bar Dips: 3 sets, as many reps per set as
    possible.

TRICEPS

Lat-machine Pressdowns: 4 sets, 12 reps.
super set [Lying Triceps Press: 3 sets, 8 reps.
Pressdowns (on lat machine, elbows held out-
    wards): 3 sets, 10 reps.
Seated Triceps Press: 3 sets, 10 reps.

BICEPS

Alternate Dumbbell Curls (warm-up with mod-
    erate weights)
Preacher Bench Curls: 4 sets, 12 reps (first set
    10 reps to warm-up). (Increases weight from
    second set, then does 6 heavy reps, and 6
    reps with slightly lighter weight, until he has
    completed 4 sets.)
Barbell Curls: 3–4 sets, 8–10 reps.
Dumbbell Curls (sometimes standing, some-
    times seated): 3 sets, 8–10 reps.
Concentrated Curl with Dumbbell (rotates
    wrist as weight travels upwards): 3 sets, 10
    reps.

FOREARMS

Reverse Curls: 4 sets, 8–10 reps.
Dumbbell or Barbell Wrist Curls: 4 sets, 10–15
    reps.

Tuesday & Friday

BACK

Lat Pulldowns (with wide handgrip, to chest): 3
    sets, 12 reps.
Bent-over Barbell Row: 3 sets, 8 reps.
Low Pulley Row: 3 sets, 10 reps.
Pulldowns (to chest, medium handgrip): 3 sets,
    10–12 reps.
Pulley Row (from top pulley): 3 sets, 15 reps.
Hyperextensions: 4 sets, 15 reps.

SHOULDERS

Seated Barbell Press (front): 5 sets, 8 reps.
Lateral Raises (with dumbbells): 4 sets, 10 reps.
Pulley Laterals (one arm at a time): 3 sets, 10
    reps.
Dumbbell Press: 3 sets, 10 reps.
Upright Barbell Row: 3 sets, 10 reps.

Wednesday & Saturday

THIGHS

Leg Extensions & Hack Squats: 4 super sets,
    15–20 reps each set.
Leg Curl: 5 sets, 20 reps.
Stiff-legged Deadlifts: 5 sets, 12 reps.

CALVES

Standing Heel Raises: 5 sets, 20 reps.
Leg-press Toe Raises: 5 sets, 20 reps.
Seated Toe Raises: 5 sets, 20 reps.
Donkey Raises: 5 sets, 20 reps.

ABDOMINALS

Roman Chair Sit-ups
Leg Raises (on incline bench or from chinning
    bar)
Seated Twists
Rope Crunches

Dave Draper's Routine

CHEST

 Bench Press: 5 sets, 8–10 reps.
Draper Flyes: 5 sets, 15 reps.
Pullovers: 5 sets, 15–20 reps.
Cable Crossovers: 3 sets, 12–15 reps.

BACK

One-arm Row (or Barbell or T-bar): 5 sets, 8–10 reps.
Special Barbell Row: 3–4 sets, 10–12 reps.
Seated Cable Row: 5 sets, 12–15 reps.
Pulldowns (1/2 front—1/2 back of neck): 5 sets, 15 reps.

SHOULDERS

Press behind Neck: 5 sets, 8–10 reps.
Laterals (or Bent-over Laterals): 5 sets, 8–10 reps.
Seated Dumbbell Press: 5 sets, 8–10 reps. (or Upright Row)

WAIST

Roman Chair Sit-ups (or Crunches): 150 reps.
Hanging Knee Raises (or Leg Raises): 150 reps.
Seated Knee Raises: 150 reps.

CALVES

 Seated Toe Raises: 5 sets, 15 reps.
Standing Toe Raises: 5 sets, 15 reps.
Donkey Toe Raises: 5 sets, 15 reps.
   (*Always vary toe positions.*)

Method

Monday, Wednesday, Friday: Chest, Back, Shoulders, Waist, and Calves.
Tuesday, Thursday, Saturday: Biceps, Triceps, Thighs, Calves, and Waist.

THIGHS

super set [
Leg Extensions: 5 sets, 15 reps.
Leg Curls: 5 sets, 15 reps.
Leg Press: 5 sets, 15 reps.
Hack Squats: 5 sets, 15 reps.
  (*Always vary foot positions.*)

BICEPS

Barbell Curls (or Alternate Curls): 5 sets, 8–10 reps.
Incline Curl and Press: 5 sets, 8–10 reps.
Concentration Curls: 5 sets, 8–10 reps. (Barbell or Dumbbell)

TRICEPS

Lying French Press: 5 sets, 12–15 reps. Finish off with Close-grip Press.
Pressdowns: 5 sets, 12–15 reps.
Seated French Press: 5 sets, 12–15 reps.
Leaning Rope Extensions: 5 sets, 12–15 reps.

FOREARMS

Reverse Curls: 4–5 sets, 8–12 reps.
Barbell Wrist Curls: 4 sets, 15 reps.
Dumbbell Wrist Curls (lean to the side): 4 sets, 15 reps.

Cory Everson's Routine

Method

She works three days on, one day off.

Day One

CHEST

Bench Press: 1 set, 15 reps; 1 set, 10 reps; 5 sets, 3–12 reps.
Incline Press: 4 sets, 6–8 reps.
Pec Machine: 3 sets, 10–12 reps.
Cable Crossovers: 3 sets, 10–15 reps.

SHOULDERS

Press behind Neck: 4 sets, 6–8 reps.
Laterals: 4 sets, 8–12 reps.
Rear Raises: 4 sets, 8–12 reps.

Day Two

UPPER LEGS

Lunges: 4–5 sets, 12–15 reps.
Leg Extensions: 4 sets, 12–15 reps.
Leg Curls: 4 sets, 12–15 reps.
Light Squats: 3 sets, 15 reps.

CALVES

Standing Raises: 3 sets, 20 reps.
Seated Raises: 3 sets, 20 reps.

ABDOMINALS

Raises, Crunches, Leg-ups, Twists in a variety of sets and reps.

Day Three

ABDOMINALS

Another session of various abdominal exercises.

ARMS

Dumbbell Curls: 5 sets, 12 reps.
Triceps Pushdowns: 4 sets, 8 reps.
Pulley Curls: 3 sets, 12 reps.
Triceps Extensions: 3 sets, 12 reps.

BACK

Pulldowns: 4 sets, 20, 15, 12, 8 reps.
Dumbbell Row: 4 sets, 10 reps.
Close-grip Pulldowns (to Chest): 3 sets, 12 reps.
Long Pulley Row: 3 sets, 12 reps.

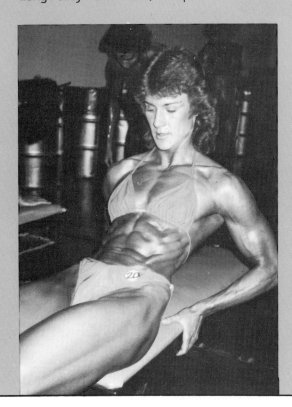

Bill Grant's Routine

Method

Monday, Thursday: Chest and back in the morning. Thighs, calves, and waist in the evening.

Tuesday, Friday: Shoulders, biceps, triceps, calves, waist, and forearms.

CHEST

Bench Press: 6–18 sets, 6–12 reps.
Incline Press (Barbell or Dumbbell): 5 sets, 10–12 reps.
Flyes (various angles): 5 sets, 10–12 reps.
Pullovers (across bench): 5 sets, 10–12 reps.
Dips: 5 sets, 10–12 reps.
Cable Crossovers: 5 sets, 10 reps.

CALVES

super set [Seated Toe Raises: 5 sets, 15 reps.
Standing Toe Raises: 5 sets, 15 reps.
Donkey Toe Raises: 5 sets, 15 reps.

BACK

Pulldowns: 5 sets, 10–12 reps. (6 reps to front, 6 reps to back)
Power Cleans: 4 sets, 8–10 reps.
T-bar Row: 5 sets, 10–12 reps.
Bent-over Barbell Row: 5 sets, 10–12 reps.
Seated Pulley Row: 5 sets, 10 reps.
   (*Before a show Bill super sets chest and back exercises.*)

SHOULDERS

super set [Presses (behind neck or front): 5 sets, 10 reps.
Laterals: 5 sets, 10 reps.
Upright Row: 5 sets, 10 reps.
Pulley Laterals: 5 sets, 10 reps.
Bent-over Rear Laterals: 5 sets, 10 reps.
Shrugs: 5 sets, 10 reps.

THIGHS

Leg Extensions: 8–10 sets, 8–20 reps.
Squats or Leg Press: 8–10 sets, 10–12 reps.
   (alternates each time)
Leg Curls: 8 sets, 8–20 reps.

WAIST

Roman Chair Sit-ups
Leg Raises
Hanging Knee Raises
   (*Doesn't count sets or reps. Works for a burn.*)

FOREARMS

Seated Barbell Wrist Curls: 3 sets, 10–12 reps.
Reverse Curls: 3 sets, 10–12 reps.
Standing Wrist Curls (weight behind back): 3 sets, 10–12 reps.

BICEPS

Machine Curls: 5 sets, 10–12 reps.
Barbell Curls: 5 sets, 10–12 reps.
Concentration Curls: 5 sets, 10–12 reps.

TRICEPS

Pressdowns: 3 sets, 10–12 reps.
Decline French Press: 5 sets, 10–12 reps.
One-arm Extensions: 5 sets, 10–12 reps.
Seated French Press: 5 sets, 10–12 reps.
Dumbbell Kickbacks: 5 sets, 10–12 reps.

Mike Mentzer's Routine

CHEST

Pec-Dec Squeezes (to failure point)
Incline Press (with barbell—forced reps)
Flyes (with cables or dumbbells)
(The above exercises are done in four cycles, with no pause between movements.)

TRICEPS

Nautilus Triceps Extension (to failure)
Weighted Dips (to failure)
(The above exercises are done with no rest between, and always to failure point. Sometimes Mike calls on a training partner for 2 or 3 forced repetitions. Usually he performs no more than 8 reps per cycle on each exercise. For his triceps Mike does 3 cycles.)

THIGHS

Heavy Leg Extensions: 1 set, 10 reps.
Leg Press: 1 set, 10 reps.
Parallel Squats: 1 set, 10 reps (as much as 475 lbs.)
Leg Curls (machine): 1 set, 10 reps.
(Sometimes the above exercises are done in super-set style. He always uses maximum poundages to failure point.)

BACK

Pullovers (Nautilus machine)
Underhand Close-grip Chins
(The above exercises are done in super-set style, for 2 cycles.)
Long Pulls (cable): 2 sets, 8 reps.
One-arm Dumbbell Row: 2 sets, 8 reps.

DELTOIDS

Lateral Raises (Nautilus machine)
Front Press (Nautilus machine)
(The exercises are done to failure point, with no rest between sets, for 2 cycles.)

BICEPS

Barbell Curls (forced reps)
Concentration Dumbbell Curls
Preacher Bench Curls
(The exercises are done to failure for 3 cycles,
    with no rest between exercises or cycles. He
    uses a partner for help.)

CALVES

Toe Raises (calf machine)
Toe Raises (leg-press machine)
(Mike uses up to 1,000 pounds in the first
    exercise and 800 in the second. Both move-
    ments are done to failure point, one set
    each.)

ABDOMINALS

Leg Raises (from chinning bar)
Crunches (leg-extension machine)
(He does super sets of the above exercises and
    works for a burn each time.)

Serge Nubret's Routine

Early Morning

THIGHS

Leg Extensions: 15 sets, 15 reps.
Leg Curls: 15 sets, 15 reps.
Hack Squats (on leg press): 10–12 sets, 15 reps.
(Before a contest, Serge adds free squats and
    does not lock knees upon rising. Up to 300
    reps per set and may go as high as 10 sets.)

CALVES

Standing Heel Raises
Seated Heel Raises
Donkey Raises
(The above exercises are done with heavy
    weights. Total sets vary between 15 and 20;
    15 repetitions each set.)

WAIST

Sit-ups
Leg Raises (in lying position)
Twists (while standing)
(Normally, he trains his waist for 30 minutes—
    45 minutes at contest time.)

Note: The actual exercises do not seem to
matter all that much to Nubret, for he tends to
change them as the mood strikes him. Some
things never change, however. He makes a
point of using only weights that allow him to
concentrate strongly on the movement being
performed. And he tries to grind out as many
sets and reps as possible within a certain time,
always striving to beat his record of repetitions
and sets. For example, if it took 45 minutes to
do 30 sets of an exercise one day, the next day
Nubret will try to squeeze 31 or 32 sets in the
same length of time.

Such movements as crossovers on the pulley
machine, pullovers with barbell, incline press
with barbell or dumbbells, and shrugs also find
a place in Nubret's ever-changing exercise
program.

The super-set principle is applied only to his
arm training.

He stays clear of heavy weights, pointing out
that most gym injuries are the result of attempting to exercise with ponderous barbells.

SHOULDERS

Standing Press (behind the neck)
One-arm Lateral Raises (lying on the floor)
Lateral Raises (with dumbbells)
(The last two exercises are sometimes dropped
in favor of other deltoid movements, but he
never drops the press behind neck.)
All movements: 10 sets each, 12 repetitions per
set.

Evening

CHEST

Bench Press: 20 sets, 12–15 reps.
Straight-arm Pullovers: 10 sets, 15 reps.
Flyes: 10 sets, 12 reps.

Day Two

Morning

(Repeats above waist and calf workout.)

Evening

BACK

Chins: 12 sets, as many reps as possible per set.
Pulldowns (from overhead pulley, 8 reps to the
front, 8 reps to the back each set): 12 sets.
Reverse-grip Pulldowns (from overhead pulley):
10 reps, 8 sets or Pulley Row from seated
position.

Day Three

Morning

(Repeats waist workout.)

Evening

ARMS

Barbell Curls (super-setted with Lying Triceps
Press)
Dumbbell Concentration Curls (super-setted
with lat-machine pressdowns). He trains his
arms for 20 minutes, working very quickly.
Approximately 10–12 sets for the biceps and
the same for the triceps.

Danny Padilla's Routine

Method

On Season:
Monday, Wednesday, Friday: Chest, Back, Waist in morning, Legs and Calves at night.
Tuesday, Thursday, Saturday: Shoulders, Arms, and Waist.

Off Season:
Monday: Chest and Back
Tuesday: Shoulders and Arms
Wednesday: Legs, Calves, and Waist

CHEST

Bench Press: 5 sets, 8–10 reps.
Incline Press: 5 sets, 10 reps.
Flyes: 5 sets, 12 reps.
super set [Cable Crossovers: 2 sets, 12 reps.
Pullovers: 2 sets, 12 reps.

BACK

Chins (1 rep front; 1 rep back; etc.): 5 sets,
    15–25 reps.
Barbell Row: 5 sets, 12 reps.
Seated Pulley Row: 5 sets, 10–12 reps.
Pulldowns: 5 sets, 12 reps.

SHOULDERS

Side Laterals: 5 sets, 12 reps.
Press behind Neck: 5 sets, 10 reps.
Rear Laterals (bent over): 5 sets, 8 reps.
Shrugs: 4 sets, reps: 50–40–30–20.

THIGHS

Leg Extensions: 10 sets, 15 reps.
Squats: 5 sets, 12–15 reps.
Leg Press: 5 sets, 8–10 reps.
Leg Curls: 5 sets, 12 reps.

CALVES

Standing Toe Raises: 5 sets, 8–12 reps.
Donkey Raises: 5 sets, 15 reps.
Seated Calf Machine: 5 sets, 12 reps.

WAIST

super set [Sit-ups (knees bent): 5 sets, 15 reps.
Hanging Knee Raises: 5 sets, 15 reps.

BICEPS

Alternate Dumbbell Curls: 5 sets, 8 reps.
Barbell Curls: 6 sets, 6 reps.
Concentration Curls: 5 sets, 8–10 reps (added 6
    weeks before contest).

TRICEPS

Lying Triceps Press (behind head): 5 sets, 12
    reps.
Pressdowns: 5 sets, 12 reps.
One-arm Pressdowns (reverse grip): 5 sets, 12
    reps (added 6 weeks before contest).

FOREARMS

(6 weeks before contest)
Reverse Curls: 5 sets, 8–10 reps.
Barbell Wrist Curls: 5 sets, 8–10 reps.

Tom Platz's Routine

Note: He splits (trains morning and evening) on Monday and Thursday. Tuesday, Wednesday, Friday, and Saturday trains just once a day. The extra work is done for contests only. Normally, Tom trains his abdominals only twice weekly.

Monday & Thursday Mornings

CHEST

Incline Press (with dumbbells): 15 sets, 4–8 reps.
(He increases poundage each set, reps decrease.)

super set [Bench Press: 4 sets, 6–8 reps (some are forced reps, with partner helping).
Flyes (on low incline): 4 sets, 6–8 reps (Normally, he uses dumbbells for last movement but shortly before a contest uses cables.)

SIDE DELTOIDS

Upright Row: 4 sets, 8–12 reps.
Lateral Raises: 6 sets, 10–12 reps.
Cable Laterals (one arm at a time): 3 sets, 10–12 reps.

ABDOMINALS

Roman Chair Sit-ups (to failure): 4 sets.
Twists and Side Crunches (as many as possible): 4 sets.

CALVES

Standing Heel Raises: 6 sets, 8 reps.
Seated Heel Raises (very heavy): 5 sets, 40 reps.
Toe raises (on leg-press machine): 6 sets, 30–40 reps.

Monday & Thursday Evenings

BACK

Wide-grip Chins: 6 sets, 10–15 reps (including half reps).

Long-range Cable Row: 4–6 sets, 10–15 reps.

T-bar Row: 6 sets, 8–10 reps. (Does some partial reps for the purpose of further stretching the lats.)

Dumbbell Pullovers (across the bench): 6 sets, 8–10 reps.

REAR DELTOIDS

Press behind Neck: 6 sets, 6–15 reps. (Decreases reps as the poundages increase each set).

Bent-over Laterals (with dumbbells): 6 sets, 10–15 reps.

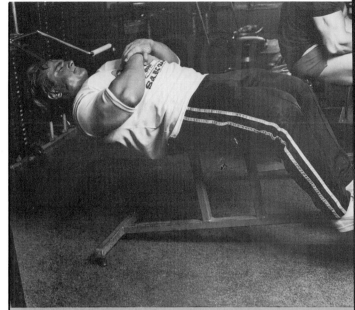

Tuesday & Friday

ARMS

 super set Alternate Dumbbell Curls: 6 sets, 6–8 reps.

Close-grip Bench Press: 6 sets, 6–8 reps (some forced reps).

One-arm Dumbbell Triceps Extensions: 4 sets, 10 reps. (Sometimes he substitutes the last exercise with seated French presses or bent-over cable extensions.)

ABDOMINALS & CALVES

(Repeat previous day's routines.)

Wednesday & Saturday

THIGHS

Squat: Warms up with 135 pounds: 10–15 reps.
5 more sets with 225: 10 reps.

275: 8 reps.
315: 6 reps.
345: 4 reps.
360: 4 reps.

(The above routine is designed to bring out extreme definition while maintaining mass.)

Hacks: 3–4 sets, 15–20 reps.

Leg Extensions: 6 sets, 15–20 reps.

Leg Curls: 6 sets, 15–20 reps. (Uses negative resistance and isometrics here. Poundages are decreased each set and repetitions increased.)

ABDOMINALS & CALVES

(Repeat previous routines.)

Gladys Portugues's Routine

Method

Trains five days a week, one body part per day. Full intensity each set.

Monday

CHEST

Bench Press: 4 sets, 6–10 reps.
Dumbbell Press: 4 sets, 6–10 reps.
Dumbbell Incline Press: 4 sets, 6–10 reps.
Flyes: 4 sets, 6–10 reps.
Dips: 4 sets, 6–10 reps.

Tuesday

LEGS

Squats: 4 sets, 6–10 reps.
Hack Squats: 4 sets, 6–10 reps.
Leg Extensions: 4 sets, 6–10 reps.
Leg Curls: 4 sets, 6–10 reps.
Standing Calf Raises: 4 sets, 6–10 reps.
Seated Calf Raises: 4 sets, 6–10 reps.

Wednesday

TRICEPS-BICEPS

Close-grip Bench Press: 4 sets, 6–10 reps.
Pushdowns: 4 sets, 6–10 reps.
Overhead Rope Pulls: 4 sets, 6–10 reps.
Barbell Curls: 4 sets, 6–10 reps.
Seated Dumbbell Curls: 4 sets, 6–10 reps.
Concentration Curls: 4 sets, 6–10 reps.

Thursday

SHOULDERS

Press behind Neck: 4 sets, 6–10 reps.
Standing Press: 4 sets, 6–10 reps.
Side Laterals: 4 sets, 6–10 reps.
Bent-over Laterals: 4 sets, 6–10 reps.
Shrugs: 4 sets, 6–10 reps.

Friday

BACK

Chins: 4 sets, 6–10 reps.
Pullovers: 4 sets, 6–10 reps.
Seated Row: 4 sets, 6–10 reps.
Hyperextensions: 4 sets, 6–10 reps.

Robby Robinson's Routine

Monday, Wednesday, Friday Mornings

CHEST

Bench Press: 8 sets, 8–10 reps.
Incline Press (machine): 8 sets, 10 reps.
Dumbbell Flyes: 6 sets, 10–12 reps.
Parallel Bar Dips (with body weight only):
    6 sets.
Cable Crossovers: 5 sets, 12 reps.
Pullovers (across bench): 5 sets, 12 reps.

BACK

Chins behind Neck: 5 sets, as many reps as
    possible.
Bent-over Barbell Row: 6 sets, 10 reps.
Long-range Cable Pull: 6 sets, 12 reps.
One-arm Dumbbell Row: 5 sets, 8 reps.

Afternoon Session

THIGHS

Parallel Squats: 6 sets, 12–15 reps.
Hack Squats (machine): 6 sets, 12–15 reps.
Leg Extensions: 6 sets, 15–20 reps.
Leg Biceps Curls: 6 sets, 12–15 reps.

CALVES

Standing Toe Raises: 8 sets, 12–20 reps.
Donkey Raises: 8 sets, 25 reps.
Toe Raises (machine): 8 sets, 8–10 reps (heavy).
Seated Calf Raises (machine): 6 sets, 25 reps.

ABDOMINALS

Roman Chair Sit-ups: 6 sets: 40–50 reps.
Seated Twists: 6 sets, 100 reps.
Leg Raises (chinning bar): 6 sets, 20–25 reps.
Crunches: 5 sets, 12–20 reps.

Tuesday, Thursday, Saturday

ARMS

Cheat Barbell Curls: 8 sets, 6–8 reps.
Seated Incline Curls: 6 sets, 8 reps.
Concentration Dumbbell Curls: 6 sets, 10 reps.
Close-grip Barbell Curls: 6 sets, 12 reps.
One-arm Triceps Stretch (lying on bench): 6 sets, 10 reps.
French Press with barbell: 6 sets, 8 reps.
Lat-machine Pressdowns: 6 sets, 8–10 reps.
Parallel Bar Dips (straight up and down): 6 sets, 10–12 reps.
(Super-setted triceps and biceps movements two weeks before the Mr. Olympia contest).

DELTOIDS

Seated Press (machine): 6 sets, 8–10 reps.
Heavy Dumbbell Laterals: 6 sets, 6–8 reps.
Bent-over Laterals (with cables): 6 sets, 12–15 reps.
Standing Press (with dumbbells): 6 sets, 6–8 reps.

CALVES

(Same as afternoon Monday through Friday sessions.)

ABDOMINALS

(As outlined earlier for Monday routine.)

Larry Scott's Routine

Monday & Thursday

CHEST

Incline Press (on machine bench at approximately 40-degree angle): 6 reps, 6–8 sets.
Dumbbell Press (on incline bench): 6 reps, 6–8 sets.

CALVES

Donkey Raises: 6 sets, 20 reps.
Seated Heel Raises: 6 sets, 20 reps.

ABDOMINALS

Sit-ups (on abdominal board, knees bent): 6 sets, 40 reps.
Leg Raises (from chinning bar): 6 sets, 40–50 reps.
Hyperextensions: 6 sets, 40 reps.

Tuesday & Friday

BACK

superset [
Seated Lat-machine Pulls (long range): 4 sets, 8 reps.
Pulldowns (from above head): 4 sets, 8 reps.
]
superset [
Chins: 4 sets, 8 reps (no weights attached to body).
One-arm Pulls (on pulley): 4 sets, 8 reps.
]
Deadlifts: 4 sets, 15–20 reps.

BICEPS

Dumbbell Curls (on preacher bench): 5 sets, 8 reps.

Reverse Curls (with cambered bar on preacher bench): 5 sets, 8 reps.
Concentration Curls (with dumbbell or barbell while lying on bench): 5 sets, 8 reps.
(The three exercises are done in tri-set fashion, with Scott resting only on completion of the last exercise. Then cycle is repeated.)

TRICEPS

Triceps Press (in lying position): 8–10 sets, 8 reps (cambered bar).
Triceps Extensions (using rope): 8–10 sets, 8 reps.
Bent-over Triceps Extensions (with dumbbell): 8–10 sets, 8 reps.

Wednesday & Saturday

SHOULDERS

Seated Dumbbell Press: 6–8 sets, 6 reps.
(Starts with 50-lb. dumbbells, works up to 90.)
Lateral Raises (one arm at a time): 6 sets, 6 reps.
Bent-over Lateral Raises: 6–8 sets, 6 reps.

THIGHS

Regular Squats (increasing poundage each succeeding set): 10–12 sets, 6–8 reps.
Hack Squats: 5 sets, 6–8 reps.

FOREARMS

Wrist Curls (with heavy barbell): 4 sets, 8 reps.
Reverse Curls (with regular barbell): 4 sets, 8 reps.

Marjo Selin's Routine

Monday

ABDOMINALS

Sit-ups: 3 sets, 20 reps.
Roman Chair Sit-ups: 3 sets, 20 reps.
Incline Leg Raises: 3 sets, 20 reps.

BACK

Lat Pulldowns: 1 set, 10 reps (150 lbs.); 3 sets, 4
  reps (180 lbs.).
One-arm Dumbbell Row: 1 set, 10 reps (70 lbs.);
  3 sets, 6–8 reps (110 lbs.).

CHEST

Bench Press: 1 set, 10 reps (95 lbs.); 1 set, 6 reps
  (115 lbs.); 3 sets, 3–4 reps (120 lbs.).
Incline Bench Press: 1 set, 10 reps (95 lbs.); 3
  sets, 8 reps (105 lbs.).
Dumbbell Pullovers: 1 set, 15 reps (40 lbs.); 3
  sets, 8–10 reps (65 lbs.).

SHOULDERS

Seated Press (behind neck): 2 sets, 10 reps (65
  lbs.); 3 sets, 8 reps (85 lbs.).
Upright Row: 1 set, 10 reps (70 lbs.); 3 sets,
  6–8 reps (95 lbs.).

Tuesday

ABDOMINALS

(Same as exercises for Monday.)

LEGS

Squats: 1 set, 12 reps (135 lbs.); 1 set, 10 reps
  (155 lbs.); 3 sets, 6 reps (185 lbs.).
Leg Extensions: 1 set, 10 reps (100 lbs.); 3 sets,
  5–6 reps (180 lbs.).
Leg Curls: 1 set, 20 reps (40 lbs.); 1 set, 10 reps
  (60 lbs.); 3 sets, 6–8 reps (80 lbs.).
Standing Calf Raises: (gradually increases
  weight for a good "burn.")
Seated Calf Raises: 1 set, 15–20 reps (90 lbs.);
  3–5 sets, 6–8 reps (160 lbs.).

Method

Warm-up sets are not included. Monday and
  Tuesday are heavy days; Thursday and Friday are medium-heavy days. Six weeks
  before a contest this is changed to a six-day-
  per-week routine.

TRICEPS

Seated Dumbbell Triceps Curls: 1 set, 10 reps (45 lbs.); 3 sets, 6 reps (70 lbs.).
Cable Pressdowns: 1 set, 20 reps (50 lbs.); 3 sets, 8 reps (90 lbs.).

BICEPS

Barbell Curls: 1 set, 10 reps (70 lbs.); 3 sets, 4–5 reps (100 lbs.).
Close-grip Curls (biceps machine): 3 sets, 10 reps (35 lbs.).
Seated Isolated Dumbbell Curls: 3 sets, 8 reps (35 lbs.).

Thursday

ABDOMINALS

(Same as exercises for Monday.)

BACK

Deadlifts: 1 set, 15 reps (135 lbs.); 3 sets, 10 reps (185 lbs.); 3 sets, 6 reps (205 lbs.).
Wide-grip Front Chins: 3–5 sets, 8 reps.
Seated Cable Row: 1 set, 15 reps (100 lbs.); 3 sets, 8 reps (140 lbs.).

CHEST

Bench Press: 3 sets, 10 reps (105 lbs.).
Inner-pec Press (machine): 3 sets, 10 reps (80 lbs.).
Cable Chest Lateral Pulley: 3 sets, 10 reps (50 lbs.).

SHOULDERS

Neck Press (machine): 3 sets, 6–8 reps (40 lbs.).
Upright Row: 3 sets, 10 reps (80 lbs.).
Bent-over Rear Deltoid Raises (cable): 3 sets, 10–15 reps (15 lbs.).

Friday

ABDOMINALS

Crunches: 3 sets, 20 reps.
Roman Chair Sit-ups with Twist: 3 sets, 20 reps.
Chinning-bar Leg Raises: 3 sets, 20 reps.

LEGS

Hack Squats: 2 sets, 10 reps (90 lbs.); 3 sets, 4–6 reps (155 lbs.).
Leg Press: 3 sets, 10 reps (290 lbs.); 2 sets, 6 reps (340 lbs.).
Leg Extensions: 3 sets, 10 reps (120 lbs.).
Leg Curls: 3 sets, 10 reps (60 lbs.).
Seated Calf Raises: 3 sets, 15 reps (115 lbs.).
Donkey Calf Raises: 3 sets, 20 reps.
Toe Press (leg-press machine): 3 sets, 15 reps (200 lbs.).

BICEPS

Scott Bench Biceps Curls: 1 set, 15 reps (50 lbs.); 3 sets, 10 reps (65 lbs.).
Seated Isolated Dumbbell Curls: 3 sets, 10 reps (30 lbs.).

TRICEPS

Seated Dumbbell Triceps Curls: 3 sets, 10 reps (60 lbs.).
Cable Pressdowns: 3 sets, 10 reps (80 lbs.).
Triceps Extensions (bench): 3 sets, 15 reps.

Kal Szkalak's Routine

Method

Monday, Thursday:
Chest, Back, Waist, and Calves.
Tuesday, Friday:
Shoulders, Biceps, Triceps, Waist, and Calves.
Wednesday, Saturday:
Thighs, Calves, and Waist.
Three months before a contest each body part
is trained three days per week. Sets remain
the same.

CHEST

Bench Press: 4 sets, 8 reps.
Incline Press: 4 sets, 8 reps.
Decline Press: 4 sets, 8 reps.
Flat Flyes: 4 sets, 8 reps.
Pulley Crossovers: 4 sets, 8 reps.
Pullovers (dumbbell): 4 sets, 10–12 reps.

BACK

Chins: 4 sets, 10 reps.
T-bar Row: 4 sets, 8 reps.
Dumbbell Row: 4 sets, 8 reps.
Seated Row: 4 sets, 8 reps.
Pulldowns (back to neck): 4 sets, 8 reps.
Close-grip Pulldowns: 4 sets, 8 reps.

THIGHS

Leg Extensions: 8 sets, 10–20 reps (increasing weight).
Front Squats: 5 sets, 15–20 reps (increasing weight).
Hack Squats or Leg Press: 6 sets, 10–15 reps (increasing weight).
Leg Curls: 8 sets, 10–15 reps (increasing weight).

CALVES

Standing Toe Raises: 4 sets, 12 reps.
Seated Toe Raises: 4 sets, 12 reps.
Toe Raises (on leg-press machine): 4 sets, 12 reps.

SHOULDERS

super set ⎡ Seated Press (behind neck): 4 sets, 8 reps.
⎣ Upright Row: 4 sets, 8 reps.

super set ⎡ Laterals: 4 sets, 8 reps.
⎣ Cable Laterals: 4 sets, 8 reps.

super set ⎡ Bent-over Cable Rear Laterals: 4 sets, 8 reps.
⎣ Bent-over Dumbbell Rear Laterals: 4 sets, 8 reps.

WAIST

Hanging Knee Raises: 200 reps.
Roman Chair Sit-ups: 200 reps.
Crunches: 200 reps.

BICEPS

Incline Curls: 4 sets, 8 reps.
Preacher Curls: 4 sets, 8 reps.
Standing or Alternate Curls: 4 sets, 8 reps.
Machine Curls: 4 sets, 8 reps.
Concentration Curls: 4 sets, 8 reps.

TRICEPS

Lying French Press: 4 sets, 8 reps.
One-arm Extensions: 4 sets, 8 reps.
Pressdowns: 4 sets, 8 reps.
Kneeling Rope Extensions: 4 sets, 8 reps.
One-arm Pressdowns (reverse grip): 4 sets, 9 reps (decreasing weight).

Ron Teufel's Routine

Note: While he has used squats for most of his training career, Ron seldom uses the movement today, since his thighs have all the mass they can carry without spoiling their symmetry. However, he recommends the various squat exercises and movements on the leg-press machine to those who still require added size in their thighs.

Note also that while Ron always trains his abdominals every day, he works his calves only four times a week, sometimes five before a contest.

Monday, Wednesday, Friday

CHEST

super set [Incline Press: 4 sets, 10–15 reps.
Dumbbell Flyes: 4 sets, 10–15 reps.

super set [Incline Press (machine): 4 sets, 10–15 reps.
Decline Flyes (pulleys): 4 sets, 10–15 reps.

super set [Bench Press: 4 sets, 10–15 reps.
Cable Crossovers: 4 sets, 10–15 reps.

BACK

super set [Chins (to front): 5 sets, 10–12 reps.
Pulldowns (to back): 5 sets, 10–12 reps.

super set [Pulldowns (to front, shoulder-width grip): 4 sets, 12 reps.
Seated Row (wide grip): 4 sets, 12 reps.

One-arm Dumbbell Row: 2–3 sets, 12 reps. (Sometimes rows with barbell)

Hyperextensions: 4 sets, 12–15 reps.

Tuesday, Thursday, Saturday

SHOULDERS

super set [Press behind Neck: 5 sets, 10–12 reps.
Lateral Raises (with dumbbells): 5 sets, 10–12 reps.

super set [Dumbbell Press (two arm): 5 sets, 10–12 reps.
Bent-over Laterals (cables): 5 sets, 10–12 reps.

super set [Upright Row (with barbell): 5 sets, 10–12 reps.
Barbell Shrugs: 5 sets, 10–12 reps.

(The last two exercises are performed once a week only.)

TRICEPS

super set ⌈ Lat-machine Pressdowns: 4 sets, 10–12 reps.
       ⌊ Triceps Extensions (with rope): 4 sets, 10–12 reps.
French Press (supine): 4 sets, 10–12 reps.
One-arm Triceps Extensions: 4 sets, 10–12 reps.
   (Sometimes uses a barbell for seated triceps extensions.)

BICEPS

Concentration Curls (with dumbbells): 4 sets, 10 reps.
super set ⌈ Two-arm Dumbbell Curls: 4 sets, 10 reps.
       ⌊ Preacher Bench Curls: 4 sets, 10 reps.
super set ⌈ Regular Barbell Curls: 4 sets, 10 reps.
       ⌊ Alternate Dumbbell Curls: 4 sets, 10 reps.

Note: While Teufel trains each body part three times weekly, he nevertheless works his triceps once a week normally—never more than twice weekly. He is satisfied that they receive enough work from shoulder and chest routines.

Tuesday, Thursday, Saturday Evenings

ABDOMINALS

Sit-ups, Leg Raises, Roman Chair Crunches.
(He does 100 repetitions for each exercise, twisting right and left at the top of each movement.)

CALVES

Standing Heel Raises: 10 sets, 15 reps.
Seated Heel Raises: 10 sets, 15 reps.

THIGHS

Single-leg Extensions (on machine): 4 sets, 15 reps.
Leg Curls (on incline): 4 sets, 15 reps.
Leg Curls (on flat bench): 4 sets, 15 reps.
Leg Extensions (both legs): 3 sets, 20 reps.
Power-driver Squats: 3 sets, 20 reps.

Ken Waller's Routine

CHEST

Bench Press: 6 sets, 10–15 reps.
Incline Bench Press: 6 sets, 10–15 reps.
Decline Bench Press: 6 sets, 10–15 reps.
Pulley Crossovers: 6 sets, 10 reps.
Special Flyes (like a press with a complete
    stretch): 6 sets, 10 reps.

BACK

Wide-grip Pulldowns (to front): 3 sets, 12 reps.
Wide-grip Pulldowns (to back): 3 sets, 12 reps.
Close-grip Pulldowns: 3 sets, 12 reps.
Long Cable Row (from high pulley): 5 sets, 12
    reps.
Long Cable Row (from low pulley): 5 sets, 12
    reps.
T-Bar Row: 5 sets, 12 reps.
Hyperextensions: 5 sets, 15 reps.

SHOULDERS

Front Barbell Raises: 2 sets, 12 reps.
Side Laterals (various hand angles): 8 sets, 12
    reps.
Laterals (starts in back of body): 4 sets, 12 reps.
Seated Dumbbell Upright Row: 4 sets, 12 reps.
Standing Upright Row: 4 sets, 12 reps.
One-arm Laterals: 4 sets, 12 reps.

THIGHS

Leg Extensions: 5 sets, 12–15 reps.
Leg Curls: 5 sets, 12–15 reps.
Machine Squats: 5 sets, 12–15 reps.
Frog Squats: 5 sets, 12–15 reps.

BICEPS

Standing Dumbbell Curls: 4 sets, 12 reps.
Concentration Curls: 4 sets, 12 reps.
E-Z Bar Curls: 4 sets, 12 reps.
Barbell Curls: 4 sets, 12 reps.
*Concentration Curls
*Barbell Curls (light)
*Barbell Curls (heavy)
*One-arm Cable Curls
*Performed as a compound set for 4 cycles of
10 reps each.

TRICEPS

Pressdowns
Reverse Dips
Kickbacks
(Due to injuries, Ken doesn't count sets or reps.
He just works as hard as he can on this body
part for 40–60 minutes.)

CALVES

Seated Toe Raises: 5 sets, 15–20 reps.
Standing Toe Raises: 3 sets, 15–20 reps.
Non-Weight Toe Raises: 3 sets, 15–20 reps.

WAIST

Seated Leg Raises: 4 sets, 25 reps.
Hanging Knee Raises: 4 sets, 25 reps.
Crunches (with pelvic thrust): 100 reps.
Twists: 250 reps.
Roman Chair Sit-ups: 500 reps.
Lying Knee Raises: 100 reps.
Decline Sit-ups: for burns.

Method

Monday, Wednesday, Friday:
Chest, Back, Leg, Calves, and Waist.
Tuesday, Thursday, Saturday:
Shoulders, Biceps, Triceps, Calves, and Waist.
Off Season: 2 exercises per body part with 5
    sets each exercise.
On Season: See above.

Rick Wayne's Routine

CHEST

Bench Press (to neck): 10 sets, 8–12 reps.
Flyes: 6 sets, 6–12 reps as weight increases.
Incline Press: 6 sets, 6–12 reps as weight
increases.

SHOULDERS

Standing Laterals: 6 sets, 12–15 reps.
Dumbbell Press: 6 sets, 6–12 reps as weight
increases.
Seated Bent-over Lateral Raises: 6 sets, 8 reps.

ARMS

super set ⎡ Barbell Curls: 6 sets, 8–10 reps.
⎣ Pressdowns: 6 sets, 8–10 reps.
super set ⎡ Alternate Curls: 6 sets, 8–10 reps.
⎣ One-arm Extensions: 6 sets, 8–10 reps.
super set ⎡ Concentration Curls: 6 sets, 8–10 reps.
⎣ Triceps Rope Extensions: 6 sets, 8–10 reps.

BACK

One-arm Row: 6 sets, 8–10 reps.
Seated Pulley Row: 6 sets, 8–10 reps.
Chins: 10 sets, as many reps as possible.

THIGHS

Squats: 6 sets, 12–15 reps.
super set ⎡ Leg Extensions: 6 sets, 12–15 reps.
⎣ Leg Curls: 6 sets, 12–15 reps.

CALVES

tri set ⎡ Donkey Raises: 6 sets.
⎢ Standing Toe Raises: 6 sets.
⎣ Freestyle Toe Raises (one leg at a time): 6 sets.
(Performed as a tri-set and does approximately
50 reps each movement.)

WAIST

tri set ⎡ Hanging Leg Raises: 5 sets, 30 reps.
⎢ Crunches: 5 sets, 25 reps.
⎣ Twists: 5 sets, 25 reps.
(Performed as a tri-set.)

Method

Monday, Thursday:
Chest, Shoulder, Arms, Waist, and Calves.
Tuesday, Friday:
Back, Legs, Waist, and Calves.

Frank Zane's Routine

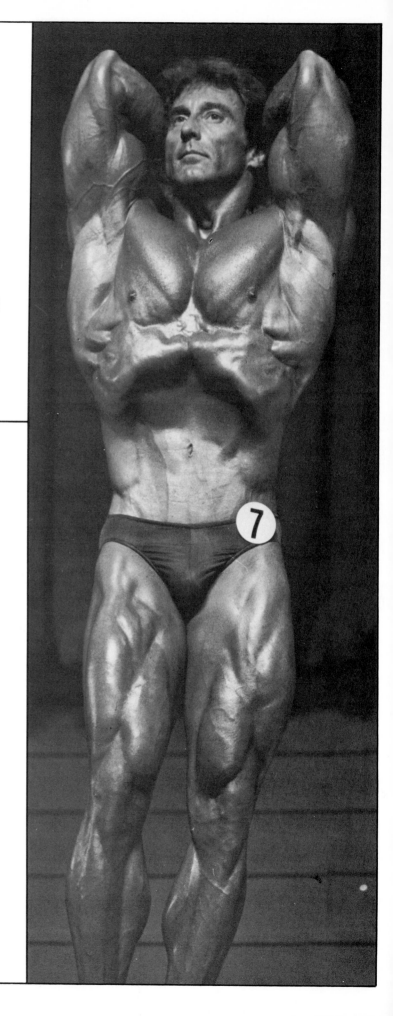

Monday, Wednesday, Friday Mornings

CHEST

Bench Press: 6–8 sets, 6–10 reps.
Low Incline Press (dumbbells or machine): 6
    sets, 10 reps.
Flyes (on decline bench): 6 sets, 10 reps.
Pullovers (across bench with dumbbells): 6 sets,
    15 reps.
(Reps decrease in some cases with increased
    weights.)

TRICEPS

Close-grip Bench Press (elbows out to sides,
    non-lock style, hands approximately 12
    inches [30 cm] apart to work outer head of
    the muscle)
Dumbbell Press (both hands, non-lock style)
One-arm Dumbbell Extensions (non-lock style)
Dumbbell Kickbacks (on incline bench in lock-
    out style)
Triceps Press (lying with head off bench, non-
    lock)
(Trains fast; performs 3 cycles of above move-
    ments.)

ABDOMINALS

Roman Chair Sit-ups: 100 reps.
Leg Raises (on incline board): 4 sets, 25 reps.

Afternoon Session

DELTOIDS

Press behind Neck (or Seated Dumbbell Press)
Alternate Front Raises
(Above movements in super-set style; he does
    8–10 reps on the first, 10 reps on the
    second. Altogether, he does 6 supersets).
Lateral Raises: 6 sets, 8 reps.
Rear Delt Raises (bent over): 6 sets, 8 reps.

ABDOMINALS

(Repeats morning routine.)

Tuesday, Thursday, Saturday Mornings

BACK

Bent-over Row (barbell or T-bar): 6 sets, 8 reps.
Low Cable Row: 6 sets, 10 reps.
One-arm Row (dumbbell): 5 sets, 8 reps.
Pulldowns (front of neck): 4 sets, 10 reps.
Pulldowns (back of neck): 4 sets, 10 reps.

BICEPS

Concentration Curls (off-center grip to work
    outer head of the biceps): 4 sets, 10 reps.
    (Supinates wrist through movement.)
Incline Dumbbell Curls (elbow in): 4 sets, 8
    reps.
Alternate Dumbbell Curls (supinating): 3 sets, 8
    reps.
Barbell Curls (90–130 lbs): 4 sets, 8 reps.

FOREARMS

Reverse Barbell Curls: 4 sets, 12–15 reps.
Wrist curls (end of bench): 4 sets, 12–15 reps.

ABDOMINALS

Same as previous routine or he might do
    instead:
Seated Twists: 1 set, 100 reps.
Hanging Knee Raises: 4 sets, 25 reps.

Afternoon Session

THIGHS

Leg Extensions: 4 sets, 15–20 reps.
Non-lock Leg Press: 4 sets, 12 reps.
Parallel Squats: 4 sets, 10 reps (135–245 lbs).
Leg Curls: 4 sets, 12 reps.

CALVES

Donkey Raises: 4 sets, 15 reps.
Standing Toe Raises (knees locked): 4 sets, 15
    reps.
Standing Toe Raises (knees bent): 4 sets, 15
    reps.
Toe Raises (toes turned in): 4 sets, 15 reps.
Seated Toe Raises: 4 sets, 15 reps.
(Trains this body part 3–4 times weekly.)

ABDOMINALS

(Same as above.)

Getting Physical: Exercises

Listed below is a variety of exercises (self-explanatory) for the *major* body parts. The potential combinations of exercises that comprise a workout for a particular body part are endless. Provided with the basic, fundamental exercises, you can design a program that fits your particular needs.

Exercise routines are obviously an individual matter. What works for one person may not work for another. Find out what gives you the best results and go for it!

NOTE: Vary the angles (flat, incline, and decline), grips (narrow, medium, and wide), positions (seated, standing, kneeling, and lying), direction (facing towards and away from the apparatus), and intensity of the movements to instantly form a brand-new exercise that will shock and stimulate the body into growth.

Abdominals

alternate knee kicks
bench leg raises
bent-knee leg raises
bent-knee sit-ups
bent-knee twisting sit-ups
broomstick twists
chinning-bar leg raises

cross-ankle crunches
crunches
decline sit-ups
decline weighted sit-ups
dip-stand "V" leg raises
dumbbell torso twists
flat-bench twisting leg raises
hanging knee-ins
hanging leg raises
heel-high sit-ups
hip rolls
incline leg circles
incline sit-ups
incline twisting sit-ups
incline leg pull-ins
jackknives
low-pulley leg pull-ins
lying leg raises
Roman chair sit-ups
rope crunches
scissors
seated side bends
side bends
side knee raises
side leg raises
sit-ups
twisting sit-ups
vertical-bench "V" leg raises
wall sit-ups
weighted chinning-bar leg raises
weighted sit-ups

Back

barbell power cleans
barbell shrugs
barbell snatches
barbell split cleans
bent-arm barbell pullovers
bent-over barbell rowing
bent-over dumbbell rowing
chins
deadlifts
dumbbell shrugs
dumbbell snatches
dumbbell split cleans
front chins
front-to-rear lat pulldowns
good mornings
high-bench barbell-lat pull-ups
hyperextensions
Kelso* shrugs
lat pulldowns (front & rear)
low-pulley rowing
partner lat stretch (with towel)
pull-ups to the waist
rear chins
reverse-grip chins
reverse-grip front-lat pulldowns
seated pulley rowing
side-to-side front chins
single-arm bent-over dumbbell rowing
single-arm cable rowing
single-arm rowing
stiff-leg deadlifts
T-bar rowing
twisting hyperextensions
upright rowing
weighted front chins
weighted rear chins
weighted reverse-grip chins

*See glossary section

Biceps

alternate Scott curls
alternate dumbbell cheat curls
alternate dumbbell curls
barbell curls
barbell preacher curls
cable curls
concentration curls
concentration curls on low pulley
dumbbell preacher curls
E-Z barbell curls
French press
hammer curls
high-bench E-Z curls
low-pulley alternate curls
pulley curls
rack barbell curls
rack dumbbell curls
reverse-grip E-Z barbell curls
reverse-grip Scott curls on low pulley
reverse-grip barbell curls
reverse-grip dumbbell curls
reverse-grip preacher curls
Scott curls
Scott curls on low pulley
single-arm curls on low pulley
single-arm dumbbell curls over incline bench
single-arm low-pulley curls

Calves

alternate donkey toe raises
alternate toe raises on leg-press machine
barbell toe raises
calf press
donkey toe raises
free-toe raises with/without block
hack-machine toe raises
negative-resistance donkey toe raises
seated barbell toe raises
seated calf-machine toe raises
seated dumbbell toe raises
single-leg calf raises
single-leg calf stretch against wall
single-leg donkey toe raises
single-leg dumbbell toe raises
single-leg toe raises with block
standing calf-machine toe raises
standing toe raises on power rack

Chest

alternate dumbbell raises
bench crossovers
bench press
bent-arm barbell pullovers
bent-arm dumbbell pullover and press
cable crossovers
chest crossovers over bench
cross-bench dumbbell pullovers
dips between stools with feet elevated
dumbbell bench press
dumbbell flyes
forward dips
front barbell rowing
high-pulley chest laterals
high-pulley pec crossovers
inner-pec press on pec deck
Kelso* shrugs
laterals
low-pulley chest laterals
machine bench press
parallel bar dips
pec-deck crunches
pec-deck flyes
pulley crossovers
push-ups
push-ups between benches
push-ups with feet on bench
straight-arm barbell pullovers
weighted dips between benches
weighted push-ups
weighted push-ups between benches

*See glossary section

Forearms and Wrists

barbell palms-down wrist curls
barbell palms-up wrist curls
barbell wrist curls (behind the back)
dumbbell palms-down wrist curls
dumbbell palms-up wrist curls
dumbbell palms-up wrist curls (behind the back)
hammer curls
hand grips
low-pulley palms-down wrist curls

low-pulley palms-up wrist curls
Olympic-plate hand squeezes
preacher-bench wrist curls
reverse curls
reverse wrist curls
rubber-ball hand squeezes
thumbs-up dumbbell curls
wrist curls on high pulley
wrists curls over bench
wrist rollers
wrist rollers over bench
Zottman curls

Neck and Trapezius

barbell shrugs
deadlifts
free-hand seated neck resistance
head-harness barbell-plate neck resistance
head-harness high-pulley neck resistance
head-harness low-pulley neck resistance
kneeling neck resistance with partner
standing towel resistance
supine barbell-plate neck resistance
wrestler's shrugs

Shoulders

alternate front deltoid raises
barbell press in front and behind neck
barbell upright rowing
bent-over cable laterals
bent-over lateral raises
bent-over laterals
bent-over low-pulley side laterals
cable side laterals
clean and press
dumbbell front raises
dumbbell front-and-side lateral raises
dumbbell press
dumbbell side laterals
dumbbell upright rowing
front barbell raises
high-pulley rear-deltoid raises
Hise* breathing shrugs
Kelso* shrugs

lateral raises
low-pulley rear-deltoid circles
low-pulley upright rowing
machine press
military press
palms-in dumbbell press
palms-out dumbbell press
pec-deck rear-deltoid raises
press behind neck
prone incline laterals
rear-deltoid raises
straight-arm barbell front raises
straight-arm dumbbell front raises

*See glossary section

Thighs

barbell jump squats
belt* squats
duck squats
dumbbell lunges
free-hand lunges
free-hand squats
front squats
hack squats
half-squats with heels elevated
Jefferson* lifts
leg crossovers
leg curls
leg extensions
leg press
leg press on sled machine
low-pulley thigh extensions
lunges
lying side scissors
reverse-direction hack squats
side lunges
single-leg biceps curls
single-leg low-pulley knee-to-chest raises
single-leg thigh extensions
sissy squats
squats
stiff-leg deadlifts
stiff-leg good mornings
Zercher* squats

*See glossary section

Triceps

alternate dumbbell triceps curls
alternate triceps extensions on high pulley
barbell extensions
barbell pullovers
barbell triceps press
bench dips
bent-over low-pulley triceps curls
close-grip bench press
dips
dumbbell triceps curls
French press
high-pulley triceps curls
incline reverse-grip triceps pressdowns on lat machine
low-pulley single-arm triceps curls
low-pulley two-arm triceps curls
pulley pushdowns
push-ups
reverse-grip barbell pullovers
reverse-grip dips
reverse-grip triceps pressdowns on lat machine
rope triceps extensions behind the neck
towel triceps curls
triceps extension on high pulley
triceps kickbacks
triceps pressdowns on lat machine

Tom Platz

Bodybuilding Tips

In this sport, one piece of information can sometimes make the difference between winning or losing, training right or wrong, growing or stagnating. Good advice is always welcome. If this is what you need, read the following tips.

Mohamed Makkawy

Abdominals
○ Keep the knees slightly bent when performing sit-ups to minimize back strain.

Back
○ The hyperextension is the only lower-back exercise that stretches the spine yet develops the spinal erector muscles.
○ When performing the deadlift, keep the back flat and the head held high as you straighten your body.
○ An effective way to enhance your V-shape is to perform wide-grip dips. Throughout the dipping motion, keep the feet forward, chin on chest, and elbows out to the sides while stretching downwards as far as possible.

Biceps
○ Curls from the end of a bench are good for building biceps with a high peak.
○ When performing biceps curls, keep the wrists locked to maximize isolation of the muscle.
○ Squeeze your biceps at the top of each curl movement for additional peak contraction.
○ As an added twist to the standard biceps curl, perform the lying dumbbell curl. The additional stress on the biceps is unbelievable.
○ While doing the Scott curl, keep the arms straight and do not bounce the weight.

Calves
○ Stretch your calves between sets of calf raises to prevent cramping and to keep the muscle loose.
○ When performing calf raises (on a block), raise the heels as high as possible and come down as low as possible.
○ Always use the three toe positions (inward, outward, and straight ahead) when doing calf raises.

Chest

- When performing straight-arm pullovers, keep the arms straight over a full range of motion to obtain maximum benefit. *Do not* use very heavy weights.
- The key to dumbbell presses is to keep the elbows back while lowering the dumbbells as far as possible.
- For incline flyes, keep the elbows low rather than concentrating on using heavy weights.
- Dumbbell pullovers are super for developing the serratus muscle.
- When performing pulley crossovers, keep pulling downwards on the cables until the hands touch in front of the hips.
- The dumbbell bench press allows a greater stretch at the bottom of the movement than does the regular barbell variation.

Shoulders

- When performing dumbbell side laterals, at the top of the movement, rotate your thumbs slightly downwards to place more stress on the deltoids.
- It is essential to shrug the shoulders both upwards and rearwards.
- Presses behind the neck are excellent for developing all three heads of the deltoids.
- To keep the tension constant during upright rows, hold the barbell away from your body.

Thighs

- Do not bounce at the bottom of the squat movement. This prevents knee and lower-back injuries.
- When performing leg extensions, hold the legs in an extended position for 2–3 seconds to really wcrk the quadriceps, then lower them.
- For leg curls, lean on your elbows to make it hard to lift your buttocks during the exercise. This keeps the stress on the hamstrings.
- Front squats place more stress on the muscles just above the knees than do regular squats.
- Squats can thicken the spinal erectors.
- Never lift a loaded bar from the squat racks unless you are completely under it, with both feet flat on the floor and evenly spaced. Your back should also be straight.
- When performing squats, if you find yourself winded before your thighs give out, try doing exercises that will increase your cardiovascular efficiency: e.g., running, cycling, jumping rope.

Triceps

- Keep elbows tucked inward to maximize the stress when performing triceps pressdowns.
- With triceps dips, stretch downwards as far as possible at the bottom of the movement. Tense the triceps at the completion of each rep.
- For maximum stress on the triceps during the lying triceps extension, keep the upper arms as straight as possible.
- Lying triceps extensions done with an *E-Z* curl bar bulk up the triceps.
- When performing lying triceps extensions, try to keep the elbows from travelling outward from the body.
- Pulley pushdowns can quickly give the triceps a "horseshoe" shape by developing the outer head of the muscle.

Workout Routines

- Vary your routines to shock the body parts from every conceivable angle.
- After a layoff, train with less intensity and gradually increase your efforts over a period of 6–10 workouts.
- Try to limit layoffs to no more than 2–4 weeks.
- When training to accomplish total muscle failure with forced and negative reps, a training partner is absolutely essential.
- Take extra time and care when attempting a new training routine.
- Be sure to warm up completely before beginning your workouts to prevent injury.

Miscellaneous

- To remove water from under the skin, it is necessary to eliminate sodium from your diet two weeks before a competition.
- Flex between sets to help rid the body of water, to harden your physique, and to aid in bringing out muscularity.
- When performing lunges, keep the trunk erect to bring out maximum flexion in the hip joint, which causes greater use of the glutes.
- Beware of lifting too much weight.
- If your elbows are aggravated during certain exercises, try using a lighter weight, changing the grip, or altering your hand spacing.
- For the most part, inhale during the easiest portion of an exercise and exhale as you complete the hardest portion of it.
- Remember, when lifting a weight from the floor, bend your knees, flatten your back, stick your buttocks out forcefully, and lift *carefully*.

Appendices

John Terilli

Directory

Nearly every address you could possibly need
is included here. Please note that your reply
would be faster if you enclose a self-addressed
stamped envelope with your letter.

a

AAU
3400 W. 86th St., Indianapolis, IN 46268

ACB Gym/Weider International, 9 Hoge Lane
B 8200 Brugge, Belgium/050-31-64-94/telex: 82169 acbgym b

AFWB, c/o Vicki Smith
PO Box 363, Niwot, CO 80544-0363

Amateur Athletic Union, AAU House
3400 W. 86th St., Indianapolis, IN 46268

American Bodybuilding Coordinating Committee
3901 W. 111th St., #1, Inglewood, CA 90303

American Drug Free Powerlifting Association
PO Box 351, Bay St., St. Louis, MO 39520

American Sports Management, 27208 Southfield Rd., Suite 3,
Lathrup Village, MI 48076/313-557-2320

Dinah Anderson, PO Box 1773
Big Spring, TX 79721/915-6731

Al Antuck, York Barbell Co., Inc.
PO Box 1707, York, PA 17405

Bill Ashpaugh
19-1/2 S. 9th St., Noblesville, IN 46060

Sherry Atton, c/o Scotty's Gym, 303 First Avenue North
Saskatoon, Saskatchewan, Canada S7K 1X5/306-244-8330

Donald Ausmus
608 Esperanza, McAllen, TX 78501

b

Josephine Baker, c/o East Coast Gym
242 Dover Rd., South Toms River, NJ 08757

Richard Baldwin, Baldwin's Body Forum
513 W. Gaines St., Tallahassee, FL 31302

John Balik
PO Box 777, Santa Monica, CA 90406

Samir Bannout
PO Box 244, Santa Monica, CA 90406

Leslie Barber
7311 Kimber, West Trenton, NJ 08628

John Barbero, Bath Beach Bodybuilding
95 Avenue U, Brooklyn, NY 11223

Michael Barbieri
8941 Provo Lane, St. Louis, MO 63123

Doris Barrilleaux
P.O. Box 937, Riverview, FL 33569

Garry Bartlett, c/o Muscle Training Illustrated
Powerhouse Publications, Inc., 801 Second Ave., New York, NY 10017

Clarence Bass
528 Chama, NE, Albuquerque, NM 87108/505-266-5858

Kay Baxter
PO Box 807, Kentfield, CA 94004/415-453-2300

Dolores Ali Beach
112 Custer St., Stamford, CT 06902

Troy Beck
18210 Promise Rd., Noblesville, IN 46060

Albert Beckles
PO Box 5005, Mission Hills, CA 91345-0005

Tim Belknap
PO Box 944, Santa Monica, CA 90406

Ulf Bengtsson, c/o IFBB Sweden
PO Box 2088, S 230 41 Bara, Sweden/40-444-86

Daniel Berumen
11150 Loch Avon Dr., Whittier, CA 90606

Better Bodies, Inc.
12 W. 21st St., New York, NY 11101/212-929-6789

Bob Birdsong
PO Box 4333, Palm Springs, CA 92263

Julien Blommaert, c/o ACB Gym/Weider International
9 Hoge Lane, B 8200 Brugge, Belgium/050-31-64-94/telex:
82169 acbgym b

Lori Bowen, Kuo International
767 Third Ave., 29th Floor, New York, NY 10017

Charles Bradshaw, c/o Bradshaw Physique Productions
PO Box 30, Oceanside, CA 92054/619-722-7486

Gene Brasher
1232 Center Point Rd., Birmingham, AL 35215/205-853-0818

Mike Bridges, Mike Bridges Systems
PO Box 5801, Arlington, TX 76011

Pete Broccoletti, c/o Icarus Press, Inc.
PO Box 1225, South Bend, IN 46624

Pam Brooks, c/o East Side Athletic Club
11322 E. 21st St., Tulsa, OK 74129/918-437-6298

Velma Buckles
115 N. Haven, Walled Lake, MI 48088

Albert Busek, c/o GmbH & Co.
PO Box 800323, 8000 Munich 80, West Germany

c

Andreas Cahling
PO Box 929, Venice, CA 90291

Roger Callard
PO Box 41, Santa Monica, CA 90406/213-306-3957

Frank Calta
4241 E. Busch Blvd., Tampa, FL 33617

Richard Cavaler
5914 12th St., Detroit, MI 48208

Cathy Chang, c/o Physique World, Inc.
1668 B South King St., Honolulu, HI 96826

Jim Charles
43 Love Lane, Oldswinford, Stourbridge, England NY8 2OH

Lydia Cheng, c/o Better Bodies, Inc.
12 W. 21st St., New York, NY 10010

Carolyn Cheshire
27 Ailsa Rd., St. Margarets, Twickenham, Middlesex, England TW1 11QJ

Mike Christian, c/o Gold's Gym
360 Hampton Dr., Venice, CA 90291

Christian Bodybuilding Association (CBA)
c/o Carlos DeJesus, 1822 Williamsburg Rd., Richmond, VA 23231

Paul Chua, President SABBF
5001 Beach Rd., No. 03-22 Golden Mile Complex, Singapore 0719

Tom Ciola, c/o The Natural Bodybuilder
2617 Genesee St., Utica, NY 13501

Barry Clothier
5285 Diamond Heights Blvd., #203, San Francisco, CA 94131/415-282-9474

Boyer Coe
PO Box 5877, Huntington Beach, CA 92646

Anita Columbu
2325 Westwood Blvd., W. Los Angeles, CA 90064

Franco Columbu
PO Box 415, Santa Monica, CA 90406

Greg Comeaux
PO Box 17556, Irvine, CA 92713

Lynn Conkwright
PO Box 4235, Virginia Beach, VA 23454/804-481-7979

Patty Cox
4600 Hyde Park Blvd., Apt. 145, Niagara Falls, NY 14305/716-284-6577

Rickey Dale Crain
PO Box 1322, Shawnee, OK 74801/405-275-3689

Candy Csencsits
R.D. 1, Box 726, Lenhartsville, PA 19534

d

Jim Dandrow
PO Box 21, Bloomfield, NJ 07003

Mario DaSilva
PO Box 36643, Los Angeles, CA 90036/213-386-9411

Steve and Ellen Davis
23115 Lyons Ave., Newhall, CA 91321/805-255-7373

Laura Dayton, c/o Strength Training for Beauty
1400 Stierlin Rd., Mountain View, CA 94043

Mike Dayton
PO Box 6410, Concord, CA 94524/415-827-5654

Greg DeFerro
PO Box 66194, Mar Vista, CA 90066-0194

Carlos DeJesus
1822 Williamsburg Rd., Suite 10, Richmond, VA 23231

Wayne DeMilia
PO Box 1490, Radio City Station, New York, NY 10019/516-997-3691/516-997-6413

Chris Dickerson, c/o Gold's Gym, Second Floor
360 Hampton Dr., Venice, CA 90291/213-399-2972

Bill Dobbins, c/o Flex Magazine
21100 Erwin St., Woodland Hills, CA 91367

Joy Dobson, c/o Demland Graphics
33 Leeds Rd., Dewsbury, West Yorkshire, England

Lance Dreher, Dreher-Marchand Enterprises, Inc.
PO Box 5, Oak Forest, IL 60452

Carla Dunlap, c/o Diamond Gym
732 Irvington Ave., Maplewood, NJ 07040/201-761-9833

Rosemarie Durfee
4167 Arrow Lane, Sarasota, FL 33582

e

George Eiferman
953 E. Sahara Ave., Suite 11-A, Las Vegas, NV 89104/702-733-1533

English Federation of Body Builders (EBFF)
72 Farmway, Alkrington, Middleton, Manchester, England

Scott Epstein, c/o Dan Lurie Barbell
149-76 254 St., Rosedale, NY 11422

John Erter
207 Lake Village Blvd., Blue Springs, MO 64010

Jeff and Cory Everson, c/o Samson and Delilah Enterprises
19001 Merion Dr., Northridge, CA 91326

f

Franco Fassi, c/o Sportman/Muscle Builder
Strada Francesca, Angolo Statale del Tonale, 24040 Zingonia (BG), Italy

Lou Ferrigno
PO Box 1671, Santa Monica, CA 90406

Bertil Fox, c/o Joe Weider
21100 Erwin St., Woodland Hills, CA 91367

Bev Francis, Kuo International
767 Third Ave., 29th Floor, NY, NY 10017

Lisser Frost-Larsen
Kaningardsvej 53, 2839 Virum, Denmark

Georgia Miller-Fudge
10113 14th St. North, Apt. 110, St. Petersburg, FL 33702

Johnny Fuller
3002 E. 20th St., Tucson, AZ 85716

Future Fitness
2828 Spreckles Lane, Redondo Beach, CA 90278

g

Cindy Gablehouse
7912 Broadview Dr., Lincoln, NE 68505

Charles Garfield
106 Evergreen Lane, Berkeley, CA 94705/415-849-0336

James Gaubert, c/o Gulf States Promotions
PO Box 2343, Lafayette, LA 70502

Vince Gironda, Vince's Gym
11262 Ventura Blvd., Studio City, CA 91604/213-980-0410

Charles Glass
742 E. 88th Pl., Los Angeles, CA 90002/213-971-4235

Mike Glass
PO Box 4587, Anaheim, CA 92803/415-533-2359

Gold's Gym
360 Hampton Dr., Venice, CA 90291/213-392-3005

Paul Graham
PO Box 27, Brighton Le Sands, New South Wales 2216, Australia

Paul and Carole Graham, c/o Paul Graham's Gym
288 The Grande Pde., Ramsgate, New South Wales 2216, Australia

Granite State Bodybuilding Association
PO Box 594, Dover, NH 03820

Bill Grant, c/o Margot, Les Grand Champs
1261 Bogis-Bossey, Switzerland (or PO Box 1493, Santa Monica, CA 90406)

Bob Green
11819-1/2 Laurelwood Dr., Studio City, CA 91604

John Grimek, c/o York Barbell Co., Inc.
PO Box 1707, York, PA 17405

Shelley Gruwell
PO Box 1329, Clovis, CA 93612

Pete Grymkowski, c/o Gold's Gym
360 Hampton Dr., Venice, CA 90291/213-392-3005

h

Lee Haney
PO Box 185, Santa Monica, CA 90406

Jackie Harrington
5502 NE Scandia Lane, #A311, Kansas City, MO 64118

Mary Hastings
14800 Robson, Detroit, MI 48227

Fred Hatfield
15343 Vanowen, #235, Van Nuys, CA 91406

Oscar Heidenstam, NABBA President
30 Craven St., Strand, London WC2N 5NT, England

Sheila Herman, c/o *Muscle & Fitness* Magazine
21100 Erwin St., Woodland Hills, CA 91367

Dan Howard, c/o Howard's Gym
17435 Newhope, Fountain Valley, CA 92708/714-556-8582

Gary Huddleston
501 N. Main, Guymon, OK 73942

i

IFBB, c/o Ben Weider
2875 Bates Rd., Montreal, Quebec, Canada H3S 1B7/517-731-3783/telex: 055-61488

International Physical Fitness
415 W. Court St., Flint, MI 48503

International Women's Bodybuilding Council, Inc.
1981 Brownsboro Rd., Louisville, KY 40206

Iron Man Gym
404 Mission Ave., Oceanside, CA 92054/619-722-7486

Bill Issac, c/o Big Island Gym
74-5605 Alapa St., Kailua Kona, HI 96740/808-329-9432

Dr. Walter Jekot
8635 W. Third St., Los Angeles, CA 90048/213-657-4481

Bill Jentz
W.S.P., Box 443, Hohokus, NJ 07423

Bob Jodkiewicz
PO Box 9461, Norfolk, VA 23505/213-820-7220

Dave Johns
PO Box 272, Pacoima, CA 91331

Cheryl Jones, Sta'Fit Health Center
133 Flagship Dr., Lutz, FL 33539

Jon Jordan
1651 Marmont, Los Angeles, CA 90069/213-650-1662/213-659-6630

Ed Jubinville
PO Box 662, Holyoke, MA 01041

k

Mike Katz, c/o World Gym East
295 Treadwell St., Hamden, CT 06514/203-281-7213

Bill Kazmaier, c/o Dynakaz, Inc.
PO Box 1974, Auburn, AL 36831-1974

John Kemper, c/o Diamond Gym
732 Irvington Ave., Maplewood, NJ 07040/201-761-9833

Robert Kennedy
Unit 2, 52 Bramsteele Rd., Brampton, Ontario, Canada L6W 3M5/416-791-8590

Dr. Robert Kerr
316 E. Las Tunas Dr., San Gabriel, CA 91776/213-285-1154/213-285-1155

Tim Kimber, c/o Gold's Gym
360 Hampton Dr., Venice, CA 90291

Jeff King
PO Box 80306, Forest Park Station, Springfield, MA 01108

Kay King-Nealy
12 E. 22nd St., #PHD, New York, NY 10010

Tom Kinney, T. K. Equipment
4 Franklin Ave., Mt. Vernon, NY 10550

Anna Knight
2807 Flakewood, Little Rock, AR 72207

Don Knipp
624 Warner Ave., #17-G, Huntington Beach, CA 92647

Susan Koch
1 Sycamore Ave., Little Silver, NJ 07739

Rod Koontz
PO Box 2288, Westminster, CA 92683

John Kuc, Kuc's Total Fitness System
PO Box 215, Mountaintop, PA 18707

l

Rich Labbe
62 Shawmut, Lewiston, ME 04240

Mike Lambert, c/o *Powerlifting USA*
PO Box 467, Camarillo, CA 93011

Edie Leen
PO Box 4577, Foster City, CA 94404

Angelito Lesta, c/o Demland Graphics
33 Leeds Rd., Dewsbury, West Yorkshire, England

Paul Love, c/o Love's Health Club
3050 Story Rd., San Jose, CA 95127/408-926-3765

Jesse Lujan
6514 Lake Ashmere Ct., San Diego, CA 92119/619-463-6443

Chris Lund
18 Craigshaw Square, Hylton Castle Estate, Sunderland-Tyne & Wear SR5 3NG, England

Dan Lurie, c/o *Muscle Training Illustrated*
Powerhouse Publications, Inc., 801 Second Ave., New York, NY 10017

Pat Luthy
PO Box 8803, Boise, ID 83707

Lisa Lyon
PO Box 585, Santa Monica, CA 90406

Mike MacDonald, Mike MacDonald Systems
15 N. Lake Ave., Duluth, MN 55802

Mohamed Makkawy, c/o Super Fitness
2110 Dundas St. East, Mississauga, Ontario, Canada L4X 1L9/416-272-4115

Ali Malla
1701 Washington Way, Venice, CA 90291

Jim Manion
140 East Mall Plaza, Carnegie, PA 15106/412-276-7771

Stella Martinez
1585 10th Ave., Suite 1, San Francisco, CA 94122/415-731-3443

Earl Maynard
520 S. La Brea, Inglewood, CA 213-673-8811

Chip McCain, McCain Productions
3100 S. Lamar, Suite 203, Austin, TX 78704

Sheritha McKenzie
2202 Pinewood Ave., #3C, Baltimore, MD 21214

Rachel McLish
PO Box 111, Santa Monica, CA 90406/213-855-1010

Julie McNew
PO Box 67276, Los Angeles, CA 90067

Matt Mendenhall
PO Box 934, Santa Monica, CA 90406

Mike Mentzer
PO Box 67276, Los Angeles, CA 90067

Ray Mentzer
PO Box 44, Santa Monica, CA 90406

John Carl Mese
17 NE 99th St., Miami Shores, FL 33138/305-757-7674

Heidi Miller
4840 Irving, #111, Irving, CA 92714

Jeff Mitchell, c/o Metro Fitness
716 Evelyn Ave., Linthicum Heights, MD 21090

Mae Mollica
PO Box 81886, San Diego, CA 92138

Carl J. Morelli
605 Third Ave., New York, NY 10158

Dr. Stan Morey
12101 N. 56th St., Tampa, FL 33612

n

John Nafpliotis, c/o *Lady Athlete*
PO Box 7235M, Lancaster, PA 17604

The National Fitness Association
PO Box 1754, Huntington Beach, CA 92647/714-979-0565

National Strength and Conditioning Association
PO Box 81410, Lincoln, NE 68501/402-472-3000

Natural Physique Center
104 Fourth Ave., New York, NY 10003/212-420-9585

Natural Bodybuilders of America
PO Box 5003, Utica, NY 13505/315-797-4191

Joe Nazario, c/o New Beginnings Health & Racquetball Club
ZM-174, Carr #2, Villa Caparra, Guaynabo, Puerto Rico 00657

Doc Neely
PO Box 490338, College Park, GA 30349/404-996-3627

Pat Neve
5031 N. 35th Ave., Phoenix, AZ 85016/602-841-1543

New Jersey Physique Committee, USA
PO Box 21, Bloomfield, NJ 07003/201-746-2019

F. A. Nicolini
4-D Somerset Dr., Suffern, NY 10901

NPC, c/o Jim Manion
140 East Mall Plaza, Carnegie, PA 15106/412-276-7771

NPC National Office
PO Box 2711, Pittsburgh, PA 15230/412-281-0400

Jack O'Bleness
3901 W. 111th St., Englewood, CA 90303/213-674-1985

Sergio Oliva
7200 North Ridge, Chicago, IL 60645

Olympic Amateur Wristwrestling Association
PO Box 247, Duluth, GA 30136

Olympus Gym
Rt. 611, Warrington, PA 18976

Phil Outlaw
5322 Trudy St., Charleston, SC 29405

p

Larry Pacifico
PO Box 14152 N.R. Br., Dayton, OH 45414

Danny Padilla
641 Brown St., Rochester, NY 14611

George Paine
PO Box 1597, GPO, Brooklyn, NY 11201/212-237-9292

Ken Passariello
PO Box 761, Orange, CT 06477

David and Peter Paul (The Barbarians), c/o Gold's Gym
360 Hampton Dr., Venice, CA 90291/213-392-3005

Bill Pearl
PO Box 1080, Phoenix, AZ 97535/503-535-3363

Tony Pearson, c/o Heavenly Bodies
PO Box 299, Northridge, CA 91328-0299

Audrey Perryman
24092 Amberley Dr., Sunnymead, CA 92388/714-653-2473

Don Peters, c/o Don Peter's Gym
18323 Sherman Way, Reseda, CA 91335/213-705-7774

Pillow, c/o Gold's Gym
360 Hampton Dr., Venice, CA 90291 (or PO Box 1076, Venice, CA 90294)

Dr. Lynn Pirie
413 N. 16th St., Phoenix, AZ 85016

Tina Plakinger, c/o Wedgewood Fitness Center
6807 W. Morgan Ave., Milwaukee, WI 53220

Tom Platz
PO Box 1262, Santa Monica, CA 90406

Benny Podda
217 Lake St., South Fork, PA 15956

Nancy Pollak
165 W. 83rd St., #41, New York, NY 10024

Gladys Portugues, c/o Better Bodies, Inc.
12 W. 21st St., New York, NY 10010/212-929-6789

Debbie Poston, c/o Athletic Fitness Center
13539 N. Florida Ave., Tampa, FL 33612/813-961-0595

Rick Poston, c/o Athletic Fitness Center
13539 N. Florida Ave., Tampa, FL 33612/813-961-0595

Peter Potter, c/o Hollywood Spa & Health Club
6712 Stirling Rd., Hollywood, FL 33024

John Powers
169 Miracle Strip Plaza, Ft. Walton Beach, FL 32548

r

Perry Rader, c/o Iron Man Magazine
PO Box 10, Alliance, NE 69301

Sandy Ranalli
2534 Reading Blvd., W. Lawn, PA 19609

Chuck Rappe
6101 Broadmoor, Mission, KS 66202

Steve Reeves
PO Box 807, Valley Center, CA 92082

Brenda Renz
10 W. Locust, Lodi, CA 95240

Bill Reynolds, c/o Muscle & Fitness Magazine
21100 Erwin St., Woodland Hills, CA 91367

Mark Ritter, c/o Muscle Training Illustrated
Powerhouse Publications, Inc., 801 Second Ave., New York, NY 10017

Mary Roberts
202 W. 20th St., Santa Ana, CA 92706/714-835-3900

Susan Roberts, c/o Roberts Health Club
930-B Carpenter Rd., Modesto, CA 95351/209-577-8661

Winston Roberts, c/o Winston's Fitness Center
4810 Jean Palon Blvd., Suite 311, Montreal, Quebec, Canada/514-622-8931

Robby Robinson
PO Box 982, Venice, CA 90291

Carlos Rodriguez, c/o Tucson Health Studios
Tucson, AZ/602-791-0489

Don Ross
11 C St., Vallejo, CA 94590

Dale Ruplinger
4611 Washington St., Davenport, IA 52806

Kathy Ruth, c/o Olympus Gym
Rt. 611, Warrington, PA 18976

s

Pete Samra, c/o Samra Nutrition
PO Box 1052, Santa Monica, CA 90406

Clark and Patty Sanchez
322 Muriel St., NE, Albuquerque, NM 87123

Ernie Santiago
PO Box 23161, Honolulu, HI 96822

Cliff Sawyer
64 June St., Worcester, MA 01602

Nina Schoenbaum
216 W. 89th St., #2C. New York, NY 10024

Arnold Schwarzenegger
PO Box 1234, Santa Monica, CA 90406

Larry Scott
PO Box 162, North Salt Lake, UT 84054

Ruthi Shaefer
3047 NW 1st, Gresham, OR 97030

Brad Shaw, c/o Eastern Lifter
PO Box 2161, Augusta, ME 04330

Sassy Shelton
3220 Gleason Dr., #68, Chattanooga, TN 37412

Peter Siegel
444 Lincoln Blvd., Suite 308, Venice, CA 90291/213-399-1963

Vicki Smith
PO Box 363, Niwot, CO 80544-0363

George Snyder, c/o Olympus Gym
Rt. 611, Warrington, PA 18976/215-343-9191

Southern Pacific Association AAU
4928 Lankershim Blvd., PO Box 6015, North Hollywood, CA 91603-6015

Bitsy Ray Spickard
2304 Bodily, Idaho Falls, ID 83402

Doug and Jeanne Splittgerber
513 E. Mitchell, Appleton, WI 54911

Oscar State
4 Godfrey Ave., Twickenham, TW2 7PF, England

John Terilli, c/o Paul Graham's Gym
288 The Grande Pde., Ramsgate, New South Wales, Australia

Russ Testo, 3 Oxford Rd., New York, NY 12180/516-274-0952

Joe Tete, c/o Tete's Nautilus Fitness Center
Coopertown Plaza, Burlington, NJ/609-386-3332

Dennis Tinerino
PO Box 299, Northridge, CA 91328-0299

Jan Todd
3212 Waverly Pkwy., Opelika, AL 36801

Mike Torchia
13 Bradhurst Ave., Hawthorne, NY 10572/914-592-8761

Kathy Tuite
PO Box 5075, Concord, CA 94524

U

United States Powerlifting Federation
PO Box 18485, Pensacola, FL 32523

United States Sports Academy
PO Box 8650, 124 University Blvd., Mobile, AL 36608

United States Weightlifting Federation, Inc.
1750 E. Boulder St., Colorado Springs, CO 80909/303-578-4508/telex: 452424

United World Bodybuilders, Inc.
PO Box 691578, Los Angeles, CA 90069

V

Joe Valdez
PO Box 5175, Whittier, CA 90607-5175

Walter van den Branden
van Waesbergestraat 50, 4561 AE Hulst, Holland

Dr. Carlin C. Venus
2666 Calle Manzano, Thousand Oaks, CA 91360/805-492-0455

Casey Viator
PO Box 314, Niwot, CO 80544

Marty Vranicar, c/o Marty Vranicar's World of Fitness
21 N. Third St., Lemoyne, PA 17043

Pete Vranicar, c/o Pete Vranicar's Health and Fitness Center
891 Eisenhower Blvd., Harrisburg, PA 17111

Ken Waller
PO Box 212, Santa Monica, CA 90405

Wally Boyco Productions, Inc.
PO Box 2378, Corona, CA 91720/714-371-0606

Russ Warner
1223 The Alameda, San Jose, CA 95126/408-293-9966

Rick Wayne, c/o Muscle & Fitness Magazine
21100 Erwin St., Woodland Hills, CA 91367

WBBG
1665 Utica Ave., Brooklyn, NY 11234

David Webster
43 West Rd., Irvine, Ayrshire KA12 8RE, Scotland

Ben Weider
2875 Bates Rd., Montreal, Quebec, Canada H35 1B7/514-731-3783/telex: 055-61488

Joe Weider, c/o Muscle & Fitness Magazine
21100 Erwin St., Woodland Hills, CA 91367

The Weider Research Clinic
Immaculate Conception Center, 4265 Papineau, Montreal, P.Q. H2H 1T3, Canada

Weightlifting Hall of Fame
PO Box 1707, York, PA 17405/717-767-6481

Steve Wennerstrom
19127 Wiersma St., Cerritos, CA 90701

Gema Wheeler
8334 Whitelfield, Dearborn Heights, MI 48127

Claudia Wilbourn
PO Box 167, Santa Monica, CA 90406

Jusup Wilcosz, c/o Sporting Gym
Olga Strasse 67, 7000 Stuttgart 1, Germany/0711-243656

Chuck Williams
1260 Tuxedo Square, Teaneck, NJ 07666/201-837-4726

Cindy Williams-Reichert
514 N. Ford Ave., #2, Wilmington, DE 19805

Jim Wilmer
204 Chell Rd., Joppa, MD 21085

Scott Wilson, c/o Gold's Gym
35 Notre Dame Ave., San Jose, CA 95113

Linda Wood-Hoyte, c/o Better Bodies, Inc.
12 W. 21st St., New York, NY 10010/212-929-6789

World Gym
2210 Main St., Santa Monica, CA 90405/213-399-9888

Dr. James Wright
7863 Grass Hollow, San Antonio, TX 78233

Frank Zane
PO Box 366, Santa Monica, CA 90406

Art Zeller
PO Box 254, Santa Monica, CA 90406

Bodybuilders' Trivia

It's interesting to learn little-known facts about the big-name bodybuilders. Did you know that . . .

Doris Barrilleaux organized the Superior Physique Association (SPA) in 1978 to promote women's bodybuilding, which later developed into the AFWB.

Tim Belknap is a diabetic.

Lori Bowen was the first woman to win the USA and American bodybuilding championships in the same year.

Gerard Buinoud and Jacques Neuville were the first French bodybuilders to ever win an IFBB amateur world championship.

Andreas Cahling was a junior national champion (in Sweden) in judo and wrestling.

Patsy Chapman is a Texas policewoman.

Boyer Coe is a codeveloper of the "Legg Shoe," which promotes development of the calf muscles.

Franco Columbu was a boxer with a record of 30 consecutive knockouts. He is also a doctor of chiropractic with a Ph.D. in nutrition.

Ed Corney trained for nearly 15 years before he entered his first contest.

Candy Csencsits was a state collegiate record holder on the uneven parallel bars in Pennsylvania.

Deborah Diana is a former rock climber.

Chris Dickerson was the first black to win an AAU Mr. America title.

Carla Dunlap was an Olympic-caliber synchronized swimmer. She is also the only consecutive two-time winner of the overall American Women's Bodybuilding Championship.

George Eiferman performed a cabaret act with the legendary Mae West.

Lou Ferrigno lost his hearing from an ear infection when he was a small child. He also played professional football for the Canadian Football League.

Ralphaela—the world's youngest bodybuilder at three years of age.

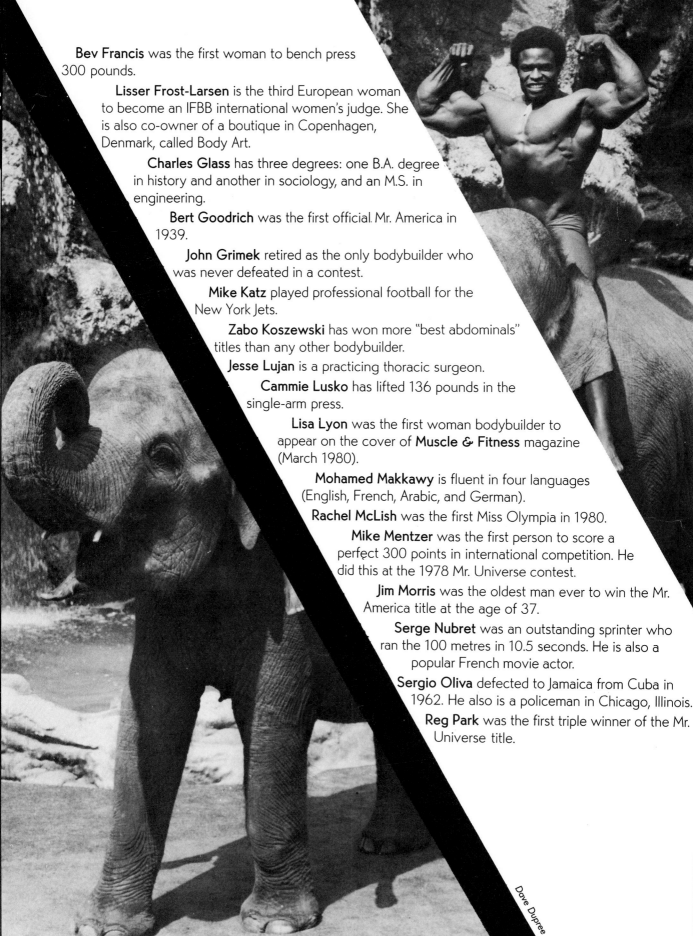

Bev Francis was the first woman to bench press 300 pounds.

Lisser Frost-Larsen is the third European woman to become an IFBB international women's judge. She is also co-owner of a boutique in Copenhagen, Denmark, called Body Art.

Charles Glass has three degrees: one B.A. degree in history and another in sociology, and an M.S. in engineering.

Bert Goodrich was the first official Mr. America in 1939.

John Grimek retired as the only bodybuilder who was never defeated in a contest.

Mike Katz played professional football for the New York Jets.

Zabo Koszewski has won more "best abdominals" titles than any other bodybuilder.

Jesse Lujan is a practicing thoracic surgeon.

Cammie Lusko has lifted 136 pounds in the single-arm press.

Lisa Lyon was the first woman bodybuilder to appear on the cover of **Muscle & Fitness** magazine (March 1980).

Mohamed Makkawy is fluent in four languages (English, French, Arabic, and German).

Rachel McLish was the first Miss Olympia in 1980.

Mike Mentzer was the first person to score a perfect 300 points in international competition. He did this at the 1978 Mr. Universe contest.

Jim Morris was the oldest man ever to win the Mr. America title at the age of 37.

Serge Nubret was an outstanding sprinter who ran the 100 metres in 10.5 seconds. He is also a popular French movie actor.

Sergio Oliva defected to Jamaica from Cuba in 1962. He also is a policeman in Chicago, Illinois.

Reg Park was the first triple winner of the Mr. Universe title.

Dave Dupree

Bill Pearl was an All-Navy champion in wrestling and a physical-training consultant for the aerospace program. He was also the biggest man (237 pounds) who ever won an international title (Mr. Universe in 1971).

Tony Pearson and Shelley Gruwell have won the IFBB World Professional Couples Championship for two consecutive years (1982 and 1983).

Lynn Pirie is a doctor of osteopathy.

Robby Robinson played collegiate football for Texas A&M. He ran the 100 metres in 10.4 seconds.

Clancy Ross was the first professional bodybuilder to ever receive a substantial amount of money ($1,000) for winning the 1948 Mr. USA contest.

Eugen Sandow's real name was Frederick Meuller.

Arnold Schwarzenegger has won the Mr. Olympia title a record seven times (with six consecutive wins).

Alan Stephan was the image on a Navy recruiting poster in the mid-1940s.

Armand Tanny was officially the first man in the state of New York to clean and jerk 300 pounds. He also designed weight-training courses for combat crews of the Strategic Air Command.

Victor Terra has won the AAU Mr. Teenage America, Teenage USA, Teen America, and Teen USA—a feat never before accomplished.

Dennis Tinerino was the first bodybuilder to be inducted into the Italian-American Sports Hall of Fame. He is also one of the founders of the Christian Bodybuilders Association.

Casey Viator was the youngest man to win the Mr. America title when he was 19 years old.

Ken Waller played professional football for the Canadian Football League.

Frank Zane defeated the mighty Arnold Schwarzenegger for the Mr. Universe title in 1968. He is also a champion archer.

Erik Hunter

Books, Magazines, & Newsletters

Mohamed Makkawy, Garry Bartlett, and Vince Gironda

Most magazines are available on the newsstands or in bookstores. Some can only be obtained through specialty bookstores; others are available by subscription only.

To get a sample copy, send the cost of one issue to the address listed. This is the best method for examining a magazine or newsletter before investing a year's subscription cost.

Bill Dobbins and Ben Weider

The books listed here are primarily of the bodybuilding, weight-training, and strength-training types.

Many of the older "physical culture" works are out of print. If you can contact the publisher (if listed), you can usually obtain a copy of a particular book. When all else fails, there are a few individuals who specialize in selling bodybuilding books. First look under "Books, Training Courses and Routines, and Magazines" subhead in the Products section, then go to the Companies section to determine exactly what persons sell bodybuilding books, and contact them for further information.

BOOKS

BODYBUILDING

Bass, Clarence. *Ripped*. New Mexico: Ripped Enterprises, 1980.

———. *Ripped 2*. New Mexico: Ripped Enterprises, 1983.

Bentley, Stacey and Fred C. Hatfield. *Toning the Body: Bodybuilding & Shaping for Women*. New Jersey: New Century Publishers, 1982.

Broccoletti, Pete. *Building Up*. Indiana: Icarus Press, 1981.

Brolus, Doug. *Developing Prize Winning Abdominals*. Michigan: Doug Brolus, 1983.

Callum, Myles. *Bodybuilding & Self-Defense*. New York: Sterling Publishing Co., Inc., 1962.

Cohn, Nik and Jean-Pierre Laffont. *Women o' Iron: The World of Female Bodybuilders*. New York: Wideview Books, 1981.

Columbu, Franco. *Franco Columbu's Complete Book of Bodybuilding*. Illinois: Contemporary Books, Inc., 1982.

Combes, Laura and Bill Reynolds. *Winning Women's Bodybuilding*. Illinois: Contemporary Books, Inc., 1983.

Darden, Ellington. *The Nautilus Bodybuilding Book*. Illinois: Contemporary Books, Inc., 1982.

Davis, Steve. *Build Huge Calves*. Nebraska: Iron Man Publishing Co., no date given.

DeJesus, Carlos. *N.I.T.: Natural Instinctive Training*. Virginia: Carlos DeJesus, 1984.

Ditillo, Anthony. *The Development of Muscular Bulk & Power*. Nebraska: Iron Man Industries, no date given.

Editors of *Consumer Guide. The Complete Guide to Building a Better Body*. Illinois: Publications International, Ltd., 1978.

Editors of *FIT* Magazine. *The Women's Bodybuilding Photo Book*. California: Anderson World Books, Inc., 1983.

Fallon, Michael and Jim Saunders. *Muscle Building for Beginners*. New York: Arco Publishing Inc., 1981.

Fodor, R. V. and G. J. Taylor. *Junior Body Building: Growing Strong*. New York: Sterling Publishing Co., Inc., 1982.

Gaines, Charles and George Butler. *Pumping Iron: The Art and Sport of Bodybuilding*. New York: Simon and Schuster, 1974.

———. *Iron Sisters: The World of Women's Bodybuilding*. New York: Simon and Schuster, 1984.

Gaudreau, Leo. *Anvils, Horsehoes & Cannons (vols. 1 and 2)*. Nebraska: Iron Man Industries, 1975.

Hatfield, Fred C. *Bodybuilding for Powerlifting*. Louisiana: Fitness Systems, 1982.

Heidenstam, Oscar. *Modern Bodybuilding*. Connecticut: Merrimack Publishing Corp., 1966.

Hoffman, Bob. *Big Arms*. Pennsylvania: York Barbell Co., 1939.

Kelly, Michael. *The Fitness Factor: Practical Body Building for Health*. New York: Arco Publishing, Inc., 1981.

Kennedy, Robert. *Beef It!: Upping the Muscle Mass*. New York: Sterling Publishing Co., Inc., 1983.

———. *Bodybuilding for Women*. New York: Emerson Books, 1979.

———. *Hardcore Bodybuilding: The Blood, Sweat and Tears of Pumping Iron*. New York: Sterling Publishing Co., Inc., 1983.

———. *Natural Body Building for Everyone*. New York: Sterling Publishing Co., Inc., 1981.

———. *Shape Up: The New Unisex Bodybuilder*. New York Frederick Fell Publishers, Inc., 1981.

———. *Start Bodybuilding*. New York: Sterling Publishing Co., Inc., 1982.

———. *Unleashing the Wild Physique*. New York: Sterling Publishing Co., Inc. 1984.

Laiken, Deidre S. *Beautiful Body Building*. New York: The New American Library, Inc., 1979

Leen, Edie and Ed Bertling. *The Bodybuilder's Training Diary*. California: Anderson World Books, Inc., 1983.

Lurie, Dan and John J. Lima. *Dan Lurie's "Instant Action" Bodybuilding System*. New York: Arco Publishing, Inc., 1981.

Lyon, Lisa. *Lisa Lyon's Body Magic*. New York: Viking Press, 1981.

Mozee, Gene. *The Secrets of Muscle Building Nutrition*. Gene Mozee Publishing Co., 1979.

———. *You Can Build 20″ Arms*. Gene Mozee Publishing Co., 1979.

Murray, Jim. *Inside Bodybuilding*. Illinois: Contemporary Books, Inc., 1978.

Paschall, Harry. *Muscle Moulding*. Nebraska: *Iron Man* Magazine, 1950.

Pearl, Bill. *Keys to the Inner Universe*. California: Physical Fitness Architects, 1978.

Pirie, Lynn and Bill Reynolds. *Getting Built*. New York: Warner Books, 1984.

Ravelle, Lou. *Bodybuilding for Everyone*. New York: Emerson Books, 1964.

Reeves, Fred. *Body Building & Reducing Course*. Connecticut: Impress House, no date given.

Reynolds, Bill. *Bodybuilding for Beginners*. Illinois: Contemporary Books, Inc., 1983.

Richardson, Bill and David Webster. *The Ultimate Physique*. New York: Sterling Publishing Co., Inc., 1984.

Richford, Carl. *The Principles of Successful Bodybuilders*. Nebraska: Iron Man Publishing Co., no date given.

———. *Upper Body Training*. Nebraska: Iron Man Publishing Co., no date given.

Ross, Don. *The Secrets of Muscle Building*. Nebraska: Iron Man Publishing Co., no date given.

———. *Size, Power, and Muscularity*. Nebraska: Iron Man Publishing Co., no date given.

———. *More Size, Power and Muscularity*. Nebraska: Iron Man Publishing Co., no date given.

Salvati, Michael. *The Production of Muscular Bulk*. Nebraska: Iron Man Publishing Co., no date given.

Schwarzenegger, Arnold. *Arnold's Bodybuilding for Men*. New York: Simon and Schuster, 1981.

———— and Douglas Kent Hall. *Arnold's Bodyshaping for Women*. New York: Simon and Schuster, 1979.

————. *Arnold's Encyclopedia of Bodybuilding*. New York: Simon and Schuster, 1984.

———— and Douglas Kent Hall. *Arnold: The Education of a Bodybuilder*. New York: Simon and Schuster, 1977.

Snyder, George and Rick Wayne. *3 More Reps*. Pennsylvania: Olympus Health and Recreation, Inc., 1979.

————. *Women of the Olympia*. Pennsylvania: Running Press, 1981.

Snyder, Lorraine. *Body Magic: The Science of Figure Contouring*. Pennsylvania: Running Press, 1981.

Sprague, Ken and Bill Reynolds. *The Gold's Gym Book of Bodybuilding*. Illinois: Contemporary Books, Inc., 1983.

Steiner, Bradley. *The Hard Gainers Bible*. New Jersey: Health Culture Publishing, 1979.

————. *Muscle Up That Waistline*. New Jersey: Health Culture Publishing, 1979.

————. *12 Keys to Bodybuilding Success*. New Jersey: Health Culture Publishing, 1979.

Walter, Denie. *Psycho-Blast*. Canada: Canusa Products, 1984.

Webster, David. *Barbells & Beefcake*. Scotland: David Webster, 1979.

————. *Bodybuilding: An Illustrated History*. New York: Arco Publishing, Inc., 1979.

————. *The Complete Physique Book*. England: Arlington Books, 1963.

————. *Physique in Focus*. Scotland: David Webster, 1964.

———— and Bill Richardson. *The Ultimate Physique*. England: Black, 1984.

Weider, Joe. *Bodybuilding: The Weider Approach*. Illinois: Contemporary Books, Inc., 1981.

————. *The IFBB Album of Bodybuilding All-Stars*. Hawthorne Books, Inc., 1979.

————. *Mr. Olympia: The History of Bodybuilding's Greatest Contest*. New York: St. Martin's Press, 1983.

————. *Training Diary*. Illinois: Contemporary Books, Inc., 1982.

———— and Bill Reynolds. *The Weider System of Bodybuilding*. Illinois: Contemporary Books, Inc., 1983.

———— and Betty Weider. *The Weider Book of Bodybuilding for Women*. Illinois: Contemporary Books, Inc., 1981.

———— and the Editors of *Muscle & Fitness*. *The Best of Joe Weider's Muscle & Fitness Training Tips and Routines*. Illinois: Contemporary Books, Inc., 1981.

———— and the Editors of *Muscle & Fitness*. *Bodybuilding and Conditioning for Women*. Illinois: Contemporary Books, Inc., 1983.

———— and the Editors of *Muscle & Fitness*. *Building Arms for Mass and Power*. Illinois: Contemporary Books, Inc., 1983.

———— and the Editors of *Muscle & Fitness*. *Champion Bodybuilders' Training Strategies and Routines*. Illinois: Contemporary Books, Inc., 1982.

———— and the Editors of *Muscle & Fitness*. *More Training Tips and Routines*. Illinois: Contemporary Books, Inc., 1982.

———— and the Editors of *Muscle & Fitness*. *Women's Weight Training and Bodybuilding Tips and Routines*. Illinois: Contemporary Books, Inc., 1982.

———— and the Editors of *Muscle & Fitness*. *The World's Leading Bodybuilders Answer Your Questions*. Illinois: Contemporary Books, Inc., 1981.

Weis, Dennis. *The Best Form of Bodybuilding*. Nebraska: Iron Man Publishing Co., 1978.

————. *Special Advice to the Bodybuilder*. Nebraska: Iron Man Publishing Co., 1982.

Zane, Christine. *The Feminine Physique: Bodybuilding for the Woman*. New York: Simon and Schuster, 1983.

DIET AND NUTRITION

Centrella, Bernard. *Dieting for Bodybuilders*. Nebraska Iron Man Publishing Co., no date given.

Coe, Boyer. *Optimal Nutrition*. California: Boyer Coe Enterprises, no date given.

Darden, Ellington. *The Nautilus Nutrition Book*. Illinois: Contemporary Books, Inc., 1981.

Mather, Don. *Bodybuilder's Cookbook*. South Carolina: Don Mather, 1983.

Neve, Vicki. *Pat Neve's Bodybuilding Diet Book*. Arizona: Phoenix Books, 1981.

Richford, Carl. *Modern Nutrition for Bodybuilders*. Nebraska: Iron Man Publishing Co., no date given.

Steiner, Bradley. *Bodybuilder's Mealtime*. New Jersey: Health Culture Publishing, 1980.

Venus, Carlin. *Diet Psyche'Ology*. California: Carlin Venus, no date given.

Weider, Joe and the Editors of *Muscle & Fitness*. *Bodybuilding Nutrition and Training Programs*. Illinois: Contemporary Books, Inc., 1981.

———— and the Editors of *Muscle & Fitness*. *More Bodybuilding Nutrition and Training Programs*. Illinois: Contemporary Books, Inc., 1982.

Zale, Norman. *Eating for Strength and Muscular Development*. Nebraska: Iron Man Publishing Co., no date given.

Zane, Frank. *Zane Nutrition*. New York: Simon and Schuster, 1984.

Zumpano, Michael and Daniel Duchaine. *Ultimate Dieting Handbook*. California: OEM Publishing, 1982.

DRUGS

Coe, Boyer and Stan Morey. *Steroids*. California: Boyer Coe Enterprises, 1979.

Goldman, Bob. *Death in the Locker Room*. Indiana: Icarus Press, 1984.

Hatfield, Fred C. *Anabolic Steroids . . . What Kind . . . How Many?* Louisiana: Fitness Systems, 1982.

Kerr, Robert. *The Practical Use of Anabolic Steroids with Athletes*. California: Robert Kerr, 1983.

L & S Research. *Anabolic Steroids and Bodybuilding*. New Jersey: L & S Research, no date given.

Mozee, Gene. *The Steroid Report*. Gene Mozee Publishing Co., 1979.

Taylor, William. *Anabolic Steroids and the Athlete*. North Carolina: McFarland and Co., 1982.

Wright, James E. *Anabolic Steroids and Sports*. Massachusetts: Sports Science Consultants, 1978.

Zumpano, Michael and Daniel Duchaine. *Underground Steroid Handbook for Men and Women*. California: OEM Publishing, 1981.

EXERCISE AND CONDITIONING

Barrilleaux, Doris. *Forever Fit*. Indiana: Icarus Press, 1983.

Benyo, Richard and Rhonda Provost. *Advanced Indoor Exercise Book*. California: Anderson World Books, Inc., 1981.

Coe, Boyer and Bob Summer. *Getting Strong, Looking Strong*. New York: Atheneum, 1979.

Boff, Vic. *You Can Be Physically Perfect, Powerfully Strong*. New York: Arco Publishing Co., 1982.

Columbu, Franco. *The Businessman's Minutes-A-Day Guide to Shaping Up*. Illinois: Contemporary Books, Inc., 1983.

——— and George Fels. *Coming on Strong*. Illinois: Contemporary Books, Inc., 1978.

Darden, Ellington. *Especially for Women*. Illinois: Contemporary Books, Inc., 1983.

Everson, Jeff. *The All Sports Training Manual*. Wisconsin: Execs, Inc., 1983.

———. *Total Conditioning: The Wisconsin Approach*. Wisconsin: Execs, Inc., no date given.

Ferrigno, Carla. *For Women Only: Carla Ferrigno's Total Shape-Up Program*. Illinois: Contemporary Books, Inc., 1982.

Gaines, Charles and George Butler. *Staying Hard*. New York: Kenan Press, 1980.

Hatfield, Fred C. *Flexibility Training for Sports*. Louisiana: Fitness Systems, 1982.

Mehteny, Eleanor. *Body Dynamics*. New York: McGraw-Hill, 1952.

Novich, Max and Buddy Taylor. *Training and Conditioning of Athletes*. Pennsylvania: Lea & Febiger, no date given.

Nyad, Diana and Candace Lyle Hogan. *Basic Training for Women*. New York: Harmony Books, 1981.

Olinekova, Gayle. *Go For It!* New York: Simon and Schuster, 1982.

Ross, Don. *Secrets of Super Fitness*. Nebraska: Iron Man Publishing Co., no date given.

Schwartz, Leonard. *Heavyhands: The Ultimate Exercise*. Massachusetts: Little, Brown & Co., Ltd., 1982.

Steiner, Bradley. *Total Fitness*. Canada: MuscleMag International, 1981.

Zane, Frank and Christine Zane. *Super Bodies in 12 Weeks*. New York: Simon and Schuster, 1982.

POWERLIFTING AND POWER TRAINING

Ashpaugh, Bill. *Powerlift*. Tennessee: The Benson Co. & Zondervan, 1981.

Boyer, Keith. *History of Powerlifting*. Pennsylvania: Keith Boyer, 1983.

Bridges, Mike. *New Dimensions in Powerlifting*. Texas: Mike Bridges Systems, 1982.

Cash, James. *The Power Bench Press*. Ohio: Power By Cash, 1982.

———. *The Power Deadlift*. Ohio: Power By Cash, 1982.

———. *The Power Squat*. Ohio: Power By Cash, 1982.

Hatfield, Fred C. *The Bench Press*. Louisiana: Fitness Systems, 1982.

———. *The Complete Guide to Power Training*. Louisiana: Fitness Systems, 1983.

———. *The Deadlift*. Louisiana: Fitness Systems, 1982.

———. *Powerlifting: A Scientific Approach*. Illinois: Contemporary Books, Inc., 1981.

———. *The Squat*. Louisiana: Fitness Systems, 1982.

Lambert, Mike. *Power Technique*. California: Powerlifting USA, 1983.

Lear, John. *The Powerlifter's Manual*. England: E. P. Publishing, Ltd., 1982.

Manners, David. *Here's Power for You*. New York: Arco Publishing Co., 1981.

Moser, Jim. *The Razor's Edge: The Complete Book of Bench Pressing*. Maryland: J & M Wholesalers, 1982.

Murray, Al and John Lear. *Power Training for Sport*. New York: Arco Publishing Co., no date given.

Pacifico, Larry. *The Larry Pacifico Training System*. Ohio: Larry Pacifico, 1980.

Roman, R. A. and M. S. Shakirzyanov. *The Snatch, The Clean and Jerk*. Nebraska: *Iron Man* Magazine, no date given.

Starr, Bill. *Defying Gravity*. Texas: Five Starr Productions, 1981

Steiner, Bradley. *Powerlifting and the Development of Strength*. New Jersey: Physical Culture Books, 1979.

———. *Powerlifting and Herculean Super Strength*. Canada: MuscleMag International, 1980.

———. *Your Guide to Success in Powerlifting: The Deadlift*. New Jersey: Health Culture Publishing, 1979.

———. *Your Guide to Success in Powerlifting: The Squat*. New Jersey: Health Culture Publishing, 1979.

Todd, Terry. *Inside Powerlifting*. Illinois: Contemporary Books, Inc., 1978.

Walter, Denie. *The Bench Press War*. Canada: MuscleMag International, 1980.

Webster, David. *How to Clean & Jerk*. Nebraska: Iron Man Publishing Co., 1965.

———. *The Two-Hand Snatch*. Nebraska: Iron Man Publishing Co., 1964.

Weis, Dennis. *Power Lift Manual*. Nebraska: Iron Man Publishing Co., no date given.

STRENGTH TRAINING AND WEIGHT TRAINING

Barrilleaux, Doris and Jim Murray. *Inside Weight Training for Women*. Illinois: Contemporary Books, Inc., 1978.

Bonomo, Joe. *Barbell System*. New Jersey: Wehman Brothers, Inc., no date given.

British Amateur Weight Lifters. *Weight Lifting*. England: British Book Center, 1975.

Carnes, Valerie and Ralph Carnes. *Bodysculpture: Weight Training for Women*. New York: St. Martin's Press, 1978.

Coe, Boyer and Valerie Coe. *Boyer and Valerie Coe's Weight Training Book*. Illinois: Contemporary Books, Inc., 1982.

Columbu, Franco. *Weight Training and Bodybuilding*. Illinois: Contemporary Books, Inc., 1982.

——— and Anita Columbu. *Starbodies: The Women's Weight Training Book*. New York: E. P. Dutton, 1978.

——— and R. R. Knudson. *Weight Training for Young Athletes*. Illinois: Contemporary Books, Inc., 1979.

——— and Richard Tyler. *Winning Weight Lifting & Powerlifting*. Illinois: Contemporary Books, Inc., 1979.

Covino, Marge and Pat Jordan. *Woman's Guide to Shaping Your Body with Weights*. New York: J. B. Lippincott, Co., 1978.

Darden, Ellington. *The Nautilus Book: An Illustrated Guide to Physical Fitness the Nautilus Way*. Illinois: Contemporary Books, Inc., 1980.

———. *The Nautilus Woman*. New York: Simon and Schuster, 1983.

———. *Strength Training Principles*. Illinois: Contemporary Books, Inc., 1983.

Ditillo, Anthony. *The Development of Physical Strength*. Nebraska: Iron Man Publishing, no date given.

Dobbins, Bill. *"High Tech" Training: Exercising with Machines/Today's Way to a Superb Body*. New York: Simon and Schuster, 1982.

——— and Ken Sprague. *The Gold's Gym Weight Training Book*. New York: Berkeley Books, 1981.

Fodor, R. V. *Winning Weightlifting*. New York: Sterling Publishing Co., Inc., 1983.

Freidberg, Ardy. *Weight Training for Runners*. New York: Simon and Schuster, 1981.

Getting Strong Book Series (10 vols.). California: Anderson World Books, Inc., 1983.

Hatfield, Fred C. *Aerobic Weight Training*. Illinois: Contemporary Books, Inc., 1983.

——— and March L. Krotee. *Personalized Weight Training for Fitness and Athletics*. Iowa: Kendall/Hunt Publishing Co., 1978.

———. *Weight Training for the Young Athlete*. New York: Atheneum, 1980.

Hoffman, Bob. *Secrets of Strength & Development*. Pennsylvania: York Barbell Co., 1940.

———. *Weight Training for Athletics*. New York: John Wiley, 1969.

Jarrell, Steve. *Working Out with Weights*. New York: Arco Publishing Co., 1982.

Kirkley, George. *Modern Weight Lifting*. England: Faber Books, 1957.

———. *Weightlifting and Weight Training*. New York: Arco Publishing Co., 1981.

Lance, Kathryn. *Getting Strong*. New York: Bobbs-Merrill Co., Inc., 1978.

Leen, Edie. *Complete Women's Weight Training Guide*. California: Anderson World Books, Inc., 1980.

———. *Strength Training for Beauty*. California: Anderson World Books, Inc., 1983.

Leighton, Jack. *Progressive Weight Training*. New York: Ronald Press, 1961.

MacFadden, Bernarr. *Building Vital Power*. New York: MacFadden Publishing Co., no date given.

Mazzei, George. *Shaping Up: The Complete Guide to a Customized Weight Training Program for Men and Women*. New York: Ballantine Books, 1981.

Mentzer, Mike and Ardy Friedberg. *The Mentzer Method to Fitness*. New York: William Morrow and Co., Inc., 1980.

———. *Mike Mentzer's Complete Book of Weight Training*. New York: William Morrow and Co., Inc., 1982.

Murray, Al. *Modern Weight Training*. England: Kaye and Ward, 1963.

Murray, Jim. *Winning Weight Training*. Illinois: Contemporary Books, Inc., 1982.

——— and Peter Karpovich. *Weight Training in Athletics*. New Jersey: Prentice-Hall, 1956.

Nagy, George. *Weight Lifting Handbook*. Indiana: Amateur Athletic Union of the USA, 1974.

Parker, Robert and John Marsh. *Sports Illustrated: Training with Weights*. New York: J. B. Lippincott, 1974.

Paschall, Harry. *Bosco Strength Notebook*. Nebraska: Iron Man Industries, no date given.

Peterson, James. *Total Fitness: The Nautilus Way*. New York: Leisure Press, 1978.

Popplewell, George. *Modern Weightlifting*. Conneticut: Merrimack Publishing Corp., 1979.

Randall, Bruce. *The Barbell Way to Physical Fitness*. New York: Doubleday, 1970.

Rasch, Philip. *Weight Training*. Iowa: Wm. C. Brown Publishers, 1966.

Reeves, Fred. *Weight Training for Athletics*. Connecticut: Impress House, no date given.

Reynolds, Bill. *Complete Weight Training Book*. California: Anderson World Books, Inc., 1976.

———. *Weight Training for Beginners*. Illinois: Contemporary Books, Inc., 1982.

Riley, Daniel. *Strength Training by the Experts*. New York: Leisure Press, 1982.

Ryan, Frank. *Weight Training*. New York: Viking Press, 1969.

Shephard, Greg. *Bigger, Faster, Stronger*. Utah: Hawkes Publishing, 1983.

Sing, Vanessa. *Lift for Life*. New York: Bolder Books, 1977.

Sobey, Edwin. *Strength Training Book*. California: Anderson World Books, Inc., 1981.

——— and Gary Burns. *Aerobic Weight Training Book*. California: Anderson World Books, Inc., 1982.

Sprague, Ken. *The Gold's Book of Strength Training for Athletes*. New York: Berkeley Books, 1979.

Steiner, Bradley. *Effective Barbell Training*. Nebraska: Iron Man Publishing Co., no date given.

————. *The Shapely Physique: How to Achieve It Through Weight Training*. New Jersey: Health Culture Publishing, 1979.

Steppe, W. D. *Better Body Through Weights*. Texas: W. D. Steppe, no date given.

Taylor, B. A. and M. E. Easton. *Physical Fitness Through Weight Training*. Iowa: Kendall/Hunt, 1975.

Webster, David. *Modern Strand-Pulling*. England: Grose, 1954.

————. *The Iron Game: Illustrated History of Weight Lifting*. Scotland: David Webster, 1976.

Weldon, Gail *Weight Training for Women's Sports*. Illinois: Weldon Publishing, 1977.

Willoughby, David and William Hinbern. *The Master Method of Health, Strength and Bodybuilding*. Michigan: William Hinbern, 1977.

Wolf, Michael D. *Nautilus Fitness for Women*. Illinois: Contemporary Books, Inc., 1983.

Zane, Frank and Christine Zane. *The Zane Way to a Beautiful Body*. New York: Simon and Schuster, 1979.

MISCELLANEOUS

Bonomo, Joe. *The Strongman*. New York: Bonomo Studios, Inc., 1958.

Darden, Ellington. *How to Lose Body Fat*. Illinois: Contemporary Books, Inc., 1983.

Ferrigno, Lou and Douglas Kent Hall. *The Incredible Lou Ferrigno*. New York: Simon and Schuster, 1982.

Gaines, Charles and George Butler. *Yours in Perfect Manhood: Charles Atlas*. New York: Simon and Schuster, 1982.

Hackenschmidt, George. *The Way to Live*. England: Health and Strength Ltd., no date given.

Ivanov, Dmitry. *The Strongest Man in the World: Vasili Alexeyev*. New York: Sphinx Press, Inc., 1979.

Karas, Jim. *Winning Naturally*. Pennsylvania: Jim Karas, 1982.

Kazmaier, Bill. *The Kaz Quests*. Alabama: Bill Kazmaier, 1981.

Krotee, March and Fred C. Hatfield. *Theory and Practice of Physical Activity*. Iowa: Kendall/Hunt, 1979.

Lamberti, Irene. *Pumping Iron Without Pain: A Preventative and Self-Care Guide to Weight Training*. New York: Leisure Press, 1983.

L & S Research. *In Quest of Size*. New Jersey: L & S Research, no date given.

Lyon, Lisa and Robert Mapplethorpe. *Lady*. New York: Viking Press, 1983.

Mentzer, Mike and Ardy Friedberg. *Mike Mentzer's Spot Body Balancing*. New York: Simon and Schuster, 1983.

Powerlifting USA. *Official IPF Rule Book*. California: Powerlifting USA, 1983.

Rosen, Trix. *Strong and Sexy: The New Body Beautiful*. New York: Delilah Communications, Ltd., 1983.

Sandow, Eugen. *Physical Culture*. England: Harrison and Sons, 1899.

————. *Sandow's System of Physical Training*. England: J. Selwin and Sons, 1894.

Serafini, Anthony. *The Muscle Book*. New York; Arco Publishing Co., 1981.

Starr, Bill. *The Strongest Shall Survive*. Washington, DC: Fitness Products, Ltd., 1978.

Venables, Gordon. *Mighty Men of Old*. Pennsylvania: York Barbell Co., 1940.

Wayne, Rick. *Pursuit of the Gods*. Illinois: Contemporary Books, Inc., 1984.

Willoughby, David. *The Super Athletes*. New Jersey: A. S. Barnes and Co., 1970.

Wright, James. *Recuperation*. Massachusetts: Sports Science Consultants, no date given.

Robert Kennedy, publisher of MuscleMag International, and Jayne Stafford

MAGAZINES AND NEWSLETTERS

American Fitness Quarterly, PO Box 15506, Columbus, OH 43215/4 issues = $12

Athlitis, 56 Panepistimiu St., Athens, Greece/Contact Andreas D. Zapatinas for details

Bodybuilding & Kraftsport, Box 45214, 10450 Stockholm, Sweden/no price given

Bodybuilding Monthly, Demland Graphics Ltd., 33 Leeds Rd., Dewsbury, West Yorkshire WF12 7BB, England/12 issues = $17/foreign = $30

Bodybuilding News, c/o John Balik, PO Box 777, Santa Monica, CA 90406/6 issues = $12

Bodypower, Multilanguage Publications Ltd., Payne House, 23–24 Smithfield St., London ECI, England. 12 issues = £13/foreign = $40

Body Talk, * c/o Doris Barrilleaux, PO Box 937, Riverview FL 33569/4 issues = $10

Crain's Muscle World, PO Drawer 700, Clayton, OK 74536/6 issues = $13/foreign = $19.50

Diet and Exercise, * 1400 Stierlin Rd., Mountain View, CA 94043/5 issues = $15

Eastern Lifter, c/o Brad Shaw, Editor, PO Box 2161, Augusta, ME 04330/4 issues = $8

Fit, * 1400 Stierlin Rd., Mountain View, CA 94043/12 issues = $14.95/foreign = $19.95

Flex, 21100 Erwin St., Woodland Hills, CA 91367/12 issues = $20/foreign = $23

Force & Beauté *, c/o Dominique Dumont, B. P. 362 R9, 67009 Strasbourg Cedex, France/4 issues = $20

The Health Letter, PO Box 326, San Antonio, TX 78292/12 issues = $19.50/Canada = $22/Mexico = $25/Central America, Caribbean, Colombia, Venezuela = $27/all other countries = $30

Health & Strength, 30 Craven St., Strand, London, WC2N 5NT, England/12 issues/year

Herkules, Šumska 50, Poštanski fah 97, 21400 Bačka Palanka, Yugoslavia/no price given

IFBB Body Builder, 9 Hoge Lane, B 8200 Brugge, Belgium/4 issues = $6/foreign = $6

The Image *, PO Box 363, Niwot, CO 80544-0363/ available to all AFWB members

International Olympic Lifter, PO Box 65855, Los Angeles, CA 90065/12 issues = $20/foreign = $20

Iron Man, PO Box 10, Alliance, NE 69301/6 issues = $10/ foreign = $17.90

Lady Athlete, * PO Box 72335M, Lancaster, PA 17604/12 issues = $15/foreign = $24

Le Monde du Muscle, Gym Riquet, 15 Rue Riquet, Paris 75019, France/no price given

Michigan Bodybuilding News, 8515 Glendale Dr., Ypsilanti, MI 48197/12 issues = $18

Muscle & Bodybuilder, Charlton Publications, Inc., Charlton Building, Derby, CT 06418/6 issues = $10

Muscle Digest, 1234 S. Garfield Ave., Alhambra, CA 91801/12 issues = $24

Muscle & Fitness, 21100 Erwin St., Woodland Hills, CA 91367/12 issues = $29.95/foreign = $39.95

Muscle Fitness, Health and Sport, c/o Paul Graham, 288 Grande Pde., Ramsgate Beach, New South Wales 2217, Australia/no price given

MuscleMag International, Unit 2, 52 Bramsteele Rd., Brampton, Ontario, Canada L6W 3M5/8 issues = $18.50/foreign = $30.00

Muscle Training Illustrated, Powerhouse Publishing, Inc., 801 Second Ave., New York, NY 10017/9 issues = $22/foreign = $26

Muscle Up, Charlton Publications, Inc., Charlton Building, Derby, CT 06418/6 issues = $10

Muscle World, Charlton Publications, Inc., Charlton Building, Derby, CT 06418/no price given

Muscular Development, PO Box 1707, York, PA 17405/6 issues = $7.50/foreign = $9.75

The National Fitness Trade Journal, Wally Boyko Productions, Inc., 2903 Gingerwood Circle, Fullerton, CA 92635/no price given

National Strength and Conditioning Association Journal, PO Box 81410, Lincoln, NE 68501/6 issues = $16

The Natural Bodybuilder, 2617 Genesee St., Utica, NY 13501/4 issues = $10

Nautilus, PO Box 160, Independence, VA 24349-9990/6 issues = $7.50/Canada = $13.50/foreign = $24

New Body, * 888 Seventh Ave., New York, NY 10106/6 issues = $8.95/foreign = $11.95

The New York Advantage, * c/o Kay King-Nealy, 12 E. 22nd St., #PHD, New York, NY 10010/the number of issues varies per year; available upon request

The North American Bodybuilder, PO Box 1490, Radio City Station, New York, NY 10019/no price given

Pleine Forme, * Gym Riquet, 15 Rue Riquet, Paris 75019, France/no price given

Power Hotline, PO Box 3238, Camarillo, CA 90311/24 issues = $28/foreign = $39

Powerlifting News, c/o Dan DeWelt, Editor, PO Box 398, Joplin, MO 64802/no price given

Powerlifting USA, PO Box 467, Camarillo, CA 93011/12 issues = $18/foreign = $24

Power Olympic Physique, PO Box 1211, Oklahoma City, OK 73101/no price given

The Right to Know, Vince's Gym, 11262 Ventura Blvd., Studio City, CA 91604/no price given

Shape *, 21100 Erwin St., Woodland Hills, CA 91367/12 issues = $20/foreign = $25

Southern Bodybuilder, c/o Bob Summer, Editor, PO Box 6322, Macon, GA 31201/10 issues = $17.50

Soviet Sports Review, PO Box 2878, Escondido, CA 92095/12 issues = $20/foreign = $24

S.P.A. News, PO Box 937, Riverview, FL 33569/12 issues = $20/foreign = $23 (this newsletter was discontinued after the July-September 1983 issue, but back issues are still available)

Sport & Fitness, Postfach 2644, 4150 Krefeld, W. Germany

Sportman/Muscle Builder (Joe Weider's Halian Edition), Strada Francesca, Angolo Statale del Tonale, 24040 Zingonia (BI), Italy/no price given

Sport Revue, Ludwig Brummer, Lindwurmstrabe 125-127, 8000 München 2, W. Germany

The Strength Fitness Newsletter, Fitness Consultants & Supply, 1610 Christine St., Wichita Falls, TX 76302/ free

Strength & Health, PO Box 1707, York, PA 17405/6 issues = $7.50/foreign = $9.75

Strength Training for Beauty *, 1400 Stierlin St., Mountain View, CA 94043/6 issues = $14.95/foreign = $17.35

Women's Physique World Magazine, PO Box 429, Midland Park, NJ/6 issues = $15/Canada and Mexico = $21/Europe = $27/Asia, Middle East, Australia, New Zealand = $30

W.S.P., PO Box 443N, Hohokus, NJ 07423/12 issues = $17

*women's bodybuilding newspapers

Glossary

a

AAU   Amateur Athletic Union

abs   rectus abdominis; abdominal muscles; stomach muscles

aerobic exercise   continuous exercise which promotes cardiovascular development by raising the pulse rate and increasing stamina and endurance; e.g., swimming, cycling, and running

AFWB   American Federation of Women Bodybuilders

amino acids   the building blocks of protein; there are 22 amino acids: the body can make 14 and 8 (called essential amino acids) must be obtained through the diet

anabolic steroids   artificial male hormones that have a tendency to build strength and muscle size; these drugs have very serious side effects and actually are in contradiction to the principles of bodybuilding and exercise; e.g., Dianabol, Winstrol, Deca-Durobolin, Anavar, and Therabolin

androgenics   pure testosterone preparations; often called anabolic steroids.

b

bar   the handle portion of a dumbbell or barbell

barbell   a form of free-weight equipment consisting of a bar, sleeves, collars, and plates; barbells can be fixed or adjustable

basal metabolic rate (BMR)   the normal speed at which the body burns calories when at rest to provide its basic energy needs

beef it   to show as much muscle as possible; also a phrase popularized by Robert Kennedy's book of the same title, which refers to upping the production of lean muscle mass via nutrition, hard work, shock-training strategies, and dedication

Bodybuilding has its own special jargon. Actually, at times, it is only discernible to those who are actively involved in it.

To become a more informed participant, jump in and familiarize yourself with the language of physical culture.

belt squat   an accessory exercise whereby a special belt is worn that is long enough to fit around the waist, rest on the hips, and also hang between the legs with a weight is attached

bench press   a chest exercise that is executed while lying flat on a bench and pushing the barbell away from the chest

biceps   the large flexor muscles at the fronts of the upper arms; also the large flexor muscles at the backs of the thighs

bodybuilding   a form of weight training used to reshape the body; this activity also tones and strengthens the muscles

body fat   the amount of fat stored in the body

bulk   the combination of muscle and fat attained through increased food intake; part of the muscle-building process

burn   a sharp sensation (i.e., a "burning") in the muscles caused by the accumulation and release of lactic acid

burn out   physical and mental exhaustion from overtraining

c

calf   gastrocnemius muscle

calorie   a unit of heat energy

carbs   carbohydrates; the most important carb is glucose

CBA   Christian Bodybuilding Association

center   establishing a balance between your stance and the weight

cheating   a very loose training style that does not adhere to strict form; using larger muscle groups to assist in performing an exercise; exercising to muscle failure is recommended before cheating is to be used

circuit training a series of exercises performed one after the other and repeated at the end of the last exercise in the series; develops strength, endurance, and stamina

clean the action of getting a barbell from the floor to shoulder level

clean and jerk weight lifted in one movement to the shoulders, then pushed to arm's length above the head

collars metal fasteners that prevent plates from sliding off the bar

concentration full mental focus sustained during performance of an exercise; see *visualization*

contests competitions held at the local, regional, national, and international levels

continuous tension a technique whereby resistance is felt by moving the weight very slowly over the full range of motion of an exercise

cool down an exercise performed after athletic activity which allows the body to return to normal

curls a bicep exercise performed with a barbell or dumbbell

cut referred to as "well defined"; muscles that are fully delineated through the skin due to the reduced amounts of body fat and water; often termed "cutting up"; see *definition* and *ripped*

deadlift lifting a heavy barbell from the floor until the body is in an upright position

definition the visible display of the musculature through the skin due to the reduced amounts of body fat and water; see *cut* and *ripped*

delts deltoids; shoulder muscles

density the hardness of muscle tissue which indicates complete muscularity

depilatory a chemical hair remover used prior to competition

Dianabol an anabolic steroid

diet a regimen for obtaining weight control; absolutely essential to the competitive bodybuilder

diuretics substances which increase urinary output used by bodybuilders to reduce water retention and puffiness; adverse effects include fluid and electrolyte imbalance, nausea, dehydration, vomiting, cramps, and diarrhea

DMSO dimethyl sulfoxide; a pain killer

dumbbell a shorter version of the barbell intended for use in one hand or with equal weights in each hand

ectomorph a person whose body is usually thin

EFBB English Federation of Bodybuilders

endomorph a person whose body often carries excess weight

exercise a physical movement to develop the body

E-Z curl bar a bar with bends in it that permits a closer grip and also prevents the hands from sliding outward during execution of a movement

fatigue muscle exhaustion

fixed weights dumbbells that have various poundages permanently welded into place

flexibility suppleness of the muscles

flexing contraction of the muscles

forced reps a training technique that allows a person to push the muscle past the point of ordinary failure to add even more intensity to any given exercise

free weights adjustable barbells and dumbbells

full range of motion the complete contraction and expansion of the muscles during exercise

genetic potential the hereditary predisposition for muscular development

giant sets four to six exercises compounded for a body part with minimal rest between the movements

glandulars tissues obtained from young animals which contain a high-quality source of nutrients (nucleoproteins, enzymes, lipoproteins, RNA, etc.) and are used by bodybuilders as food supplements to help increase muscle mass; e.g., raw orchic, prostate, adrenal, liver

glutes gluteus maximus; buttocks muscles

gynecomastia the excessive development of the male mammary glands; commonly referred to as "bitch's tits"

hack squat a regular squat performed with the barbell held behind the thighs

hamstring biceps femoris; back thigh muscles

hardcore bodybuilding a phrase popularized by Robert Kennedy's book of the same title, which refers to the ultimate degree of weight training which allows an individual, via hard work, dedication, and pain, to push past his/her limits

hard gainer an advanced bodybuilder only able to add 2—3 pounds of muscle mass per year

heavy-duty training a method which encourages the use of very heavy weights and high-level intensity to obtain maximum size and strength; a phrase popularized by Mike Mentzer

Hise breathing shrug an exercise performed by shouldering a very heavy poundage and hunching it upwards while taking deep breaths to build bulk and power

hypertrophy muscle growth

IFBB International Federation of Bodybuilders; governs amateur and professional bodybuilders

instinctive training the performance of exercises based on individual interpretation and feel

intensity the amount of work done by a muscle during exercise

intercostals muscles between the ribs

iso-tension a technique to enhance muscularity and density; this is done by flexing each muscle very hard in a variety of positions for 8—10 repetitions for approximately 5—10 seconds

Jefferson lift a lift whereby an individual straddles the barbell to pick it up

Kelso shrug a system of movements designed to isolate the muscles of the upper body and use the natural flexibility of the shoulder girdle to develop the entire trapezius area, lats, pecs, and build overall body power

knurling the cross-hatched grooves on the sleeves of a bar that makes gripping the bar easier

lactic acid the waste product that causes the sharp sensation in the muscles referred to as a "burn"

lats latissimus dorsi; back muscles

laxative a bowel stimulant used for temporary relief of constipation used by bodybuilders to dehydrate the body and also to prevent a bloated abdomen; adverse effects include abdominal pain, nausea, dehydration, and potassium loss

layoff a break in training

lifting belt a thick leather belt worn to protect the lower back and abdomen from injury when lifting weights

lipids fats

mass the size or fullness of a muscle

max maximum; working the muscles to the limit

mesomorph a person whose body is muscular and athletic

minerals chemicals that are found in the soil and are passed to humans via plants and animals; vital to life in small amounts; e.g., sodium, calcium, potassium, iron, and magnesium

muscle-priority training intense exercising of a weak or lagging muscle group first in your workout session

muscularity synonymous with definition; see *definition*

n

NABBA   National Amateur British Bodybuilding Association

Nautilus   equipment developed by Arthur Jones which allows the user to make significant muscle gains by training harder, slower, briefer, and over a full range of motion; concepts and principles also popularized by Mike Mentzer and Ellington Darden

NBBA   Natural Bodybuilders of America

negative reps   raising the weight at normal speed, then lowering it at a much reduced speed

NPC   National Physique Committee

o

obliques   side abdominal muscles

Olympic lifting   an international competitive form of weight lifting consisting of the snatch and the clean and jerk

overload   a level of stress or intensity that is greater than normal

overtraining   when too much exercise is performed without sufficient recuperation time; usually results in a cessation of bodybuilding gains

p

peak contraction   an exercise movement at its most strenuous point

peaking   a competitive bodybuilding technique that attempts to gradually intensify training while strictly reducing the diet, resulting in a loss of all body fat which allows the muscle groups to be vividly displayed beneath the skin

pecs   pectoralis major; chest muscles

plates   flat, cast iron or vinyl-coated concrete discs with a hole in the center which fit on barbells or dumbbells to increase the weight

posing   the art of displaying the physique

potpourri routine   a routine consisting of a series of six or more exercises for each muscle group, with each being performed for only one set

poundage   the actual weight of a dumbbell, barbell, or weight machine used in an exercise

powerlifting   a form of weight training composed of three lifts: the squat, bench press, and deadlift

pre-exhaust   the constant working of a specific muscle with an isolation exercise followed by a combination movement; e.g., incline flyes (isolation) and incline bench press (combination); invented by Robert Kennedy

progression   a gradual increase in the amount of resistance per exercise to promote muscle growth

proportion   the relationship between the size of the various body parts

psychoblast   a technique utilizing mind control, sheer dedication, motivation, and inspiration to develop great strength and muscle size; popularized by Denie Walter's book *Psychoblast*

pump   an action that occurs when blood collects in a particular muscle area

pumping iron   weight training which uses barbells, dumbbells, and machinery; popularized by Charles Gaines's book *Pumping Iron*

pyramiding   progressively increasing the weight while decreasing the repetitions with each succeeding set

q

quads   quadriceps femoris; front thigh muscles

r

rack   stand used to store dumbbells

reps   repetitions; the number of times an exercise is performed

resistance   the actual weight utilized in an exercise

rest interval   a pause between sets of an exercise

ripped   synonymous with cut; the state whereby muscularity is vividly displayed through the skin because of the reduced amounts of fat and water in the body; term popularized by Clarence Bass

routine   a complete program of exercises

SABBF Singapore Amateur Bodybuilders Federation

sanction an official authorization from a governing body (NPC, IFBB, AFWB, etc.) to hold a contest

serratus the quadrilateral muscle situated between the ribs and scapula at the upper and lateral parts of the chest

set a specified group of repetitions

sleeve a hollow metal tube fitted over the bar of a barbell or dumbbell which helps the bar to rotate in the hands more easily

snatch weight lifted from the ground in one pull to arm's length above the head

SPA Superior Physique Association

specialization a manner of working a particular area very hard and regularly, while reducing the number of other exercise movements for the rest of the body

splitting performing half of a workout one day and the other half the following day with a rest period the third day before repeating the cycle

spotter a person who watches you during your workout for safety purposes

squat a deep-knee bend exercise for the thighs

steroids see *anabolic steroids*

sticking point when no further progress is made in training by adding weight or there is no visible occurrence of muscular gains

stretching a movement that promotes flexibility of the body; these exercises are usually done in a warm-up routine

striations individual fibers along a muscle which show up in great detail when ultimate muscularity is achieved; these are seen on an individual with outstanding definition

supersets the rapid alternation of two exercises—one pulling and one pushing; e.g., biceps curls with triceps extensions

supplements concentrated vitamins, minerals, and proteins in tablet, powder, or capsule form

symmetry the shape and contour of the body

testosterone the male hormone responsible for secondary sex characteristics

thyroid the gland which regulates the basal metabolic rate; in bodybuilding, it refers to a preparation of synthetic or dessicated animal thyroid gland containing active amounts of thyroid hormone which aids in burning stored fat more readily; adverse effects include cardiac arrythmia, weight loss, headaches, and loss of lean muscle tissue

traps trapezius; upper-back muscles

triceps the three-headed muscle at the back of the upper arm

triset three exercises compounded for a body part with minimal rest between the movements

Universal multi-functional machines that permit exercises for every muscle group and can allow six or more athletes to train simultaneously

up and down the rack a system of using a light set of dumbbells to perform a certain number of repetitions and then moving up to the next heaviest weight until the resistance is too much; at that point, the person starts coming down the rack using progressively lighter dumbbells

vascularity the prominent appearance of veins on individuals who have achieved a low level of body fat

visualization a mental technique which consists of imagining the body exactly as you want it to be and practicing this technique for a few minutes every day; a mind-body link

vitamins organic substances that play a vital role in the metabolism of carbohydrates, proteins, and fats, acting as biochemical catalysts; e.g., A, C, E, B_1, D, K, etc.

WABBA   World Amateur British Bodybuilding Association

warm-up   an activity that prepares the body for athletic exercise by loosening up the muscles

WBBG   World Body Building Guild

weightlifting   a form of weight training whereby persons compete against each other in the amount of weight they can lift in either powerlifting or Olympic lifting

workout   an exercise program

workout partner   an individual who works with another as a spotter or as a source of encouragement and motivation

Zercher squat   a squat which entails grasping a barbell against the lower chest by holding it in the crook of the arm before beginning the exercise

Picture Credits

The illustrations in this book display the products and photography of many people and business organizations. Represented among them are the following: Ariel Computerized Exercisers, Inc., Fig. 52 (exercise station); Billard Barbell Co., Fig. 1 (neoprene waist trimmer), Fig. 2 (sauna suits), Fig. 4 (weightlifting gloves), Fig. 10 (dumbbells), Fig. 21 (barbells), Fig. 34 (E-Z curl bar), Fig. 35 (hand grips), Fig. 37 (chest expander), Fig. 40 (jump ropes), Fig. 41 (scissors "V" builder), Fig. 42 (wrist roll-up), Fig. 44 (triceps bomber), Fig. 45 (wrist and ankle weights), Fig. 46 (iron boots), Fig. 56 (barbells), Fig. 66 (power twister), Fig. 68 (leg-lift bench), Fig. 69 (triceps-pushdown attachment), Fig. 73 (barbells), Fig. 80 (dumbbells), Fig. 85 (barbells), Fig. 88 (multi-purpose bench), Fig. 91 (barbells), Fig. 102 (barbells); Boss Gym Equipment, Ltd., Fig. 63 (side-delt machine), Fig. 89 (calf machine), Fig. 92 (hack-squat machine), Fig. 93 (Scott bench), Fig. 96 (leg-extension machine), Fig. 97 (leg-curl machine); Bricker Labs, Fig. 24 (vitamins/supplements); Creative Health Products, Fig. 30 (skinfold caliper); Edward, Gregory, Leigh, Fig. 9, (Tunturi rowing machine and home cycle), Fig. 29 (Tunturi rowing machine), Fig. 33 (Amerec running machine), Fig. 38 (Tunturi jogger), Fig. 54 (vital-signs monitor); Fowles Company, Fig. 59 (Camstar abdominal twist machine), Fig. 79 (Camstar bench-press machine), Frank Calta Super Fitness, Fig. 65 (forearm machine), Fig. 84 (leg-curl machine), Fig. 98 (cable crossover), Fig. 101 (Roman chair and hyperextension); Future Equipment Co., Inc., Fig. 6 (leg-press machine), Fig. 18 (calf machine), Fig. 20 (hack-squat machine), Fig. 61 (dumbbells and rack), Fig. 62 (calf machine), Fig. 71 (Scott/preacher bench), Fig. 72 (Olympic incline bench), Fig. 75 (Olympic decline bench), Fig. 77 (cable crossover); Hoggan Health Equipment Co., Fig. 19 (Camstar military-press machine); Keiser Sports Equipment, Fig. 8, 58 (arm-curl machine), Fig. 70 (leg-press machine), Fig. 78 (lat-pulldown machine), Fig. 90 (leg-press machine), Fig. 95 (leg-extension machine); *MuscleMag International*, Fig. 11 (hack-slide machine), Fig. 51 (Weight-gain formula), Fig. 82 (workout bench); Pacifico Enterprises, Fig. 5 (weightlifting belts); Pillow, Fig. 7 (She-Beast products); Quality Designs, Fig. 17 (cambered bench-press bar); Queststar, Fig. 16 (the Water Machine); Universal Supplements Corp., Fig. 23, 49, 50 (vitamins), Fig. 26 (protein supplements), Fig. 47, 48 (protein drinks); W. C. Leathers, Fig. 3, 99 (waist belts); Weider International, Fig. 12 (Slim Bells), Fig. 15 (Body Blaster Bench), Fig. 22, 31 (Mega Pak vitamins), Fig. 36 (chest expanders), Fig. 43 (Herculean Power Builder), Fig. 100 (vinyl barbells); Weight Lifter's Warehouse, Fig. 39 (lifting gloves), Fig. 57 (knee wraps), Fig. 60 (power belt), Fig. 87 (wrist straps); York Barbell Co., Fig. 13 (preacher bench).